WHAT PEOPLE SAY

"An incredibly powerful book t
entrepreneur grappling with the
this book has already helped m
purpose, and understand the patl

and my business. I can't recommend it highly enough. A must read
for anyone wanting to lead with impact in this increasingly crazy
world."

Amazon *** Review**

"A contemporary masterpiece in the leadership literature. Jankel
synthesized decades of research and models into an alliterative
work of art that lay persons needing change and transformation
can discover wisdom for their choices in this confusing and chaotic
time."

Amazon *** Review**

"As a transformation guru, Nick Jankel uses his unique voice and
powerful insights to inspire. His ideas are as relevant to the newest
start-up as they are to the oldest public company."

**Special Advisor to President Obama & Former
Head of White House Office of Social Innovation**

"An outstanding framework with powerful tools. Huge impact!"

President, Kellogg Company

"At the forefront of thinking about creativity, sustainability, and
entrepreneurship and communicates with authority, conviction,
and on the basis of personal experience."

**Directorate General for Enterprise and Industry,
European Commission**

"Nick Jankel goes deeper and clearly made an impact on me and on others. Looking forward to seeing the seeds grow in my mind and my organization."

EVP, Merck

"I've recently been struggling with my role as a leader - feeling stuck in a rut and oddly powerless to make any significant change - but this book, full of insight and practical theory, has really helped me identify some of the blockages that were holding me back from my leadership potential and I now truly believe that I have the tools I need to overcome them."

Amazon *** Review**

"A pronounced and profound impact. Exceptional."

CEO, HSBC South Africa

"Nick Jankel is engaging, humorous, and strategic—inspiring people to have a strong commitment."

Director of Strategy, UK Government

"Nick Jankel inspired us to work on ourselves as leaders and lead the change."

SVP, SAP

"A challenging synthesis that demands serious consideration."

Amazon *** Review**

"The business world has only a few people who think deeply about things, and fewer still that have decades of experience. Jankel is both. Has radical new ideas for organizations that are thoughtful and tested in the biggest companies in the world."

Amazon *** Review**

NOW LEAD THE CHANGE

NICK JANKEL

Library of Congress Cataloging-in-Publication Data

Library of Congress Control Number: 2020936334

Jankel, Nick Seneca 1974–

Second Edition, November 2020
California, United States
Switch On Books

412pp.
Leadership. Smart Thinking. Transformation.

Printed in the United States and wherever books are sold.

ISBN 978-1-9997315-6-4 (print book)
ISBN 978-1-9997315-7-1 (ebook)

Switch On Books London & Los Angeles

www.switchonnow.com

Discounts are available on quantity purchases by corporations, associations, and others.

For details, contact the publisher through the website above.

ABOUT THE AUTHOR

With a Triple First from Cambridge University in Medical Science and Philosophy of Science—and over 20 years hard-won experience advising world-class blue-chips, start-ups, scale-ups and non-profits on the front lines of disruption—Nick Jankel is one of the world's preeminent practitioners, keynote speakers, and theorists of transformational leadership.

Nick is the lead architect of neuroscience-driven and heart-led change, innovation, and leadership methodology Bio-Transformation Theory & Practice®; and advises conscious entrepreneurs and C-Suite executives of ambitious organizations on how to transform themselves, their enterprises, and the systems they are part of to be sustainable, purposeful, and regenerative.

When not expanding the theory, he designs and facilitates programs for individuals to transform in life, love, and leadership. He invites you to visit his companies' websites at *switchonnow.com* and *wearefuturemakers.io*.

OTHER BOOKS BY NICK SENECA JANKEL

Switch On: *Unleash® Your Creativity And Thrive With The New Science And Spirit Of Breakthrough*

The Book of Breakthrough: *How to Use Disruptive Innovation To Create A More Thriving World For All*

Become A Transformational Organization: *Galvanize Agility Without Losing Stability To Survive And Thrive In The Digital, Disrupted, And Damaged World*

Spiritual Atheist: *A Quest to Unite Science and Wisdom Into a Radical New Life Philosophy to Thrive in the Digital Age*

For my father:

Thank you for showing me the power in courage, dignity, and commitment; and the potency of giving up comfort and convenience to truly care about our world.

In everyday life there are many people who have what it takes to be a leader, although their gifts are not always apparent. Their greatness lies not in their ability to respond adroitly to superficial social changes but in their strength of character, in their capacity to remain true to themselves. When life's dramas are being played out at the very deepest level, it is these people who come forward, whose modest strength is suddenly recognized.

[H]ere, perhaps, lies humanity's greatest hope: great deeds can be accomplished by simple, ordinary people.

Vasily Grossman

CONTENTS

Contents

PROLOGUE
FORGE OR FAIL THE FUTURE

Three unprecedented and seismic drivers of change in the outside world are putting intense environmental pressure on *every* organization to adapt both radically and rapidly internally. Enterprises and institutions that do *not* transform what they do and how they do it— not just once, but many times over the coming years—will find they are a mismatch for the future. Therefore, they will inevitably fail.

This is simply the eternal truth of evolution: a truth that many leaders have forgotten after decades of success in markets that were stable, predictable, familiar, and clear; and where existing organizations controlled access to the means of production and distribution so few competitors could challenge that success. All this has now changed, accelerated by the Covid-19 pandemic that, at the time of going to press, has shaken our world to the core. No organization or institution on Earth can hide from intense and dramatic evolutionary pressures to adapt fast and frequently.

The great challenge is this: leading adaptation is very different from managing Business as Usual. In fact, successfully transforming a business model, organization, or system just once is the hardest task a leader can take on. Being able to lead and land *continuous* transformations to adapt your products and processes to stay in step with the relentlessly changing world is the capability that all leaders must strive for.

It is likely that if you are reading this book, you have developed decent skills at managing projects (and if you haven't, no worries; this book will support you too). You can get stuff done to time, on budget, and to a suitable level of quality for your sector or space. The challenge you face is that this is no longer enough to ensure you make it; either as individuals within your career, or as an organization. It is the same for our crisis-hit world. To future-proof your enterprise, your career, and our shared world, you must be able to respond creatively, empathically, and consciously to the three seismic shifts threatening us all.

However, 20th Century management science, theory, and tools—including line management, performance management, reward systems, KPIs, balanced scorecards etc.—were designed to enable people to solve known and knowable problems fast. From kindergarten to an MBA, managers and leaders are trained to use such tools to get to the 'right' answers as quickly as possible. This means downgrading people's innate creativity and adaptability in favor of stability and predictability.

Much of this made sense in the Industrial Age: the last thing that anyone wanted from a soldier in a trench or a factory worker on the production line was 'variance', questioning assumptions, refusing 'received wisdom', or challenging authority: what we now call innovation, disruption, and agility.

20th Century management tools and training were very useful, if rarely empowering, when the mission for all managers was to deliver predictable returns by improving production or service levels incrementally (in stable, predictable, familiar, and clear environments). But the world in which we operate is becoming less stable, predictable, familiar, and clear by the hour. We are in a volatile, uncertain, complex, and ambitious (VUCA) reality and it's only going to get more confusing and overwhelming.

Whether seen in uncontrollable forest fires and spontaneous trade wars, or rapidly spreading pandemics causing economic meltdowns, VUCA is the new normal. We must still manage our projects and get stuff done. But we must also be adaptable, agile, ingenious, and nimble. Managing projects and performance is now merely a hygiene factor for any leader and enterprise. We must step up beyond our management comfort zones to *lead the change* that the market and the environment are demanding from us. We must lead our teams and our enterprises in, through, and out of what I call the Triple Threat.

The first threat is from *digital* technologies: from AI and automation to blockchain and 3D printing. These technologies are rapidly making legacy business models—most invented in the Industrial Age—seem tired, ill-fitting, and uncompetitive. Digital technologies can scale up the provision of everything from homes to bank accounts without scaling up the traditional costs and challenges that come from building hundreds more factories and employing tens of thousands more people.

Digitally-powered products and services can deliver more value for less, with a better user experience, too. Simply put, business processes, practices, products, and models developed in the Machine Age of the 20th Century (and even earlier) are struggling to stay effective and profitable in the Digital Age of the 21st Century, where ideas and ideals can travel the world at the click of a mouse. If the core of your business isn't digitized and data-driven in some fundamental way, it is only a matter of time before your enterprise is no longer fit for the future.

At the same time, AI, automation, and machine learning are now better than many human beings at both repetitive *and non-repetitive* analytical tasks. The deep-learning algorithm that beat the world's best human at the complex game of Go became exponentially better—100× better—than he was at his peak just two years later. In the near future, machines will be able to do almost all of our analytical tasks better than we can.

Not only will they do these things better than human beings, but they will be able to do them without the foibles that human beings have, like cognitive bias, fatigue, and being sick with a virus. As managers, we all have to find ways not to be made redundant by technology— figuratively and literally—by future-proofing our careers. This only happens when we step up as leaders who have mastered our innate capacity to be collaborative and creative; and our humane capacity to be compassionate and caring.

Exacerbating the challenges we face as leaders is the second massive threat to every organization. I believe it is even more important than the plethora of digital technologies discombobu-lating business: the dramatically *disrupted* needs, wants, desires, and pain points of *emerging* customers and employees. The vast majority of your workforce, and soon your customers, are Millennials or even younger. Born after the fall of the Berlin Wall, empowerment, equality, and ethics are part of their generational DNA.

They demand from their leaders, and the brands they buy from: meaning (a genuine purpose); mastery (autonomy and creativity); majesty (dignity and respect); and membership (belonging, without being cultish). If we don't know how to offer them this value—as well as manage their performance and productivity—they get over-whelmed, jaded, confused; and they disengage.

Research by Gallup shows that roughly two thirds of all employees are disconnected from their work and managers, costing US companies alone $550 billion a year; and that six out of every ten employees are burning out on the job. Teams with the highest levels of engagement because of meaning, mastery, majesty, and membership are 12% more profitable and show 60% less employee churn.

Radical social and cultural changes mean that markets—the people who buy and make products—are changing far faster than most organizations are. The resultant mismatch is making it hard for organizations that do not embrace continuous transformation to attract, keep, and serve *emerging* customers and workers. Remember that while business makes profit for shareholders, it can only do so when it solves problems for large groups of people who *cannot solve the problems themselves.*

In a world where younger people are empowering themselves more and more—using digital ideas and peer-to-peer and sharing ideals—businesses need to find real pain points to resolve or they will find the number of customers willing to pay them is far reduced. If we offer no value, there is no transaction and so no profit. If we forget that we need to find and serve *new* types of customers, by having deep and empathic insights into emerging needs and resolving them creatively and elegantly, then we will have no business. Period.

As if this were not enough, we are *all* facing a third threat: the threat from fundamentally *damaged* global systems. Our ecological, societal, organizational, and psychological structures are at breaking point after many years of constant stress. Some are already imploding with the novel coronavirus pandemic that has swept across the world, exposing social inequalities, financial frailties, and worrying weaknesses in our global socio-economic system. There is a 'perfect storm' of crises brewing that will test our individual and collective resources, resilience, responsibility, and resolve for years to come.

I believe there are four distinct crises within the overall damaged ecosystem with which *every leader* must grapple to some degree (which I will investigate in much more detail later in the book): The Industrialization Crisis (more than 3 billion people might live in unbearable heat due to climate change by 2070). The Inequality Crisis (50% of human beings live one paycheck or crop failure away from destitution; and 40% of all US citizens have less than $400 in their checking account for emergencies). The Illness Crisis (for three consecutive years life expectancy has dropped in the USA and there have been more than 600,000 extra deaths just among people aged 45 to 54). The Identity Crisis (almost 4 million guns were sold during March 2020 in the USA alone and 2019 saw the most mass killings on record).

Every organization must, at minimum, grapple with the intense risks each of these crises brings to their existing business and operating models. Ideally, every organization should find ways to transform one element, or more, of each crisis into business opportunities: authentically serving people and planet by resolving unmet needs through their business *purpose*. As I will demonstrate later, each crisis interplays with the other three; and each reveals much about the state of our material and conscious worlds.

For example, the Covid-19 pandemic has already killed hundreds of thousands of people and may go on to kill many more. Yet the outsized impacts of the tiny SARS-CoV-2 virus (the official scientific name of the Covid-19 pathogen) on lives and livelihoods were utterly predictable because they are the result of *existing* weaknesses and frailties in both our global and local systems. Such damages manifest as the four crises I describe above.

The Covid-19 pandemic is exposing preexisting 'maladaptations' across businesses and society as a whole. It is magnifying and amplifying the intensity and importance of the digital, disrupted, and damaged drivers of change. It also seems to be a foreshadowing of far more intense threats from a climate gone haywire due to industrialization; and a society riven apart by inequality, ill-health, and conflicts over identity. For organizations, the pandemic has accelerated preexisting, and generational, disruptions away from physicality to virtuality; and from carbon-releasing consumer comforts and conveniences to the *essentials* of health, wellbeing, and community.

These already existed as weak signals: for example, in the climate protests in schools and in the philosophy of Extinction Rebellion. As planet-negative airlines—that spent the last decade of record profits paying out enormous exec bonuses and funding exuberant share buybacks—ask for massive government bailouts to prevent their bankruptcy, future-fitting organizations like streaming services, delivery companies, and bicycle makers are booming. Why? Because they have already adapted to 'weak signals' of their future in the present.

The writing has been on the wall for decades about pandemics spreading around the globe through extensive mobility, migration, and air travel. SARS, MERS, Ebola, and the everyday flu are features of our concrete present. Scientists have been suggesting that we develop a coronavirus vaccine for years. People have ignored the global risks and the warnings; just as they keep ignoring the cacophony of scientific alarm bells ringing about climate change, pollution, inequality, antibiotic resistance, mental ill-health, physical ill-health, and intense rises in sectarian conflicts and extremist politics.

The novel coronavirus is demonstrating that societies that prioritize productivity, consumer addictions, and GDP above all else lack the psychological and physiological resilience—and healthcare and welfare 'redundancies' (excess capacity to cope with surges)—needed in a profound and prolonged crisis. Poor leadership has been the cherry on the cake of maladaptation and failure that has caused much needless suffering.

Despite an increased understanding of the importance of leadership in long-term organizational performance—and consequently increased investment in leadership development—most leaders are maladapted when it comes to making tough decisions and solving complex problems in challenging VUCA environments. Few are equipped to deal with the disasters of the damaged world; let alone find ways to mitigate their impacts with innovations driven by a genuine social and ecological purpose.

Leadership development programs often serve to shore up the tired and outdated thinking used by senior managers—and their favorite management consultants—rather than seeking to empower leaders to challenge that thinking wisely and strategically. Budgets for leadership development are often cut in times of crisis—even as leaders struggle to cope with the adaptation requirements of such crises.

The good news is that, in the original Greek, a crisis is simply a 'turning point': an opportunity to pause, take stock, understand the future in the present . . . and then transform. However, we cannot transform our organization just once and hope all will be well. The Triple Threat facing us all—digital tech, disrupted societies, damaged systems—is so fervid and so complex that we cannot run a *single* digital transformation, business model innovation, or restructure program and be match fit for the future.

This kind of linear, silver bullet, thinking might have worked in previous decades; but the external world today is changing so fast that every organization must be able to *continuously* transform itself time and time again to adapt and stay competitive.

The only way to enable continuous transformation in our business models and processes is if we have *people* within our organizations that can themselves continuously transform. Constant Transformational Challenges driven by a radically-changing VUCA world cannot be 'off-shored' to a management consultancy to solve, no matter how brilliant they are. They have to be owned and engaged with *by the people within the organization*. For it is they that must seek out, design, and implement successfully transformational solutions time and time again as the future unfolds.

The skills and capabilities to transform over and over again must be developed within an organization. Otherwise it will not be able to adapt to every crisis and leverage every turning point. I found this out the very hard way in my first start-up consultancy supporting large organizations to innovate. Nine times out of ten, the organizations I worked with ignored, shrunk, or poorly executed game-changing ideas that competitors would later disrupt them with. This was not because of a lack of capital, technology, or resource. It was always because of a lack of leadership.

Years of research—and decades of my own experience—tells us this: you cannot succeed as an organization beyond the level of consciousness of your people, especially your leaders. At least, not for very long. As Bob Anderson puts it: "The organization simply cannot outperform the collective effectiveness of its leaders."

As every organization has access to similar technology and production capabilities, you can't rely on 'stuff'—even the very latest machine learning (ML) algorithm—to defend you any longer. Technology is obsolete the day it is shipped; the more so given that anyone in any country can compete with the largest companies in the world through employing white-label labs and factories.

You can't control what your competitors do and you can't control how technologies become more or less in vogue. You can't control your customers, stop them changing, or prevent them from going elsewhere. You cannot control a pandemic from killing customers and shutting down markets. You can't control fires, flooding, and methane pulses (that may also release viruses frozen at a time when primates were yet to exist) in the Arctic. The only thing you can control—although 'master' is a more accurate word (in terms of virtuosity, *never* domination)—is how you sense, feel, think, and act; and how you inspire and guide others to sense, feel, think, and act.

The elemental truth around which this book evolved is this: in fast- and dramatically-changing environments, our *consciousness* as leaders—how we sense, feel, think, and then act—is our main driver of competitive advantage and the only factor in our (almost) complete control. All my everyday work advising some of the most successful and inspiring organizations in the world to adapt, innovate, and lead transformation and supporting tens of thousands of individuals and leaders to transform themselves is premised in the same truth.

How we feel and think within determines how our organizations succeed (or not); and whether our society works for us and anyone else. Therefore this book is focused on providing you, as a leader, with a methodology, philosophy, principles, toolset, and a practice-set that can help you switch on your inner consciousness to then step up to lead transformations in concrete matter (that really matter). When you can masterfully shift your own consciousness you can shift anything and everything about the material world of your teams, products, and businesses.

Although the start point for all transformation is to attend to gritty external challenges thrown up in the tangible outside world, leaders who understand how transformation works rapidly return to their own inner world to start leading the change from the inside-out: inside their consciousness. Our consciousness is a sophisticated fusion of nuanced thoughts, beliefs, and assumptions; inspiring and disabling stories, frames, and narratives that generate meaning; fragmented yet often intense and traumatic memories that we often deny or repress only for them to return in unusual ways; myriad subtle and complex emotions that can take years to fully understand; and rich yet fleeting and capricious sensory experiences that we are often unaware of.

We have to find ways to transform all of these if we want to behave differently. We cannot sense, feel, think, and act the same as before and expect different outcomes and outputs from a day at work. To expect to stay the same while somehow transforming our teams and organization is, as many have said, the definition of madness. We must change within in order to take charge of change outside us—rather than be left behind by it.

All business models and empires crumble eventually. New, more adaptive innovations always emerge to take their place. The dissolution of old and outdated habits of thought and action will always occur. New ones will always take their place. Some things will be lost (which we may realize that we do not need after all.) Much will be gained.

The transformation of the old can happen *to* us and be very, very painful; or it can be consciously led by us and we can play a role in forging a future that we ourselves envision. Whereas management and transactional forms of leadership are all about *maintaining* the status quo, we need a kind of leadership that can *disrupt* the status quo with as little pain, and as much elegance, as possible. This is transformational leadership.

The version of transformational leadership that I explore in this book goes far beyond the notions of it mooted in earlier, and less exciting, times. Rather than focusing on just our 'followers', I believe the times we live and work in demand that we focus our entire mind and body on ensuring our organizations—and the systems we are part of—remain match fit for the future.

Transformational leaders learn to see every major external change—from blockchain to climate change and from global pandemics to the needs of Generation Alpha—as *an invitation to transform* something within their enterprise that is a mismatch for the way the future is emerging. The transformational leader adapts to fast-changing environments by transforming products/services and the process and practices that underpin them; not just once but many times, as the environment demands.

The virtuoso transformational leader embraces and owns external changes—and then *metabolizes* them into value-generating ideas. As a cell takes in food and extracts the nutrients to create value in our body, the transformational leader takes in external realities that they do not control and smelts them, in heart and in mind, into value-creating products and services with which they can forge the future. The most powerful solvent for transmuting crises into creativity is, as we will see, a sense of deep connection— dare I say 'love' (and I do!)—in our consciousness.

Transformational leaders are able to manage the existing business by continuously improving established best practices, ensuring their teams are motivated to solve technical problems quickly and efficiently; even as they spend most of their energy and passion forging the future by inventing next practices for their function, sector, and industry.

They ensure that their teams can support the metabolization of changes in the external world into creative ideas that are deployed through their enterprise as 'disruptive innovations,' 'digital transformations,' and 'agile processes.' Sensing weak signals of the future in the present, transformational leaders are as concerned with rapid adaptations that remove unnecessary treacle and reduce frustrating friction from internal processes as they are with leading the seemingly more glamorous business model innovations and award-winning user experiences that adapt the business to emerging customers and their needs.

The transformational leader never sees constant evolutionary pressures as a burden or inconvenience. They do not fall into habits that see them despair, moan, or get angry (for long, at least); and they do not allow their teams to do so, either, once a new threat has been spotted and the shock has been processed properly. They do not let their own blinkers ignore warning signs and weak signals.

They do not leave the change for someone else to take care of; nor do they talk a lot but fail to walk the walk. They do not discuss the change endlessly nor bemoan the loss of the old. They do not allow their desire for comfort have them block adaptation and the emergence of new ideas. They do not allow their teams and colleagues to have 'interesting conversations' that do not move the enterprise firmly onward.

They do not retreat into nailing the best ever spreadsheet or the most perfect strategy document as a way of feeling in control and productive. They do not rely on their technical expertise to get them through. They never focus solely on the illusory comforts of

Business As Usual (even as they manage the existing business and ensure it pays for the development of future ones).

They do not ignore the "Transformational Challenges"—when you see a term in speech marks like this, it means it is a transformational term I will use to distinguish an important idea or concept—thrown up by the fast-changing world and instead pay attention to the 'easy' technical problems that are familiar and clear.

The transformational leader attends and attunes her/his *entire* being to engage fully in rapid and dramatic changes in the environment. Without any resistance or refusal, the leader explores ways the organization can turn on a dime to adapt with purpose and power to resolve Transformational Challenges fully and completely.

To the transformational leader, every crisis—whether at the local team level or at the global economic level—is a "bifurcation point". With each bifurcation point, we get to *choose* to transform our way of working and the things we sell and market consciously . . . or we allow things to decline and break down—and we deal with the consequences. These are the *only two options in a VUCA world*, where nothing stays the same for long.

Doing nothing, hoping to tweak our existing products and models indefinitely with performance upgrades and efficiency fixes, may look smart and feel safe but simply ensures that we will decline eventually. By refusing the constant invitations to transform, we will manage our enterprise to fade from relevance . . . and fail the future.

The transformational leader knows, cognitively and deep in their guts, that the only way to contribute their most creative and adaptive ideas—and agile and progressive actions—each day of work is by *mastering* their own body and mind. They understand that the only way to metabolize a Transformational Challenge thrown up by rapid external change is to take it into their mind and body fully; and so alchemize what appears to be dirty, worthless coal into pellucid, priceless diamond with the searing heat of purpose.

By choosing to expand their own consciousness, transformational leaders free themselves from: cycling fear and stresses that lock them into outdated management techniques that are ineffective in this era; perceived limitations that trap them in banal and uncreative thinking that blocks innovation; and addictions to old business models and the assumptions that underpin them, which prevent the birth of new ones.

Instead of locking into past strengths, the transformational leader remains poised at their "Leadership Edge", ceaselessly dealing with relentless challenges with agility and panache. Such leaders can always find their way back to being free, fluid, and on fire so they can endlessly turn challenging problems into concrete and creative solutions that ensure their teams, organizations, careers, and human civilization are future-proof.

There is one enormous barrier blocking you from becoming a truly transformational leader: your own biology. Your mind and body evolved to scan the world constantly for threats. If one is spotted, fear is triggered and your body is flooded with stress hormones. This gets you to move away, or confront the threat, fast: way before your cognitive smarts have kicked in. This stress response has saved your life and enabled you to be here, reading this. It has enabled you to develop strengths that have gotten your needs met, allowed you to succeed in the world, and enabled you to rise as an entrepreneur, manager, or project leader.

However, it is these very patterns of sensation, emotion, thought, and action that will get in the way of your forging the future of your career, your industry, and our crisis-hit world. You must master this biology if you want to be able to change your consciousness and so lead and land business transformations that keep your enterprise match fit for the future.

Since studying medicine and philosophy on the path to becoming a psychiatrist, I have spent my entire career asking and answering a single question: how do we reliably achieve the hardest task in life: transforming our biology—and so our patterns of thought and action—in order to transform the world? Over perhaps a 100,000 hours—of committed study, experiment, and practice—I have co-developed a theory of transformation called Bio-Transformation Theory & Practice (BTTP).

BTTP is both a theory of change; and a methodology, toolset, and practice-set (practices that allow us to be the change, not just talk about it) for delivering it. BTTP is a theory grounded in scientific evidence but it is not limited by what science has had the time, desire, method, and finances to prove. It is as much inspired and animated by timeless human wisdom; and practical hacks for concrete change. By weaving together the three great threads of human genius—science, wisdom, and practice—BTTP can support you to lead and land transformations where it counts.

To fully actualize the power of BTTP, I have studied (and continue to study each week) cutting-edge knowledge from the latest science, particularly neurobiology, animal behavior studies, experimental psychology, and the study of complex systems. I have then consciously (re)united these scientific truths with life-changing wisdom from the great philosophical traditions—like Stoicism and Buddhism—that provide us with crucial insights into how to change our consciousness that science simply cannot deliver (by nature of its focus on objective facts, not subjective experience).

I have then spliced into this body of work the hacks, tips, and tools I have gained over a quarter of a century on the front lines of change as a practitioner (supporting over 100 blue-chip companies, scores of government departments, multiple global non-profits, and many leaders and everyday citizens to become transformational). Finally, over many hours of simplification, illustration, and teaching, I have architected Bio-Transformation Theory & Practice into a coherent, cohesive, and communicable methodology that actually works.

In this book I lay out seven elemental principles that lie at the heart of BTTP; and show you how these 'gems' can help you lead and land continuous adaptive transformations that future-proof your career, enterprise, and our world. They are:

1. How your one unified mind and body works

2. The two modes of consciousness at your disposal and how to use the right one to fit the moment

3. The Third Way of creative harmony that gets you out of simplistic and oppositional dualities

4. The four elements that make up every leadership and organizational habit; and how to break through these patterns to create the change you want to see

5. The five stages of transformational development we can inhabit as leaders; and how to consciously evolve yourself to make the most of your one short life

6. The six spirals of transformational action that enable you to embrace and solve any problem from the inside out: from self-transformation through self-mastery, right up to leading systemic change

7. The seven steps of how to lead transformations in yourself, your team, your organizations, and your systems by moving along the Transformation Curve

Along the way we will explore: how to discern technical problems from Transformational Challenges (and how to treat them very differently); what occurs on the path of the Breakdown Decline if we repress or reject the invitation to transform that crises constantly present us with; why sometimes doing nothing as we metabolize a Transformational Challenge into a creative solution is better than acting fast (and why this is way harder that it sounds); the vital importance of sensing and acting upon weak signals before perfect data arrives; how to use all mistakes for "triple-loop learning"; and how to arrive at clarity in decision-making in complex settings using 4 vital forms of guidance.

We will gain insights into: how to harness your leadership purpose to ground you in uncertain environments and deliver value to society; why many people resist change and transformation and ways to liquify this resistance; eight principles to stay resilient in the tough times ahead; how the Connection Solution opens up our transformative potential; why we should all develop reconnection practices as leaders; why the patterns we develop in our early career both help and hinder us; twelve classic leadership archetypes that bring much benefit but also have major limitations that must be transcended if we are to rise to more evolved stages of leadership; and how the Covid-19 pandemic affords us a unique opportunity to bring a more adaptive world into reality today.

Given there are likely to be even greater existential threats on the horizon—from droughts and flooding to rising sea levels corroding the shores of our cities—Covid-19 is simply the latest call for leaders to wake up to the crises we all face and lead the change *now*. Devastating though it is (and I have lost much-loved ones to it), it is but a drill for the challenges ahead. Without truly transformational leadership, the four crises of the damaged world will turn into the Four Horsemen of the Apocalypse.

Yet seen from the lens of transformational leadership, the dangers and existential risks we face—and technologies and innovation opportunities we can seize—are material world realities that are calling us to upgrade our consciousness within: to wake up; switch on; and step up.

The four crises—as well every business fail driven by a lack of proactive adaption to digital technologies and to disruptive user needs—are all underpinned, and exacerbated, by a different pandemic: *a critical absence of transformational leadership.*

Transformational leaders—in business, society, and politics—always ensure that their organizations/societies are future-proofed. They always have adaptive options available to meet global risks head on by creating value-generating products and services that solve emerging needs (supported by technological innovations). A problem is always an opportunity for a transformational leader.

Now is not the time to step back in fear, false modesty, or ennui. Suffering is everywhere. Those whose homes and livelihoods are destroyed by floods, cyclones, and droughts are calling. The tribes, animals, and forests devastated by palm oil and fires are calling. The tundras releasing methane that might make global warming unstoppable are calling. The bleached, dying coral reefs that are radically reducing our fish stocks are calling. The dying bees that we need to ensure we can all eat are calling.

Our customers and employees dying decades before their time, from addictions and disease, are calling. The millions of anxious teenagers—many from the most privileged homes—who are burning and cutting their skin daily are calling. The subsistence farmers whose food we enjoy but who are one crop away from destitution are calling. Our colleagues and co-workers with stagnant incomes, stressed-out lives, and unaffordable healthcare are calling. Our friends, loved ones, and team members are calling for our support, inspiration, and guidance.

It matters not what domain of life or sphere of activity you want to lead and land transformations in. The theory, methodology, thinking, practices, and tools of Bio-Transformation Theory & Practice that you will find in this book are as relevant to leading a family or local community as they are to leading a global corporate or entire nation.

If you choose to master the science and wisdom of transformational leadership you can harness these life-changing and world-changing insights to transform outdated thoughts and unskillful habits that are leading to missed opportunities in your career; irrelevant and obsolete processes and products in your organization that are leading it to fail; and the suffering that everyone, and the planet on which we rely for everything is experiencing.

The time has come for us all to lead the change, now. Because, our career, our organizations, and our crisis-hit world really cannot wait.

PART 1
THE TRANSFORMATIONAL
LEADERSHIP IMPERATIVE

Natural selection acts solely through the preservation of variations in some way advantageous, which consequently endure . . . But we may go further than this; for as new forms are produced, unless we admit that specific forms can go on indefinitely increasing in number, many old forms must become extinct.

Charles Darwin, *On the Origin of Species*

Competition is between the new species with a small population adapting fast to new conditions and the old species with a big population adapting slowly.

Freeman Dyson, Theoretical Physicist and Mathematician

1
THE VUCA WORLD

The world around us is changing fast and furiously. The transformations in all areas of our lives are both intense and dramatic. The world is changing at a rate with which few can keep up. Not only is the world around us changing, but the very nature of the change is changing, too. Changes are occurring quicker than ever; they impact us in more challenging ways; and the changes don't stop or settle down—so life remains unpredictable and uncertain. The environment in which we'll be operating in just a few years' time is not only difficult to predict, it's often beyond our imagination.

We see this when we look at business. For example, a decade ago, who could have predicted that:

- The autonomous driving unit of Google, called Waymo, was considered by analysts to be worth more (as a component of Alphabet, Google's parent company) than the world's most valuable car companies like Toyota, GM, and Ford. It has few products in the market; and little to no revenue after ten years.
- Uber, a company that only launched in 2009, would become the world's largest transport company without owning cars,

trains, planes, or buses. Then, in the year after its IPO, it lost almost half its value—in part because its ethics as a business did not fit with the way the world was heading

- The world's largest hotel company, Airbnb, owns no hotels. It hasn't paid for a single brick to be laid or had to train a single housekeeper. It never has to deliver a single hot room-service meal, yet it sells more nights of hotel stay than the largest hotel groups in the world. More interestingly, had you heard of it over a decade ago when people like me were putting our houses on it to rent?

- The world biggest media company, Facebook, gets its users to create the content and does not pay them a cent; nor does it take them out for lunch to hip new restaurants in Los Angeles, Manhattan, or London.

- The world's biggest retailer, Amazon, has only a few hundred physical stores; and it makes c.63% of its revenues from selling cloud computing services to corporations.

Would any of us been able to predict this in the year 2000? When we understand how drastically the world is changing, it becomes clear that the management techniques developed over half a century ago to generate predictable returns in stable markets are no longer entirely fit for purpose to ensure businesses make it in the world that is rapidly emerging. In the 20th Century, managers operated in environments that were relatively stable, predictable, familiar, and clear.

In fact, management science was built on the premise that the world in which every organization operated was stable, predictable, familiar, and clear. Leaders learned to use tools to manage production processes and teams that were predicated on a stable, predictable, familiar, and clear reality. 10-year or 5-year strategies, line management, KPIs, yearly planning processes, Gantt charts, balanced scorecards, performance reviews, 60-minute meetings, and many more all emerged as tools to generate efficiencies, and so consistent profits for shareholders, in the Industrial Age; the age of machines.

Such tools, which originated in processes for making machines ever more efficient, only work optimally to manage organizations if the environment is stable, predictable, familiar, and clear and so all you need from your people is to do what they always did but a bit better, and a bit more efficiently, each year. Continuous improvements were enough to generate single-digit growth, particularly if it was through cost reductions that generated the same or more output but with less overhead (flashy offices, workers, managers).

But the 21st Century environment is anything but stable, predictable, familiar, and clear. In fact, it is quite the opposite. It is volatile, uncertain, complex, and ambiguous. These four terms form the acronym VUCA, coined in the late 1990s by the US military to describe the nature of the environment that soldiers find themselves in today. It is increasingly being applied to the conditions all leaders must perform in within our fast- and furiously-changing world. Simply put, VUCA makes Industrial Age management tools ineffective at best; damaging at worst.

To explain VUCA: Our world is more and more *volatile*: things change very quickly, even overnight, and often for the worse. We can see this in the America-China trade wars, in the rise of populist movements, in the confusion of Brexit, and in the meteoric spread and explosive impact of Covid-19. Volatility has become a part of our existence, and it makes things difficult to plan for or control. The world around us is also increasingly *uncertain* (uncertainty is about 'unknown unknowns' as opposed to risk, which entails 'known unknowns' that can be figured out with metrics): the near future, even next month, is unpredictable. We don't know the long-term impact of AI, blockchain, or robotics; we don't know how new generations will affect the existing work force and the future of work; none of us know how quickly our world is going to heat up, how fast sea levels will rise, and what the implications are in terms of the price of homes, or our access to nutrition. No amount of data, which is always about the past, can help us with this uncertainty—it is unmeasurable and unknowable; rather than estimable and knowable and so be calculated in financial risk models.

We're also experiencing more *complexity* than ever before: there are more connections among different systems—organizational, economic, social, and scientific—than any human being could ever get their head around. Even the CEOs of the world's largest companies, and the presidents and prime ministers of the most powerful nations, cannot understand the complexity in their own system, let alone how their system interacts with so many others. Finally, the world around us is also fundamentally *ambiguous*: give different data to different people and they will take different things from it, creating different narratives and different levels of meaning. This makes getting clear information and insight into the future virtually impossible for any organization, however smart its strategy team is.

As leaders of any entity—of nations, of organizations, of community groups, of families, of relationships, of ourselves—we have to be able to upgrade how we make sense of this new kind of crazy in order to make decisions that future-proof our enterprise. The first step is radically to improve our sense-making apparatus so we can make sense of the major forces that are driving such profound changes in our shared human reality without overwhelming our brains with thousands of data points, and scores of urgent trends, that we simply did not evolve to make sense of.

2

THE 3D FUTURES FRAMEWORK

Geologists call our current era the Anthropocene. It is the first geological time period to be named after a species: *anthropos*, humankind. We are the only species to have impacted the geology and structure of the planet so profoundly. However, much as we have changed the planet, the material 'hardware' with which we have to work—the wetware of our brain and nervous system—is barely more developed than that of our ancient ancestors.

The late, great physicist and philosopher Freeman Dyson wrote: "It has taken 200,000 years for our species to evolve biologically from its origin in Africa until today, [but] it has taken only about 200 years of cultural evolution to convert us from farmers to city dwellers and to convert a large part of North American forest to farmland." We all have to deal with Anthropocene angst (AI, Millennials, climate change, Covid-19, recessions, profound inequality) with Neolithic neurons.

Where our ancestors only had to hunt every few days, pick some berries, and tell stories to each other around a fire (and fell the occasional beast), we have to use the same hardware to deal with 300 emails, 6 meetings, and a to-do list the size of Greenland

7

every single day. Not just that: we have to get everyday business done even as we must invent the future of our industry; and reinvent ourselves in the process.

The dubious honor of having a geological time period named after us can be seen as a mass wake up call for every human on Earth to use this turning point to adapt and recalibrate the software running on our biological hardware so we reduce stress and suffering; and increase equality, peace, and sustainable prosperity. Time is running out.

The fast and furious fluxes and fluctuations of the VUCA world can be bewilderingly labyrinthine; and intensely overwhelming. As I will go on to explore more fully, our brains and our bodies experience change, chaos, and uncertainty as painful. Without some kind of organizing framework to make sense of the vast shifts that are dissembling, and then reassembling, everything we know and hold dear about life and a future on this planet, we can easily get defensive and resistant. Instead of embracing the changes so we can forge the future we want to see, we push them away, discount them with a righteous-sounding narrative, and ignore them even as our organizations lose competitiveness, and our leadership style becomes obsolete.

To prevent us locking into a defensive position driven by our innate biological responses to confusion and complexity, I have developed an organizing framework that helps us make sense of the changes by making them simpler but not simplistic. It's called the 3D Futures Framework and I have been piecing it together over the last twenty years of being a professional futurist and scenario planner.

It upgrades our consciousness to help our Neolithic neurons catch up with the endlessly tangled knot that is our Anthropocene Age. Rather than try and deal with a thousand trends in our business strategy—trade wars, crypto tokens, opioid deaths, gender fluidity, lean manufacture, fake news, veganism—the Framework allows us to parse the radical complexities of our era into three key domains: The Digital World. The Disrupted World. The Damaged World.

Almost all the changes you will encounter over the next few decades that demand transformational leadership will fit into these three domains. Rather than be constantly bamboozled by yet another trend or fad to which someone draws our attention, we can now peer at the world through three distinct lenses to gain insight on how it is changing. But, as I will explain in later chapters, we can then transform each lens into a prism to focus our creative genius through. Our minds become laser-like in both inventiveness and focus so we can then adapt our business models and operating models in a cohesive and congruent way.

In essence, the three intense and potent drivers and domains of change—the digital world with fast exponential technologies; the disruptive world with massive social changes; and the damaged world with global existential risks—are a "triple threat" that each of us must engage with as leaders if we want to future-proof anything.

3
THREAT 1: THE DIGITAL WORLD

The impact of the Digital World on our lives and businesses is hard to underestimate. Kodak, Blockbuster, and even tech company Nokia were all disrupted out of business by digital technologies. So, in many ways, was President Mubarak in Egypt's "Arab Spring" and Hillary Clinton by Trumpian tweets. Any organization that doesn't grok the threats and opportunities of the digital world cannot play a foundational role in the future.

The core possibility that digital technologies unlock is the capacity to scale ideas globally, into peoples' homes and businesses, rapidly, and with very little additional cost. You don't need to build a new factory to go from selling ten apps to ten million. Leaders can scale their offerings exponentially: 10× or 100×. This means they can scale their ROI exponentially, too. This is what 'unicorns' are focused on: growing to be worth a billion dollars or more in years not decades.

The exponential growth potential of digital tech can be brilliantly illustrated by the time it took different technologies—some analogue and some digital—to reach 50 million users (the kind of numbers a multinational needs to serve to be worth getting out of bed for). It took the telephone 75 years to spread to 50 million people. It took 68 years for air travel to become a mass-market phenomenon. It 62 years to go from the first few automobiles bought by the wealthy to 50 million people owning their own car. Radio took 38 years to spread to 50 million people and analogue TV took 14 years. In contrast, the internet took just four years to reach 50 million users. Facebook took just over 3 years. Twitter took 2. Instagram just over 1. The Angry Birds app took *just one month* to reach 50 million downloads.

This ability to scale an innovation through digital technology to reach this many paying customers or needy citizens so quickly is unprecedented in human life. As is said in Silicon Valley: software is eating the world, especially Industrial Age processes and business models. Digital technologies allow ideas and innovations to spread faster than our brains can often grok. They do not grow in a linear way, taking many years to scale and reach mass penetration. They follow what is known as an *exponential* growth curve: the speed of growth gets faster as time progresses, reaching extraordinary numbers very quickly. Digital technology spreads ideas, products, services, and even cultural 'memes' and ideals, exponentially.

Everywhere we look, we can see digital technology—now expanding from just the internet to technologies like blockchain, AI, the Internet of Things, and 3D printing in what is called the 4th Industrial Revolution—that would have been considered science fiction just thirty years ago. For example:

- In May 2019, design studio Fuseproject unveiled plans to build the world's first 3D-printed housing community in an impoverished part of Latin America

- In 2018, Walmart started deploying blockchain to track the journey of foodstuffs so it could identify a source of food contamination and potential illness in just seconds instead of weeks.
- An experiment was conducted in 2017 pitting Artificial Intelligence against trained lawyers to review legal contracts. The results revealed that AI was 30% more accurate than the human lawyers, and completed the 92-minute task in just 26 seconds.

With the help of digital technology, we can now build houses in 24 hours instead of 24 months. We can use the driverless public vehicles, robotics, chatbots and gene editing. We can even print body parts for amputees. No one person can possibly understand the long-term impact of just one of the 4th Industrial Revolution technologies on organizations, let alone the combined effects of all the technologies landing: The Internet of Things; Big Data; wearables; sensors; 5G telephony; Artificial Intelligence (AI) and Machine Learning (ML); Artificial Life (ALife), CRISPR gene editing, nanotech, and bio-printing; robotics, machine-to-machine communication and automation; blockchain based platforms and currencies; the distributed web; chatbots; Augmented Reality (AR), Virtual Reality (VR) and Mixed Reality (MR); human-machine interfaces; manufacture-on-demand; advanced hacking and cybercrime . . . the list goes on.

Digital technologies are increasingly all around us. They are in our homes, our offices, our fridges, our doorbells. We carry them with us in our phones. We wear them on our bodies. They sense things around us that we cannot sense and create a virtual reality that we can barely detect. To survive, let alone thrive in, the digital world, we must transform the way we organize, produce, market, work, and lead.

However, this does not mean following the management temptation to shove new technologies into our existing business models and value chains just because we can. I have witnessed many organizations do this and fail to generate value—exponential or otherwise. Digital transformation requires more. Much more.

Instead, we must explore the unique potentialities for value-creation that each platform opens up in the "adjacent possible"—the space for new possibilities that arises around existing realities—and leading our teams on a journey of transformation to discover how we can deliver our unique business purpose and brand propositions through, and within, digital technologies. We are looking for unprecedented ways to provide value to new and emerging customers—and help them resolve real pain and problems that matter as the future unfolds.

Young or old, whether we have vertical power in the systems and organizations we operate in or not, the ever more digital world changes everything. Our own careers are at stake. We all have to contend with the advances of automation, robots, and AI into the workplace. Human irrelevance and obsolescence loom large.

If an AI *already* has a board position in a Venture Capital firm with an equal vote to the five human executives, where does that leave us? Where do we go from here if we want to compete for roles with the technologies we have invented?

Even if we retreat into the supposed safety of 'perfect management'—optimized data models, brilliant number-crunching, epic report-writing, etc.,—AI algorithms that have taught themselves how to do routine *and non-routine* analyses far better than we can (and without our cognitive biases, frailties, sickness, and need for sleep) will eventually expose us as less good than they are at mechanistic thinking. We cannot hide in spreadsheets and charts.

4

THREAT 2: THE DISRUPTED WORLD

The second driver of dramatic change is an enormous shift in social and cultural mores and customs—particularly our ideas and ideals about how we live and work—driven by intense *generational* change. I see this shift being even more important for leaders to understand than the advent of exponential digital technologies. This is because whatever technologies we use to make and scale our products, they only succeed if people want them, need them, and value them.

Consumer perceptions of their pain points and needs are changing fast. Customers are becoming more empowered than in the past—and so able to meet their own needs without a business being involved. So leaders have to pay attention to new customer and employee types and needs even more than they do to digital technologies. Making this more challenging is that generational cohorts are getting shorter in length and are disrupting society sooner, and more radically, than generations in the past. So-called Millennials now make up the largest percentage of the workforce and are challenging every leader to step up and shape up. Generation

Z, the generation that is now entering the workplace, is already disrupting companies with emerging needs as customers and employees. Gen Alpha, the generation coming after, will disrupt again.

For example:

- Whereas 60% of Baby Boomers (say those on the Board of a business) think having a tattoo shows questionable personal morals, 40% of Millennials (who make up the majority of staff and possibly customer-base too) have one.
- Of Generation Z, 70% have a Netflix subscription and 25% have already earned money online. In addition, 1 in 4 of them have already self-harmed—cutting (mainly girls) or burning (mainly boys) themselves—by the time they are 14. And those are just the reported numbers.
- Of Generation Alpha, those currently in elementary/primary school, 20% have already been to a protest and 50% have made a video online already. The oldest of them became 8 in 2020.

These emerging generations have a fundamentally different outlook on the world. All of us in positions of leadership need to understand what it is if we want to lead them as team members or the customers we must interest in our products. Most perspicaciously, we must understand what motivates them if we are to design and deliver work experiences and product experiences that tap into their deepest ideals.

The Millennials, and those younger, seem to have a fundamentally different set of motivations than the generations that went before them. Or, at very least, they are clearer and more empowered around their non-monetary demands from their employers, from the companies they buy from, and the brands they are loyal to. I call these the 4Ms of Millennial Motivation (and everyone else who is authentic about their genuine human needs beyond subsistence):

- Meaning—in their work, in their life, and in their cultural constructs. They seek this meaning through working for companies that have a genuine societal purpose; working on projects that have a reason for existing beyond making profit; through buying brands that take a social and environmental stand; and by constructing narratives about life that bring a sense of fulfillment

- Mastery—of themselves, their potential, and their capacity for leadership. They seek experiences, projects, and people that help them develop their skills and capabilities. They want to work in environments that are empowering, where there is useful and clear feedback, and a coaching orientation that allows for rapid personal development

- Membership—of communities of practice and of groups of affinity that feel safe and supportive. They want to *belong* to communities, in the workplace, in social life, and online. They want to join brand communities that get them. They want to collaborate with peers and learn from it. They want to transcend the loneliness and atomization of modern life with deeply meaningful connection

- Majesty—in terms of dignity, courtesy, and equality. They seek leaders and systems that treat all colors and classes with equal respect; and that value their existence and contribution as a human being no matter their age, gender, race/ethnicity, sexual orientation, religious choices, income, or education level

These four demands—for meaning, mastery, membership, and majesty—are not new; but they are more important to, or simply more demandable by, the current generation and those coming after them than any previous generation. The 5th 'M' is money.

For these people, not being groped on the subway or hit on at a team away day is simply a cost of entry into basic humankind. They can see through power plays, attempts by management at polished coercion, and most brand bullshit (including the "purpose-washing" of many businesses).

Many are more interested in working on projects where they can collaborate, innovate, experiment, and learn than they are keen to secure additional bonuses and fancy job titles (though they can always be offered it all!) As customers, they want speed and convenience, yes; but they also want empowering, humanizing, and insightful user experiences that treat them as valued individual human beings, not just as abstracted numbers in a database.

How we motivate, empower, inspire, guide, manage perfor-mance of, and train these generations has to transform. How we innovate products and services for them, and the kinds of models in which we believe, must also change. If our users of the future have needs, wants, ambitions, and aspirations that are transforming, so too must the ways in which organizations deploy (digital and analogue) technologies and capabilities to serve them.

5

THREAT 3: THE DAMAGED WORLD

The digital and disrupted worlds are bringing about a time of massive change. We are entering this challenging time at the same moment as being hit by a full-scale environmental and social emergency. Human beings are changing their environment in unprecedented ways, damaging the civic and ecological systems that all organizations rely on for succor.

After centuries running Industrial Age production and manufacture processes that create pollution, waste, and carbon—and disempowered and disengaged workers with stagnating incomes and diminishing quality of life—our systems are at a breaking point. It is easy to forget that there can be no booming economy without a thriving ecology. In fact, it is not too melodramatic to state that the damage we have inflicted on our ecological, social, and psychological systems is threatening our existence as a species.

Our planet is suffering from rampant climate change. As sea levels rise and we experience more extreme weather, much about our current lives and livelihoods is at risk. Intense weather events such as wildfires, hurricanes, and flooding will mean that insurance cover could quickly become unaffordable for ordinary citizens. It has been estimated that up to a third of global wealth could be lost due to coastal property becoming uninsurable because of rising sea levels. People can live in it but it will be worthless because it cannot be insured. The potential loss of global GDP caused by the worthlessness of this property has been predicted to be the biggest economic shock our world has ever seen. It would make the financial crisis of 2008 or the Depression of the 1930s look like a walk in the park.

It is estimated that we are losing 2.5% of our critical crop pollinators every year. Within a century, all the pollinators we rely on for all our food could vanish. We are dealing with an ecological system with as few as 50 growing seasons left to grow our foods. A shortage of fertilizers could have major consequences for our ability to feed ourselves. Pollution is causing an international health emergency. In China, an estimated one million people a year are dying from the effects of pollution and it could be even more in the US and UK.

In cities, our children are growing up with levels of pollution that affect not only their long-term physical and mental health, but their intelligence and ability to learn. Dirty air in urban areas causes high blood pressure, diabetes, and other respiratory illness and will lead to a higher overall death toll from the coronavirus. Pandemics will hit the world in ways never see before; and we may soon run out of antibiotics because of over-prescribing and their use in animal feed.

50% of all human beings today are only one medical bill or crop failure away from destitution; and 40% of citizens of the richest country on Earth, the USA, have less than $400 in their bank in case they are laid off. For the first time in recent history, a generation of children may have to accept a less prosperous life than their parents. Many of those within the emerging generations—Millennials, Gen

Z, and Alphas—will experience lower earnings, limited workplace benefits, 'zero-hour contracts', and working in a precarious 'gig economy' with no healthcare. Many will have to repay the trillions of dollars of student debt that they are accruing, often by gaining degrees that may not help them gain much financial reward.

The challenges we face are not only physical. Anxiety is now the fastest growing illness in young people in many countries, with one in four teenage girls admitting to self-harm. In the UK, 72% of young people say they've experienced a 'quarter-life crisis'—a crisis of meaning and purpose in their twenties. Suicide is now the biggest cause of death in young men in the US and UK. Stress and depression are costing the economy billions; and 'deaths of despair' are killings tens of thousands across the most advanced economies in the world. Stress is the number one burden on global health today. Developed counties lose one percent of GDP each year to backache, of which over 80% has no clear biophysical cause. The amount of pain felt by the average American has gone up in the last decade even as 100 billion pain meds are prescribed each year in a country of 250 million people.

These physical and psychological symptoms are a result of an increasingly damaged world. Add to these the acidification of oceans, massive political instability, the rise of populism, large-scale migration and volatile unemployment, and you have a melting pot of threats to our survival as a species. Our existence is on the line. The planet is sure to survive without us; but at what cost to billions of living, breathing, feeling, and aspiring human beings?

The 3D Future Framework: Invitation to Engage

Q. Which of the threats—digital, disrupted, or damaged world—are the greatest danger to your organization's business model?

Q. If you were paid to ensure your organization survives these threats, to what would you pay most attention (guess what, you are!)?

Q. Which of these threats are most pertinent and poignant for yourself as a human being; and for those you care about most?

6

THE FOUR CRISES OF THE ANTHROPOCENE AGE

Within the damaged world, there are four kinds of major existential threats to our livelihoods and lives. They have the potential to become Four Horsemen of an Anthropocene Apocalypse: the Industrialization Crisis, the Inequality Crisis, the Illness Crisis, and the Identity Crisis.

The Industrialization Crisis shows up in phenomena like: a massive rise in atmospheric carbon. Global air and sea temperature increases (each day, heat equivalent to 400,000 Hiroshima bombs is added to our oceans). Radical increases in air pollution in our cities is killing millions and damaging the brains of millions more. Microplastics—now found in air, water, and the cells in our bodies—are potentially lethal to all life. More than half the summer sea ice in the Arctic has disappeared. There are mass extinctions of thousands of species, many of which have not yet been named. The bleaching and collapse of coral reefs is threatening at least 1/5 of all ocean life and with it tens of millions of livelihoods. There have been enormous drops in biodiversity—for example, a 2.5% reduction each year in the numbers of pollinators like bees—reducing our capacity to feed ourselves. Lasting changes to the planet's water system is leading to droughts and fires in some areas; and floods in others.

The Inequality Crisis shows up in phenomena like: the most extreme levels of economic inequality ever seen in advanced liberal democracies with ever-rising child poverty, homelessness, and in-work destitution. Globally, the richest 1% of people took 82% of new wealth created in 2018. Just over a dozen men have more wealth than the entire female population of Africa.

Even in 'communist' China, the labor/capital split has gone from 43/57 to 38/62 in the last decade. Tens of millions of farmers that feed humanity live just above subsistence. This has forced many to push into animal habitats that open up pools of zoonotic viruses. Hundreds of millions of kids across Asia and Africa still do not go to school; and, for those that do, many have no money for books. Malaria, a mostly preventable disease when people have access to appropriate resources, kills around 50 children per hour.

In the wealthy West, things are equally challenging. In 1979 there were just under 20 million well-paid manufacturing jobs in the US. Now there are c.12 million, but the population has doubled in the same period. In one county in coal country, 60% of males are either unemployed or living on disability payments. As capital has taken ever more of the profits of industry over the last four decades, many people are earning the same or less than they did in the 1970s in real terms.

Lower- and middle-income earners in rich countries have lost out the most on globalization—with approximately zero income growth between 1988 to 2008—as manufacturing jobs were moved to countries with lower wages so companies could make far higher profits. The average industrial worker in the US earned 9% *less* in 2015 than the average worker in 1973 even as the economy *grew* by 200% in the same period. During roughly the same period, the tax payments of America's billionaires have *dropped*, as a percentage of their wealth, by almost 80%.

During a ten year period of cheap debt fueled by fiscal policies like quantitative easing that arose after the 2008 recession (but have never been fully switched off)—and after generous tax cuts for corporates in the last few years—US companies spent around a trillion dollars on share buybacks.

Hitting another (predictable) recession, many are now asking the government for billions in pandemic funding to stay in business. Yet workers have to spend double what they used to on healthcare (even after employer insurance schemes); and rent takes over half of their earnings each month for the majority. 78 percent of workers in the US live paycheck to paycheck; 3 in 4 are in debt; and most believe they will always be indebted.

In the UK, over 50% of care workers who put their life at risk during the novel coronavirus pandemic are paid less than the living wage. They are four times more likely to be in the 'precariat'—without a fixed-hour contract or having access to company benefits—than the average worker. The Covid-19 pandemic has led to millions of US workers losing access to healthcare at a moment when more people need coverage than ever. A young African-American man lost his life from the Covid-19 virus in one of the richest cities on Earth—Los Angeles—because he was refused treatment as he had no health insurance.

Roughly half of all those going to food banks in the USA have someone in their home who works full time; and about a quarter of homeless Americans have jobs. In the UK, the largest food bank operator has recorded a rise of 300% in the number of people regularly getting help to eat since 2010; a period that saw dazzling stock market gains. According to studies at Harvard, 92% of Boomers earned more than their parents (after adjusting for inflation). Within Gen X, only 50% earn more than their parents did. Because of all this, the average Western worker has experienced a precipitous drop in their sense of majesty (dignity, esteem, and respect), membership (working class men tend to find their community at work), mastery (of skilled tasks in the technological economy), and meaning.

This is only set to get more painful for low-skilled workers made redundant by the Covid-19 pandemic; and, in the near future, automation, robots, and AI. A job—once a guarantee of dignity, mobility, and security—no longer reliably plays this role. As Thomas Picketty made clear in his masterpiece *Capital in the Twenty-First Century*, without major redistributive forces, the growth of capital far outstrips the growth of wages (and the economy in general). This causes the richest to gain ever more wealth; and most others are reduced to living hand-to-mouth.

The Illness Crisis shows up in phenomena like: the relentless increase in post-industrial, non-communicable 'mismatch' diseases like obesity, cancer, diabetes, and heart disease. Most of us will die from diseases like these that were very rare before the Industrial Revolution. Covid-19 kills many more people who suffer from heart disease, obesity, and high blood pressure than those without such conditions (although it does kill young people without preexisting conditions). We are in a period where future pandemics will become more common because of both human lifestyles and the over-use of antibiotics.

In the US and UK, life expectancy has been dropping driven by the explosion of 'deaths of despair' from alcohol and opioid addiction (legal and illegal) and suicide. The death rate for forty-something white Americans without a college degree has risen by 25%; and fallen by 40% for those with a college degree. Black people without a degree in the US are 40% less likely than their white contemporaries to die from suicide, alcohol, or drug overdoses. Meanwhile, according to Gallup, 67% of all US workers feel burnt out; costing an estimated $125 billion to $190 billion in health-care spending each year.

There is a rampant rise in mental health diseases like mood disorders (e.g. depression and anxiety) and personality disorders (e.g. narcissism and borderline) that are destabilizing families and leading to systemic ill-health across entire classes and generations. Depression is now the number one burden on ill-health worldwide. Kids in the US have more changes in family set-up than children in any other wealthy country, leading to growing rates of attention and behavioral disorders and ever more corroded communities. This costs society billions while generating untold suffering.

A fifth of all people in the UK are abused before they are 16. 700,000 kids are abused each year in the US. Four out of five cases of all abuse are by parents; over 90% of sexually abused children are molested by someone they know. Anxiety is the fastest growing illness in teenagers in the UK. Just under 50% of Americans feel lonely and left out; and believe their relationships are not meaningful. Only half have meaningful social interactions on a daily basis. Loneliness is as great a risk to physical health as obesity and smoking.

The Identity Crisis shows up in phenomena like: a return to the intense tribalism that many thought was a relic of the past. Populist politicians have been elected across the world, from Brazil to Hungary. Extremist ethnic tensions and hatreds are sparking killings in Portland, Pennsylvania, and Palestine. Polarized political debates are rife with incredibly inflammatory language that leads citizens to act in hateful and murderous ways. There were 434 mass shootings in the US in 2019 alone. There has been a global increase in neo-Nazi, Far Right and Alt-Right activities: white nationalist hate groups have grown 55% in the US since Trump took office.

There has been a widespread Western return to colonial jingoism and imperial arrogance: 1/3 of Britons think less-developed countries were better off when they were colonies. Nationalist nuclear proliferation is occurring again, with intense concerns about nuclear issues in Iran, North Korea, and Syria. The US still has almost five thousand nuclear missiles in its stockpile.

Schisms over identity politics, gender, ethnicity, religion, sexuality, trans-rights, and more are taking over campuses and media outlets—and are causing internecine breakdowns and uncivil war. There are endless culture conflicts over what is true and what is fake (news), which is influencing pandemic protections and mass safety. Vitriolic online trolling and bullying is triggering people to commit suicide. And there is still a massive gender and ethnic pay imbalance—with few women and minorities in multi-national Boardrooms.

The Four Crises: Invitation to Engage

Q. Take a minute to pause and reflect on these realities, closing your eyes and feeling into how you experience them; and where in your body and mind you sense these feelings.

Q. Which of these crises touches you in the most intense way?

Q. In which areas does human or planetary suffering break your heart most?

7

CRISES IN THE TIME OF CORONAVIRUS

At the time of press, the Covid-19 pandemic has accelerated how rapidly we must engage with, acknowledge, own, and transform each of the four crises of the Anthropocene. It has also magnified how each crisis interacts with the other three to generate the symptoms of suffering and decline that are a feature, not a bug, of our current outdated global system (and the vast majority of individual organizations within it).

Scientists in the field of 'planetary health' think that it is our *industrialized* destruction of natural habitats and associated reductions in biodiversity—for urban development needed for the emerging middle classes, for palm oil needed in beauty products, for fossil fuel extraction to power our conveniences—that creates the conditions for new viruses, such as SARS-CoV-2, to arise. Millions of people are in regular contact with millions of bats, which carry tens of thousands of new viruses. In 2015, a research team found that 3% of people from four rural Chinese villages close to bat caves had antibodies that indicated a previous encounter with SARS-like coronaviruses.

Of 335 new diseases that emerged between 1960 and 2004, estimates show that at least 60% of them were zoonoses (I.e. they came from animals). Industrial agribusiness increases the chances of humans being impacted by viruses that live in animal populations; and the cultivation of land has pushed human populations deeper into pristine natural environments. It also appears that the vast majority of deaths from the novel coronavirus have occurred in the most polluted regions of the most advanced industrial economies. Air pollution may be a key factor in whether a person develops acute respiratory distress syndrome (ARDS) when infected by the SARS-CoV-2 virus.

Inequality of access to good quality healthcare, wages, and nutrition means those who are poorer are more likely to be impacted by the pandemic, lockdowns/shutdowns, *and* their impacts on existing healthcare and welfare systems. Many viruses, like Ebola and HIV, cross over to humans in wet markets, and through trade in bushmeat, that is driven by an insatiable desire for flesh; together with inequality causing many to be unable to afford hygienic supermarket food. It has emerged that those of Asian and African descent in the UK have much higher rates of serious illness and death from Covid-19.

While the super-rich jet off to island fortresses and have antibody tests done in private clinics, millions across the world cannot afford to go to hospital when sick; and many more must work in low-paid but high-risk healthcare, retail, and delivery jobs serving those on the front lines of the fight against the virus. Gig economy and zero-hour contract workers have to work in places where they have a sustained risk of exposure even as white-collar executives work from home. It is a luxury to be able to self-isolate and to socially-distance. The most deprived areas of the UK have had double the number of deaths per 100,000 people than affluent areas. Those most in poverty lose the most.

People with preexisting *ill-health* from post-industrial lifestyles—from lung diseases and diabetes to high blood pressure and obesity—are much more likely to die from Covid-19. We are yet to understand what leads some people to have such deadly experiences of the virus whilst others have no symptoms. However, data from other viral diseases show that preexisting mental ill-health and Adverse Childhood Experiences can play a major part.

Conflicts have erupted around the novel coronavirus between those with different *identities*. Rather than collaborate on health protocols and vaccines, countries have put the entire global population and economy at risk by competing. Within federal Europe and the United States, states have competed with each other for scant ventilators. In Singapore, foreign workers crammed into extremely small dwellings were not treated with the same respect and care as nationals, which caused a second wave of the pandemic. President Trump tried to bribe German scientists to give him exclusive use of a potential vaccine (presumably to boost his re-election campaign).

Protesters of all kinds have risked infection to fight for their passionately-held—and, in the case of African-Americans, systematically discriminated against—identities. In the UK, people have committed hate crimes by coughing intentionally into the faces of people from other ethnicities. Many were healthcare workers. A train operator and woman of color, working in London's Victoria Station, was spat on like this. She died from Covid-19 (even though police believe the perpetrator did not have the virus). An official inquiry, published at the time of press, has found that structural racism and everyday discrimination suffered by Britain's black, Asian and minority ethnic people has contributed to the high death rates from Covid-19 in these communities.

8

A NEW HUMAN OPERATING SYSTEM

The picture may seem bleak, but it is bursting with opportunity for positive change—and pregnant with possibilities for genuine transformation. The reality is that the Triple Threat of the digital, disrupted, and damaged world is not going anywhere no matter how much we might want it to. None of us gets a choice in this: we all have to deal with them to some degree, even if we are just about to retire. Nowhere on Earth is safe from freak weather, global pandemics, or tanking pension funds. What is more, these drivers of change will hit us at the same time. They are not just trends to manage. They are destabilizing and disrupting the fundamental 'Operating System' (O.S.) of our world.

Just like a computer has an O.S. upon which we build software, humanity also has an O.S. upon which we build societies. Our human Operating System is being transformed by the Triple Threat. The 'apps'—businesses, institutions, political parties—built upon the old O.S. will not be fully adapted to, or optimized for, the emergent O.S.. It is highly likely that your business or institution either needs rapid upgrades to work on the new O.S.; and/or you need to build new 'apps' that make full use of the possibilities that the digital, disrupted, and damaged world brings.

The new O.S. that is emerging has no precedent in human history. Briefly, we have moved through several key operating systems in the history of our species: from tribes, to hierarchies/ aristocracies, to enterprises and markets, to the emerging era that is dominated by digital technologies and the global/local networks they afford us. This is not meant to be a history that is true and eternal; just a useful way of understanding the evolution of humanity; society; and organizations.

In *pre-modern* Tribal O.S., we have an intimate relationship with nature and each other. Small communities are the source of our identity and also our physical and psychological surviving and thriving. Each tribe member has a deep sense of belonging that holds them safe. Trade is local, occurring mainly through a network of people who have developed trusted relationships with each other.

On the other hand, brutality is rife. Rampant xenophobia drives violence based on whether you are in the group/tribe or not. Slavery of conquered peoples is common. Naive and disempowering myths about our genesis and purpose lock us into false certainties. In Tribal O.S., the strongest, angriest, or most loyal man (it is, and always has been, usually a man) wins.

In *early-modern* Institution O.S., educated and powerful people such as priests and aristocrats (and then scientists and scholars) are afforded the time needed to generate legal entities and encode laws that write down what the rules, responsibilities, and rights are that we must follow to survive and thrive within the state. These structures provide 'citizens' of these institutions—whether guilds/clubs or nation-states–with stability and security. Trade evolves to allow the exchange of goods, value, and ideas between people separated in space and time.

On the other hand, nationalistic, religious, colonial, and class-based ideologies lead to the oppression and suppression of those of a lower class or ethnicity. People of the wrong education, gender, or color are diminished and demeaned, subject to poverty, penal servitude, and state-sponsored violence. Mercantile capitalism makes vast profits for the elites, often through the suffering of those in colonies. Those at the top of the pyramid, who maintain their hierarchical power through (usually self-serving) laws, rules, and customs win.

In *late-modern* Enterprise O.S., reason, rigor, and a right to liberty are prioritized. Critical thinking and scientific knowledge are used to undermine priestly dogma and aristocratic power and replace them with provable certainties and meritocracies. Analysis and logic are used to trump ideology and religion. The mechanistic thinking of cause-and-effect enables machines to be built that replace human labor. Free-market capitalism and the liberal order allow people to scale innovations, driving major returns on capital invested and improving the lives and living standards of billions.

On the other hand, the focus on competition over compassion—and measurement over meaning—generates social alienation and consumer addiction. Extractive and accumulative greed leads to rampant inequality and ill-health; and environmental destruction and degradation. Those who are most competitive, ambitious, and algorithmic (using science to predict, control, and dominate) win.

In *post-modern*—or, more accurately, 'metamodern'—Network O.S., digital and real-world networks allow for unprecedented co-creativity, collective wisdom, sharing (of private physical and intellectual property), peer-powered services, mutual aid, and mass creativity. This O.S. affords citizens the ways and means to criticize and disrupt all claims to truth and power, whether by science, politics, or capital.

Regenerative thinking—circular, conscious, life-affirming, and holistic—allows capital to innovate healthy social and economic systems that promote human flourishing; and alleviate the suffering of all sentient beings. Those who are most co-creative and collaborative—and digital and agile in an interconnected system—win; or rather *thrive*: because the aim of the game has changed from *winning* in a zero-sum game to *flourishing* as a network.

On the other hand, a desire for forced equality and flatness in Network O.S. can generate a tyranny from below. The relentless need to criticize and deconstruct previous ideologies and institutions can erode certainties; and so lead to rampant negation and nihilism (such as deaths of despair). In the absence of purpose and compassion, Network O.S. can enable an abstract and technocratic—as opposed to an empathic and connective—form of globalization that reduces rootedness and local self-reliance.

Of course, the three older Operating Systems still exist in our current metamodern world even as the new Network O.S. comes online. Some companies and societies operate under the thrall of strong men. Some exist with steep hierarchies where those with most wealth, status, or education maintain power. Some really believe in meritocracy and the survival of the fittest/smartest/highest achievers. A few businesses and communities are, slowly, exploring how to make most use of Network O.S. Many organizations and institutions use all four in different departments, functions, and localities.

I believe that each organizing approach has a role to play across most organizations and nations, depending on the moment; but that we must all be looking to make the most of Network O.S.—as rapidly as possible—to mitigate the threats, and unlock the opportunities, of the digital, disrupted, and damaged world.

If we want to harness the unique and exceptional opportunities of Network O.S., while mitigating the existential threats of the Four Horsemen of a potential Anthropocene Apocalypse—the Industrialization Crisis, the Inequality Crisis, the Illness Crisis, the Identity Crisis—we will need to adapt ourselves and our organizations fast.

Otherwise, we will be using habits and ideas developed in an old O.S. to try to thrive in a new one that is characterized by unparalleled levels of digitalization, disruption, and damage. This cannot be anything other than a failure because of the elementary law of evolution: adapt . . . or die.

Operating Systems: Invitation to Engage

Q. Which O.S. does your organization predominantly run? What are the benefits? What are the costs in both human and economic terms?

Q. Which O.S. do you prefer? Why do you think this might be?

Q. What have you optimized in yourself to win in this O.S. that you prefer?

9
ADAPT OR DIE

The human Operating System of the Industrial Age—the age of mass production and consumption through machine-enabled economies of scale (and no care for carbon)—isn't adapted well to the emerging reality in which we find ourselves. What got us here might not get us there: surviving and thriving in the digital, disrupted, and damaged world. The organization (or leader) optimized for the Industrial Age does not function well in the digital, disrupted, and damaged world. This is why enterprises are struggling to remain competitive and innovative in the marketplace—and find it hard to generate attractive places for employees to spend the majority of their time in; and energy on.

If we as leaders remain locked in our old way of thinking, and the patterns of behavior that go with it, we start to lose *fit* with the world around us. There's nothing moral in this loss of fit—it doesn't mean we're bad people or fundamentally flawed—but over time it means that we fade from relevance. We become mismatched, maladapted, and so eventually irrelevant. When an organization loses its fit with the world, it starts to fade from significance and relevance. Usually this begins slowly; but it can be very quick, too.

Just ask the much-admired business *WeWork*. However, usually the warning signs are there for many years. But senior leaders ignore the signs; repress them actively; or, more likely, simply cannot see them for what they are within their existing mindset. This is understandable as we will see. Our biology is geared to have us see the world not as it is, but as we want to see it, until we switch on and awaken from our slumber.

Many think that the warning signals of maladaptation are hard to spot. But to the transformational leader, the signals and symptoms fading from fit are clear: our organization focuses on boosting accounting profits (bottom-line growth) instead of generating value for emerging customer types (top-line growth). Enterprises create products and services that become quickly commodified as margins race to the bottom rather than seeking sources of value in the future to capture with exponential ideas and innovations. We see little real growth in the value we add to the world even as armies of people work ten-hour days to produce returns.

We become vulnerable to competition from start-ups and up-starts, often from outside our traditional industry. We have to grow through expensive, and often misguided and mismatched, mergers and acquisitions rather than drive forward home-grown transformational innovations. And we find ourselves churning out carbon, waste, and pollution; extracting resources without a thought to the costs; and accumulating capital as if climate change and rampant inequality were not major risks to Business as Usual.

We might find ourselves in a position where, although our legacy KPIs are being met, we cannot seem to bring about positive change. We find that our customers are unhappy and churn. They're not served well by our products and services and so they complain, often leaving to go elsewhere. Our employees complain, too, as the "offer" to them starts to fade from relevance. They, too, leave, and it becomes harder and harder to attract and retain the most creative, agile, and inspired talent.

We rely on byzantine processes—that have accreted over time to control people and avoid costly errors—to make business work even as they now create endless friction and drag. We maintain policies that were well-intentioned but now just frustrate and demean our people and suppliers. The hierarchies we've built that seem powerful and important within the enterprise aren't quick enough to make use of new insights that would win us new customers and generate new value. We have a sense of constant overwhelm that paralyzes people. We might discover that, no matter how much we say we want to empower our teams, co-workers find it hard to step up after a lifetime of being told what to do and what not to do.

The enterprise ends up with many managers but few genuine leaders. Managers might be reluctant to move beyond their technical expertise and step up to the transformational plate. Outdated behaviors and beliefs—like thinking we need to know more than our employees or micro-managing them even as we say we are delegating—loses us the trust of our teams. Without trust there can be no genuine transformation, as it is the lubricant of effective change. We find it harder to motivate people using the old levers of promotion, power, and profit because these assets simply don't appeal as much to younger team members.

Perhaps we retreat into micro-detail, creating the ultimate spreadsheets and the best reports, rather than spending time forging the future. We may get hung up on having perfect data for decisions about an unknowable future. We might focus on hustling continuous tweaks to existing products—whether construction or code—instead of building a culture where people feel sufficiently empowered and passionate to innovate value-creating products and service at the edges of the enterprise, where our emerging customers are.

All these phenomena, and many like them, are not the problems themselves. If you recognize your organization or yourself in them, each is evidence that you have yet to crack Transformational Challenges that are inviting you to resolve them through adaptation. They are symptoms of a deeper mismatch between how you think and feel and the way the world is becoming. Simply put: there is no guarantee your organization has a right to exist in the future. There is no right to continue to be a senior, powerful leader or awesome entrepreneur.

The constant change in the outside world means that *everything* we do as leaders is either becoming more or less valuable *but it is never staying the same.* 20th Century mindsets tend to see stasis where, in fact, there is constant flux. Our processes, procedures, products, and people are either becoming valuable more day by day because they fit the future world better as time goes on; or they are becoming less valuable with each passing day, *but they are never static.*

Please read the last sentence again, as it's so key. If we stay the same and continue to do what we've always done, the changing world around us will make us obsolete in time. The period in which we can stay complacent is getting shorter and shorter. If we keep our products and services, the way we manage, even the way we do our expenses constant—or just tweak them with small improvements to the same basic model—we will find ourselves going backward because the world is moving so fast. The proof is in the pudding.

The average age of a company has gone from 75 years in 1937 to just 10 years in 2019. This is predicted to drop to just 7 years by the end of the 2020s. In other words, the time in which a company can create a business model and find a way of generating value from it before competitors, or changing customer needs, disrupt it is now under a decade. This is why a professor at Yale Management School has predicted that between 50% and 75% of Fortune 500 and FTSE 100 companies will be replaced by the year 2027.

We don't have to look far to see this happening already. The UK department store Marks and Spencer, once a stalwart of the FTSE 100 and one of its original members, has dropped out of the FTSE 100 altogether. Not only this, but many of its fellow originators of the FTSE 100 either no longer exist or are no longer in the top 100 companies of the UK. In 2018, over 20 companies left the Fortune 500. Only 60 companies that were in the Fortune 500 in 1955 were still in it in 2017.

What economist Joseph Schumpeter called "creative destruction"—the death of old businesses and business models because of the innovation of new, better adapted ones—is speeding up. Human beings took three centuries to create and optimize the wheel. Apple releases (often breakthrough) new products every few months to stay in step with its fast-changing customers' needs, wants, and expectations (like privacy, for example).

We cannot try to stay neutral in the digital, disrupted, and damaged world and hope to get out of the workplace into retirement. We all have to deal with the Transformational Challenges and global crises at hand. There is nowhere to hide because even in a villa by the sea in Carmel or Provence, sea waters will rise, extreme weather will hit people, pension funds and stocks will dive with every pandemic, and descendants will look to us for answers. Therefore we either play our part in fitting the future that is emerging or we fail, whether through underperformance or obsolescence.

Any failure to adapt in step with the rapid changes in the external world will cost the organizations that pay us, the teams that rely on us, the loved ones who care about us, and the children for whom we are responsible. Failure can be spectacular, like bankruptcy or a fall from grace; or it can be more insidious, such as a long, slow decrease in competitiveness; or a gradual loss of value and relevance as an individual in the workplace.

Not only are our own enterprises at risk, but so are all the livelihoods that are reliant on them; and the various forms of social and economic capital stored within them. Our species is really at risk if our leaders—and that means you and me—blindly, blinkers super-glued on, speed up a socioeconomic system that works for very, very few (and even they aren't really helped much by a polluted, hot, wet, sea levels-rising, virus-laden, highly stressed out world).

Our social and economic system is fading from relevance and the pain of this is showing up everywhere. Simply put, we cannot accelerate the absolutely necessary Great Transformation to a regenerative global socioeconomic system without deep adaptation of *every* enterprise. It is adapt or die at the level of our entire species; and all the civilizations we have developed to date.

The only way out is to adapt in step with the world. Then we do not just fit the future, but we can actually play a part in forging the future. We can leverage our insights as transformational leaders to guide the systems we are part of to manifest our vision of a better world: a vision based on genuine heartfelt purpose and not just craving for accumulation and extraction of profit. If not, the way out will just bring us back in again.

However, we can only forge the future we want to see if we are prepared to not just improve how we do things incrementally but also transform how we do things exponentially. We cannot tweak the old model, based on the old rules, indefinitely and expect to lead the change. Of course we need to continue to drive best practices in our teams and organizations; and ensure efficiencies improve on legacy activities. Yet we also must be prepared to transform *everything* we do continuously. We must be ready to invent next practice constantly. We will all need to transform protocols, policies, processes, and products *many times* in the years to come.

Adapt Or Die: Invitation to Engage

Q. Which signals or symptoms of mismatch do you recognize in your enterprise and your career? Which energize you most to transform?

Q. Which signals or symptoms of mismatch do you recognize in your industry, sector, or system? Which energize you most to transform?

Q. Which customer and employee complaints might be cause for a moment for reflection to ask: is what I do, and how I do it, a fit for the way the world is going?

10

THE TRANSFORMATION IMPERATIVE

In a world that is rapidly transforming, with a new Network Operating System emerging—powered by digital, disrupted, and damaged drivers of change—we must stop thinking about innovation as something that someone else in the business 'should' do, sporadically, within specific projects in order to make short-term gains with as little risk as possible. We must no longer think of innovation as anything other than a special case of continuous transformation and adaptation. We must see innovation as something *everyone* in the organization does, continuously and relentlessly, to ensure that all our products, processes, and people stay relevant and match fit for the future. This is the Transformation Imperative.

While managers want to maintain predictable returns by optimizing the existing (business/operating/delivery/financial/talent) model, leaders must be guiding products, processes, and people to adapt to fit the world as it is emerging. We can't transform everything at the same time, but we must be constantly seeking insight from customers and other users about where our products, processes, and people are not fitting, and then prioritize where transformation is needed most.

We must develop skills in how to spot what is 'breaking down' and is no longer a good fit for the world, even if it was of value in the past; and what is 'breaking through' and therefore shows that there is a source of value in the future. These insights, which arise naturally when we open-mindedly and open-heartedly acknowledge that something is not working—and then seek to penetrate the hidden order of things to find out why—fuel the creativity, agility, and passion we need to adapt our products, purchases, and people in real time to stay in tune with the changing world.

This Transformation Imperative is not new. It's just a new way of articulating what we've known from Charles Darwin and decades of evolutionary science: all organisms/organizations must continuously adapt or they die. This is perhaps the fundamental law of biology. However, over the last few decades, most people in medium and large organizations, and enterprises in stable or government-protected industries, have been protected from the stark realities of evolutionary pressures.

Modern Industrial Age institutions, with access to land and capital—and so the means of production and the means of distribution of products and services—have prevented new entrants into markets. Lobbying activities have been focused on maintaining privileged access to markets. Rightly or wrongly, power and regulations have created a defensive wall around the people who work in organizations, sheltering them from environmental pressures. This has been going on for so long in some cases that the people within haven't got much muscle in agility and adaption. Many managers have spent their days focusing on performance, following the rules (both of the market and line managers), and playing power games to rise up the corporate ladder.

Suddenly, with the digital world allowing new entrants to disrupt market after market—and with fickle customers and consumers changing their loyalties based on not just product quality but purpose quality, too—everyone in every institution is now feeling the fierce force of evolutionary pressures, whether they are a President or a PA. Pandemics and climate change add to the challenges. The defensive walls that once protected institutions from competition are crumbling, allowing in nimble upstarts; but also fresh insights.

This means that every leader, within every organization, is now impacted by the rapidly changing environment; and the pressure to adapt that comes from the three drivers of the digital, disruptive, and damaged world. Every organization and every leader is exposed—without exception—and must now enact continuous transformations to stay fitted. As IBM's CEO Ginni Rometty has put it, "The only way you survive is you continuously transform into something else. It's this idea of continuous transformation that makes you an innovation company."

The sooner people awaken to the reality that it is adapt or die at an unprecedented scale, at every level of society, the sooner they move from fear and resistance to enthusiasm and action. If we can't embrace the Transformation Imperative, there is only one ending: a descent, whether slow or rapid, into underperformance, irrelevance, and ultimately obsolescence. There is nothing good or bad, moral or immoral, about this. It just is the nature of things. And the quicker we get our heads around it, the better off we and our organizations will be.

Those of us who are not willing or able to adapt to the radical changes in our ecology and culture through the process of continuous transformation will find themselves irrelevant and obsolete. We know from evolution that, when species do not adapt fast enough, they die out. Natural history is littered with species that weren't able to adapt, including various hominids. We are forcing more than a few to extinction with Industrial Age thinking.

A failure to adapt has top execs fired for sexual abuse or financial 'irregularities'; media personalities deselected for using racist tropes; senior leaders sidelined and made redundant for remaining social and ethical dinosaurs; and our politicians fail adequately to limit carbon to prevent runaway climate change. This led Barack Obama to say, "If you look at the world and look at the problems it's usually old people, usually old men, not getting out of the way." We need to get out of the way of ourselves by shifting our mindsets and embracing new ways of thinking. Only by doing this, sometimes many times a day, can we act on the transformation imperative and do our very best to stay both surviving and thriving. We may not make it. But at least it won't be because we were not willing or able to adapt.

In the corporate world, an unwillingness to adapt leads companies to fail, most spectacularly when they crumble and fall. Not that long ago, when I consulted with them on innovating retail experiences, Nokia had over 40% of the global mobile phone market. Almost one in two phones on the planet were Nokias. Within just a few years it was only selling $10 'dumb' phones. Why? It failed to respond to changes in customer needs and desires that companies like Apple and Samsung tapped into when they perfected the design, marketing, and app-led ecosystems of the smartphone. Nokia failed to adapt willingly and fast enough. Period.

It does not work to leave transformation to the last minute. In the immortal words of the late General Electric CEO Jack Welch (one of the 55 companies still in the Fortune 500 from 1955): "Change before you have to." If we leave transformation until it is too late—and environmental pressures develop into full-blown crises—we usually no longer have the time, resources, will, energy, resilience, and trust needed to land the transformations that are needed. The concrete world of process, service experience, and product changes lags far behind the world of beliefs and feelings. Therefore companies need to have a consciousness shift that fully recognizes the Transformation Imperative *before* their problems become full-blown crises that threaten their existence. Otherwise, they are unlikely to have the time needed to embed change. Even more useful is for leaders to respond to their Transformation Imperative so early—and with such foresight—that they develop "preadaptations." Preadaptive transformations become increasingly valuable as the world continues its relentless march towards being ever more digital, disrupted, and damaged. Preadaptations 'inoculate' the organization against failure—and allow it to forge the future instead. This is what has allowed the tech giants to thrive so extraordinarily through the pandemic and beyond.

It is still risky to transform and innovate. Creative responses to emerging changes will never be perfect the first time. New ideas always need iteration, testing, and development. But in this VUCA world, I firmly believe that it is now riskier *not* to adapt, transform, and innovate proactively. The writing is on the wall for all processes and products that evolved in a world that no longer fully exists.

Transformation Imperative: Invitation to Engage

Q. What is the nature of the Transformation Imperative in your industry or space?

Q. What is your organization doing about it?

Q. What are you doing about it?

11

TRANSFORMATIONAL CHALLENGES

The typical responses of an established organization to our dramatically changing VUCA world is to do what it has already done, just faster and better. In the motor industry, GM and Ford responded to the decline of car purchase and car driving among younger generations by employing a youth advertising agency (MTV's off-shoot) and marketing the Fiesta in the US, respectively. Neither of these did much to resolve the problem because the steady decline of drivership among Millennials, and younger generations, is not a 'technical problem' to fix with known solutions (advertise more, make smaller cars, etc.) but a "transformational challenge."

The only way to resolve such a challenge is to metabolize it willingly into transformational solutions (like car-sharing, ride-sharing, cycle-sharing). But the mindsets of senior leaders in the automotive industry stopped them from seeing the real problem beneath the perceived problem. They were hampered by their blinkered and limited consciousness. This is why Ronald Heifetz and Marty Linksy wrote in their book, *The Practice of Adaptive*

Leadership, "the most common cause of failure in leadership is produced by treating adaptive challenges [Transformational Challenges] as if they were technical problems."[1]

Kodak had the same issue: even as photo-sharing sites like Instagram were blossoming, smartphones were being given away with digital cameras, and people were becoming less interested in printing images, Kodak spent a fortune installing ten thousand printers in retail outlets across the US. The mindsets of senior managers could not see that the issue was not a technical problem— how to get conventional printing solutions to people—but a Transformational Challenge: what are mass-market consumers going to want and need in the sphere of 'imagery'?

While Instagram was being created by less than 10 people in a year, Kodak—with all its smart executives and management consultants—spent a decade managing the decline of a Fortune 50 business because their mindset, their consciousness, could not see or embrace the issue as a Transformational Challenge. All they saw, with all their intelligence, was a technical problem to solve with known solutions. Leaders in every organization need to relook at technical problems to see if they are actually Transformational Challenges in disguise. Are the symptoms of a lack of fit with the market solvable with existing fixes or do they need adaptive, creative, transformational responses?

Ironically, the number two in the photographic film market, Fujifilm, saw the decline of film photography as a survival threat and embraced it as a Transformational Challenge. It embarked on a multi-year major transformation journey that has resulted in them growing into a $20 billion business with its imagery expertise transformed into products and services across healthcare to consumer electronics. In fact, you are probably a customer of Fujifilm because its technology is in most smartphones. What of Nokia and its smartphones? The tragedy at the heart of the fall of Nokia is that just as Kodak invented the digital camera in 1974—but told the inventor not to tell anyone about it—Nokia also invented the very technology that disrupted them: the smartphone! This ably demonstrates that it is not access to technology or capital that is the most important factor in forging the future of our digital, disrupted, and damaged world. The crucial factor is having *people* whose mindset, whose consciousness, can harness emerging technologies *and adapt them to the fast-changing human beings who must use, buy, sell, and value them.*

Nokia had the technology it needed to forge the future of the smartphone market. It didn't have the mindsets, and culture, necessary to make it happen. While the consciousness of Nokia's leaders *assumed* the smartphone was a phone first and then some extra features, leaders at Apple saw it as a full-spectrum portable computer; with added phone features. This simple transformation in consciousness—that showed up as a powerful consumer "insight" into the future of the mobile space—led to a profound transformation in a global market that has impacted billions.

Whereas industry experts saw through the same lens as Nokia's leaders—one Bloomberg analyst said that "[t]he iPhone's impact will be minimal. It will only appeal to a few gadget freaks. Nokia and Motorola have nothing to worry about"—Apple and Samsung were inventing a new industry. Nokia and Motorola failed to adapt in time. Where Nokia saw technical problems, Apple embraced a Transformational Challenge: how to engage people all over the world with a mobile computer that was a delight to use and full of value-creating software.

At the time of writing, the coronavirus has rippled through the world sending people to their death and stocks crashing. Western governments responded with unprecedented fiscal stimuli and social changes. Yet most did not act decisively until mid- to late-March 2020. Both Donald Trump and Boris Johnson were cracking jokes about it, and shaking hands with people, well into March; even as hundreds were being reported dead in Wuhan, China. The prestigious medical journal, *The Lancet*, published a peer-reviewed research study by Chinese scientists on January 24th 2020, stating that the Covid-19 "infection caused clusters of severe respiratory illness similar to severe acute respiratory syndrome coronavirus and was associated with ICU admission and high mortality."[2] In several papers, scientists talked about the importance of protective equipment; and trace and testing capability.

Having been criticized by the world for not sharing data on SARS, Chinese scientists took the time to collect the data and publish the study in a foreign language, in a Western journal, even as the crisis was hitting them. Yet the consciousness of Western leaders—and their most senior scenting and medical advisor—simply did not see this as the Transformational Challenge that it was/is. They saw it as a technical problem that could be solved with actions developed to deal with the seasonal flu.

Add to this the low-level consciousness that delivers Trumpian hubris and outdated American exceptionalism—and Johnsonian buffoonery and outdated British exceptionalism—and we had/have a recipe for disaster. As I write, the world is struggling to adapt to the crisis physically, medically, socially, and economically; and a few will see it as the invitation for the total socioeconomic transformation that it is. Maintaining a leadership consciousness that denies or ignores transformation challenges in favor of focusing on familiar technical problems costs lives and livelihoods. The editor of *The Lancet* went on to state that our leaders "missed opportunities" and made "appalling misjudgments" that led to "the avoidable deaths of tens of thousands of citizens."

Transformational Challenges illustrate that there is a source of value in the future that we can explore and exploit *if we can transform our consciousness*—our ideas and assumptions—sufficiently to then transform our actions, decisions, and models. If we react to such challenges by denying, dismissing, or diminishing them (and despairing), we will not be able to transform our activities and enterprises in time. We refuse the call, the invitation, that shows up in the signals and symptoms of a mismatch: between what we do and how the world is.

It is only by shifting our mindset from seeking to find and fix technical problems—which may feel safe within our comfort zone—to being curious about Transformational Challenges, that we can rise to the unique Transformation Imperatives of our organization and system.

Transformational Challenges: Invitation to Engage

Q. What Transformational Challenges might your organization be treating as technical problems? What Transformational Challenges for your career might you be treating as technical problems?

Q. Where is your organization like Kodak? Where is it like Fujifilm? What is this costing your organization and your career?

Q. What could speed up recognition of Transformational Challenges in your organization and in yourself?

12

TRIPLE-LOOP LEARNING

What prevents leaders from recognizing and then solving Transformational Challenges is their *own* outdated beliefs and assumptions about what is right and wrong for their market, space, or career. These outdated assumptions are locked in place by the emotional desire to feel right, in control, and clever. This desire can easily become an addiction which then prevents insights from colleagues, and emerging customers, from challenging our assumptions.

'Smart' managers are so convinced that they are right—about their business model, political ideology, or the meaning of life—that they cannot adapt, change, and grow as times change. Conventional intelligence—rational, technological, and analytical—is exactly what we *don't* need when we try to solve complex Transformational Challenges; at least, not until the time has come for technical expertise and operational execution to implement fresh thinking.

Professor Sydney Finkelstein, who wrote a book called *Why Smart Executives Fail*, studied over 50 organizations that have declined into irrelevance and how managers were reposing for this. His summary is clear: "failures are caused by flawed executive mindsets [assumptions] that throw off a company's perception of reality, and delusional attitudes [craving being right] that keep this accurate reality in place."

As I will explain in more detail later, locking in old and outdated beliefs are always emotions: wanting to feel right, fear of change, needing to be in control, anger from the past, and many more emotions that swirl around our bodies and distort everything they touch. By transforming emotions through developing wisdom, leaders can change how they think, developing further complexity in their intellect. Then leaders come up with the insights, intuitions, and innovations their systems/communities/enterprises need to transform, adapt, and thrive into the future. Leaders support what is already seeking to emerge from a complex, adaptive system.

At the heart of every breaking down organization, market, or system—in decline because it does not fit with the changing world—is a set of ideological, political, and psychological assumptions in our consciousness. These are then anchored in by powerful emotions, such as those that stem from trauma. The assumptions help us feel safe, in control, and 'right'. Plato called such comfortable and convenient assumptions 'noble lies'. They are wrong and misguided. But they are noble because they serve a purpose, usually one of cohesion and control.

Such assumptions lock us into mismatched products, services, and business models because when we hold onto them we cannot think new thoughts. We end up developing strategies and plans from within our assumption-base—this is best practice from years of experience solving technical problems—which then fail to solve the Transformational Challenges. As the saying goes, assumptions are the mother of all . . . mistakes. Every fail has within it a kernel of an assumption that no longer fits the dramatically changing world.

To rise to a Transformational Challenge fully, we must question *all* our assumptions, no matter how cherished. This is what I call "triple-loop learning." Building on the organizational thinker Chris Argyris' work with single-loop and double-loop learning, I believe that every fail/mistake we make or witness can be learned from in three ways; through three learning loops:

1. What the fail/mistake tells us about how to optimize a specific process, policy, or product to solve a technical problem that remains an issue (for example, how Kodak could get printing technology to people, or how government can stop disease transmission as fast as possible).

2. What the fail/mistake tells us about whether there is a Transformational Challenge our enterprise or organization can solve with value-creating and digitally-driven innovations that forge the future (for example, how Fujifilm saw the need to adapt rapidly away from printing technology and into imaging innovation, or how a government can maintain livelihoods in a VUCA reality with innovations like Universal Basic Income).

3. What the fail/mistake tells us about whether our entire industry or system has a Transformational Challenge to respond to within the ever more damaged world which is leading us off an existential cliff (for example, how an imaging business might help resolve blindness driven by an explosion of diabetes, or how the G20 might recalibrate capitalism in the wake of failure to cope with climate change or a pandemic).

At the core of the four crises of the Anthropocene—that are threatening everything we hold dear—are a series of assumptions whose veracity and fit with reality need challenging in order to allow transformation to occur. The Industrialization Crisis is caused and/or exacerbated by a series of assumptions such as: the idea that there are limitless raw materials for industrial usage; the scaling of linear production processes that see social and environmental footprints as 'externalities' outside of balance sheets; the privileging of economies of scale that drive GDP growth over care work (nursing, social work, teaching etc.); the belief in manipulative marketing to scale unnecessary desires to meet expanding supply (fueling industries like Fast Fashion, which consumes 25% of worldwide chemicals and drives 20% of worldwide water pollution); the idea that we are only ever enough with the 'right' luxury brand, holiday home, or car; the belief that fossil fuels—which have enabled a sustained population explosion—are cheap and abundant with no social or environmental costs; and the notion that human beings are simply self-interested maximizers of their individual reality rather than collaborative optimizers of a shared reality.

The Inequality Crisis is caused and/or exacerbated by a series of assumptions such as: the ideal of meritocracy that locks people into working long hours to make it in a game that evidence shows has been rigged from the start; an ideological belief in *laissez-faire* and trickle-down economics spreading wealth and wellbeing without the need for redistributive and progressive taxes; the idea that businesses exist solely to return short-term profits for shareholders and should do whatever they can, within the law, to avoid paying taxes; the creation of debt by banks that allows rentiers to grow wealth without work; outdated (and frankly racist) ideas of what different classes, races, and ethnicities should expect from life; and the relentless ideological logic of a form of globalization decoupled from human dignity and connectivity.

The Illness Crisis is caused and/or exacerbated by a series of assumptions such as: the idea that low-fat, high-carbohydrate food is healthy; the notion that cheap sugars should be sold to people via advertising-triggered addictions; that the sedentary lifestyle of late-modernity is an ideal to aim for; that education should be about facts rather than about life skills and wisdom; that productivity and wealth-creation are more valuable than community and health-creation; that money is more important than meaning and convenience more important than connection; and that productivity from technologies takes priority over parental presence; that power, profit, and prestige trump care, connection, and compassion.

The Identity Crisis is caused and/or exacerbated by a series of assumptions such as: colonial mindsets and closed minds; a fear of, and aggression towards, the Other that can only be neutralized by an expansion of our caring and compassion; a mass desire to migrate—fueled by economic inequality, climate change, and oppression—destabilizing ethnic identities and a sense of a cohesive community; resentment due to a loss of dignity after long-term wage stagnation, endless rises in the cost of living and learning, and the advent of meaningless jobs; arrogant elitism and inequitable power/ knowledge dynamics from professionalized expertise leading to a mistrust of elites and experts; the belief that the nation-state is an appropriate source of identity—and unit of organization—in a networked world; and the unmitigated costs of a globalization agenda that is blind to meaning, membership, mastery, and majesty.

There will always be signs and signals that a set of assumptions are no longer a fit with the way the world is (if indeed they ever were). If we leaders ignore them, with willful arrogance or unconscious ignorance, we will block the transformation that is possible in the space. Pressure will build up and eventually burst in the space in the form of an emergency. This is just how nature works. Transformation is "biodynamic": it is responsive to the live changes within in a living system. We don't get to choose when transformation needs to occur. But we do get to choose how we act/react in the moment to the failures, signals, and mistakes that are in front of us. We either block the biodynamic emergence of future-proofing transformations with our outdated beliefs. Or we can 'get out of the way' of ourselves and the transformation by letting go of the noble lies that resist it.

Triple-Loop Learning: Invitation to Engage

Q. What mistake has your organization made recently that provides useful insight about how to optimize a specific process, policy, or product to serve existing needs and customer types?

Q. What mistake has your organization made recently that provides useful insight about how to transform a specific process, policy, or product to serve emerging needs or customer types?

Q. What mistake has your organization made recently that provides useful insight about how to transform your entire industry to future-proof it—and shift our world to a regenerative economy where everyone thrives?

13

LEADERSHIP CONSCIOUSNESS IS KING

Our individual assumptions as leaders, and our collective assumptions as an organization or society, are what block natural evolutions and biodynamic transformations from taking place. However, it is how we emotionally guard these assumptions that causes the most problems as others—whether team members, collaborators, vendors, or customers—with different views and perspectives are ignored. Assumptions are maintained because people, particularly senior managers, love *feeling* right.

In *Ringtone: Exploring the Rise and Fall of Nokia in Mobile Phones*, the authors state that "[those] who experienced Nokia's decline first-hand described to us how negative emotional dynamics at the very top harmed communication and strategic decision-making. An authoritarian culture of fear pervaded multiple levels of management, producing a shoot-the-messenger mentality and rampant defensiveness. Fearing for their jobs, managers stayed quiet when top leaders latched onto losing strategic options."

Redundant, mismatched, outdated leadership assumptions prevented a top-ten global brand from adapting. This was a mindset issue not a physical or technological issue. This was a failure of leadership consciousness. Likewise, Western governments' tardy, reluctant, and weak responses to the Covid-19 pandemic was a failure of leadership consciousness not technical capability or operational power.

The "outer game" of organizational competence—strategy, innovation, tactics, operations, marketing—is a direct result of the "inner game" of its people, most importantly its leaders. I learned this the hard way. For years, my business just did strategic innovation and business model invention for companies. We would take a brief about a market that an organization had ambitions to grow within. We would identify with the lead client a suite of Transformational Challenges that its enterprise could solve. We would go off and find "weak signals" of the future in the present through precedents from other markets and through lots of insight-generating ethnographic, qualitative, and quantitative research.

Then we would run sophisticated innovation and design thinking workshops to turn future-forward insights into innovation ideas. We would turn those ideas into fully-fledged concepts. Then we would design rich user experiences and business models around each concept. We would look at feasibility and profitability forecasts for each to help make investment decisions. We would prototype innovations with smart experiments. We would work out how best to market and brand complex ideas to customers not used to them. Finally, we would come back to the business and present innovation road maps to senior leaders that included incremental changes, significant changes, and transformational innovations that could —together and over time—fully forge the future.

Then . . . 9 times out of 10, nothing much would happen. This became such a consistent experience that I realized it was a Transformational Challenge for me as a leader. Engaging in triple-loop learning, I realized I needed to transform our business model and the Theory of Change that underpinned it. I also realized through this process that the innovation consulting industry was hastening our social and ecological demise by generating 'unmet needs' driving consumer addictions; and by generating endless carbon/waste to satisfy these needs.

The deep insights I garnered from leadership reflection and introspection included the fact that, without leaders who can feel new feelings, think new thoughts, and act new actions, organizations cannot forge the future. In more than 20 years of advising some of the world's most interesting and ambitious organizations, I have seen time and time again that, without the right leadership culture and capabilities, most transformational initiatives fail.

Teams solve technical problems that involve no breakthroughs rather than Transformational Challenges, so the problems persist. Sometimes they solve Transformational Challenges but then find they do not have the leadership skills, and organizational culture, necessary to transform their enterprise. Around these, and other, insights we built the leadership development offers of *Switch On* and the regenerative business offers of *FutureMakers,* They both help organizations drive transformational outcomes in innovation and strategy that leave the world better—more sustainable, equal, healthy, united, and regenerative—*through the transformation of leaders, teams, and culture.*

In *Mastering Leadership: An Integrated Framework for Breakthrough Performance and Extraordinary Business Results*, Bob Anderson and William Adams put hard data behind my 'soft' insights. In an enormous research project, studying 50,000 leaders around the world, they discovered that, at most, only 20% of leaders are creative, responsive, and anything close to what I would call "transformational." However, those that are, drive incredible real-world results: 600% of the concrete business outcomes of 'average' leaders. That is 6x the impact. That is exponential. Read another way, the data suggest that leadership—whether good or bad, innovative or stagnant—is a driver of 38% of the results of any organization. Instead of investing in expensive IT systems or reorgs—that often fail to return significant value in a VUCA world—organizations can drive a 40% increase in performance by transforming how their leaders lead. In fact, leaders only have their own consciousness under their complete control in a fast-changing landscape. Therefore the *only* determinant of an organization's *long-term* competitive advantage, in the VUCA reality, is actually the consciousness—and so the capabilities—of its leaders.

In the same study, carried out with the Mendoza School of Business at Notre Dame, the researchers discovered that when over 70% of leaders in an organization were 'creative'—on the path toward becoming truly transformational—then revenue growth, profitability, and the stock price were in the top ten percent of the market. If most leaders were 'reactive'—controlling, blocking change, ignoring Transformational Challenges, abdicating responsibility—then business performance was in the bottom per cent of the market. If that is not a business case for transformational leadership development, I am not sure what is!

What this study also shows is that, at the very least, a full 80% of the leaders of most enterprises are out-matched by the VUCA world. They cannot respond adequately to the digital, disrupted, and damaged drivers of change. This implies that the average organization is less than half as productive as it could be if its leaders were truly transformational. As Adams and Anderson make clear, no organization cannot outperform the capabilities of its leaders (for very long). Likewise, our society cannot outperform the consciousness of its leaders, corporate and political.

In the old world, if you owned the means of production and distribution, then you could defend your market with competent managers delivering efficient outputs. But in a world where more and more people have access to new technologies, and can invent and implement disruptive business models through attracting Venture Capital, management is not enough. Only creative, adaptive transformational leadership can ensure you make it. The great secret in 21st Century business success, that they don't teach at the 'best' MBA programs is this: whomever 'owns' the vitality and agility of the culture, is responsible for fostering psychological safety and genuine empowerment, determines the style and skills of leadership needed, and ensures that transformational leadership is embodied and embedded, holds the keys to the kingdom of the future.

This will become ever more true because the speed of change outside an organization is getting faster than the people within it can process and cope with. Every product line and business function will have to re-invent itself continuously: i.e., not just one disruptive innovation program or agile process change to last a few years; but continuous transformation at all times, and forever, to adapt.

Yet most organizations do not invest nearly as much in leadership programs as they do in process and strategy upgrades. There are very few (perhaps zero) CEOs who were once HR or Learning & Development professionals in their early careers. Many HR folk who buy in leadership programs do not go on the leadership programs they buy in; so many are risk-averse and outdated in their thinking. Companies continue to buy in management programs that masquerade as leadership development but simply recapitulate the Industrial Age thinking that they evolved to serve.

Even when leadership development is taken seriously, there are still way too many classroom-based programs teaching theories and practices alone, rather than experiential journeys that upgrade leadership consciousness *at the same time as* getting leaders delivering genuine transformations to deliver exponential results.

14

THE LEADERSHIP INVITATION

Every Transformation Imperative therefore includes within it a Leadership Invitation. The invitation is simple: are you willing to look the issues you face in the eye, see them as Transformational Challenges rather than downgrade them to be technical problems, and challenge the assumptions that are locking you in place?

It doesn't matter how smart you and your executives are, how many Ivy League MBAs are in the team, how many genii are put on a strategy project, how many Oxbridge-led management consultancies are paid to help, or even how clever the strategies you develop are: if the people within your organization don't have the level of consciousness needed to respond creatively to Leadership Invitation—challenging outdated assumptions and discovering future-forward insights in their place—then your enterprise will not stay relevant. As we will soon see, we need something other than smarts to make it in the VUCA world.

In the 1980s, McKinsey, the leading management consultancy for strategy development (with many of the smartest people in the room) was paid $5 million by AT&T to develop a strategy to dominate the future of the telephony industry. McKinsey predicted that cell phone adoption by the year 2000 would be less than a million. The actual number was over 100× more: 109 million. AT&T was maladapted for the future and was disrupted by mobile-first rivals. It has arguably never recovered.

In 2000, the very smart CEO of Kodak said to very smart investors that we have "a great brand, a great balance sheet, cash flow. This is very *smart* time to be in the picture business" [my italics]. It then took 15 long, and I am sure very painful, years for Kodak to go from a $30 billion dollar business with $16 billion in annual revenues . . . to bankruptcy. During this time there were scores of intelligent and well-meaning people whose entire ten (or twelve) hour days was focused on digging Kodak out of the maladapted hole it was in. Even with reorgs and strategies resets, it failed to rise to the Transformation Imperative. During this time Kodak's share price steady declined from $92 per share to 36c.

Meanwhile, the Japanese CEO of Fujifilm rose to the challenge and accepted the invitation. Rather than keep on trying to solve an illusionary/delusional technical fix—keep people printing photos at all costs—he chose to take the business on a serious and significant transformation journey. He made a conscious choice to transform and invested a massive effort in building an innovation culture. He centralized R&D and led the company on a journey to interrogate emerging customer needs and matching each need to existing and potential capabilities. He ensured that the organization reconceived itself as in a different business sector, and invested heavily in transformation.

As transformation takes time, short-term profits dropped (but less than Kodak). In 2011, shares lost 1/3 of their value. The CEO had "many, sleepless nights." It would have been easy to drop the invitation and give up or try and go back. But he persevered and Fujifilm pioneered products in biotech, cosmetics, chemicals, and

Liquid Crystal Displays. Between 2000 and 2010, Fujifilm revenues practically *doubled* from 1.4 trillion yen to 2.2 trillion. In the same period, the bigger, stronger, more respected Kodak saw it halve from $14 billion to $7 billion.

This kind of result can only be delivered when we accept the invitations that the VUCA world offer each of us as leaders. You will be given many such invitations in the digital, disrupted, and damaged future in which you must lead. To accept the invitation, you need to metabolize the Transformational Challenges with which you are faced and turn them into value through the transformation of your consciousness. The invitation brings you to a "metabolization moment" or "MetaMo": a decision point where the path of your organization and career bifurcates into two.

To not choose transformation is a choice. To hope you can survive with tweaks to the existing model(s) is as much of a decision as investing time, energy, and resources in transformation is. In a MetaMo you have two options: The first is to recognize the reality that you must adapt; and then step up as a transformational leader to make adaptation happen. The other choice is to procrastinate, defend the current model, commission a report, and/or to delay, dismiss, or downgrade the nature and urgency of the Transformation Imperative. As the CEO of Fujifilm said of his once stronger competition: "Kodak was the premier company for so long. This, I believe, made it slow to adapt. From the outside, it appeared that Kodak deep down *just really didn't want to*." My italics.

Most senior leaders I meet recognize the need for more conscious, creative, and collaborative leaders; and more agile, adaptable, and transformational cultures. But few want to pay for them; or take the time to implement them properly. Senior managers often expect people and culture to change as easily as machines and code do. Many have little patience for how much time, energy, money, and commitment it takes to cultivate truly transformational leaders. Few CEOs want to deal with messy, complex human beings (which we all are!) It seems much easier, and more concrete, to measure progress in productivity, process implementation, or planning than it does in culture-change and leadership development. So that's where the big bucks go . . . even as the business loses its competitive edge year after year because many MetaMos are missed.

This truth has been very humbling for me. As I pivoted my entire business and career around my own Leadership Invitation to transform, I went from being in my twenties jetting around the planet running high-profile innovation projects for the world's most successful companies. . . to being in my late forties running mistakenly-called 'training' workshops in low-cost hotel rooms. It's much less glamorous working in leadership development and culture-change than innovation and strategy consulting. Budgets are far, far smaller and much harder to get hold of. C-Suite airtime is far less; and senior leaders often pay you less respect (until they go through a program, that is).

But the elemental fact is that, without consciousness shifts in leaders, then concrete transformations—like that exhibited by Fujifilm—cannot occur. They don't teach you this in Management School (at least not the ones at which I have lectured). Few on the Boards of most organizations seem aware of this abiding truth (until they are humbled, too, by external events). Most management consultants, selling shiny new process architectures, digital transformation programs, agile processes, new IT systems, and restructures, think the idea anathema (which is why so many of these change programs fail to make a lasting difference). I have even discovered that many of those in HR have not yet realized how important and powerful they are in future-proofing their organization.

However, it is never too late to switch on to the power of leadership and reinvent an enterprise with it. Nokia again proves a fertile example. While reactive and arrogant leadership at the top contributed fundamentally to its humbling downfall, a shift in leadership culture created the conditions for its current path to reinvention. In 2012, the Chairperson and much of the Board were replaced. The new Chair realized that he needed to instill a culture of radical openness. He led by example, cascading transformational principles from the top down: such as 'no news is bad news, bad news is good news, and good news is no news'.

As he said: "If the board is a place where the management comes with knees trembling, a single solution in their mind, that they need to sell to the Board, there is no way for the Board to contribute." While not returning quite to the heights it achieved in its heyday, Nokia is now back delivering transformational innovations to the world, predominately in mobile network equipment. It even placed in the Forbes Top 100 Digital Companies in 2019.

Leadership Invitation: Invitation to Engage

Q. Where might assumptions about what business you are in, and what business model is 'right', be holding you and your organization back?

Q. Where is your leadership consciousness becoming mismatched and outdated?

Q. What might the invitation be for you to step up your leadership consciousness to deliver organizational competence?

15

TRANSFORMATIONAL LEADERSHIP

There are many, many types of leadership; probably as many as there are leadership coaches and 'trainers'. I find this word troubling as great 'training' does not train people but instead cultivates the conditions for them to lead and land change themselves precisely because they have been untrained (and so are limitless). Having been in the leadership 'industry' for almost two decades, I believe that *transformational leadership* includes yet transcends all others. It is perhaps the ultimate form of leadership. It is certainly the most well-adapted to the current VUCA environment.

Transformational leadership is the only form of leadership that can make the most out of the opportunities of the Network O.S. and so help our species enact the Great Transformation before it is too late. Transformational leadership is what we need to engage fully and wholeheartedly with the four crises that impact us all: Industrialization, Inequality, Illness, Identity. Transformational leadership is what we need to mitigate the serious risks each crisis entails; and to also seize the many opportunities for exponential value creation each opens up so we can together co-create a regenerative world where life flourishes.

The unique challenges of our era demand that many more leaders switch on and step up to become truly transformational. Without transformational leadership, your best efforts at adaptive strategies, agile processes, disruptive and business model innovation, net-positive sustainable supply chains, deep culture-change, digital transformation, purposeful businesses, and ecosystem-wide innovations will fail; or at least fail to deliver on their potential for exponential returns. Given the fast- and furiously-changing environment, with all its endless and troubling evolutionary pressures, if you are not consistently working to deliver continuous transformations across products, processes, and people—as opposed to managing predictable returns through tweaking the existing model with incremental changes—then there is no leadership. If there is no need for transformation, then there is no need for leadership. Management will suffice.

Yet, as you hopefully see, management is necessary but not sufficient to avoid being disrupted in the VUCA reality; or to execute disruption yourself. As the *Wall Street Journal* put it: "market-leading companies have missed game-changing transformations in industry after industry not because of 'bad' management, but because they followed the dictates of 'good' management." 'Good' management maintains and improves existing best practice. It was never designed to invent and experiment with possible next practices. Management theory evolved to maximize the outputs of machines (and people considered to be like machines). It did not evolve for rapid adaptation and creative responsivity. Management tries to improve what has already worked, not challenge assumptions and explore new ways that might solve bigger problems in more value-creating ways.

This is why managers at Kodak kept optimizing the hell out of the film photography and printing model—assuming customers had constant and stable pain points around wanting to print out their images—rather than inventing a new model that solved new pain points—like how do I connect with people using images—as the old business model became obsolete. As a former Senior Vice-President of Kodak admitted: "Kodak management didn't fully recognize that the rise of digital imaging would have dire consequences for the future of photo printing . . . they could have tried to compete on capabilities rather than on the markets it was in, but this would have meant walking away from a great consumer franchise. That's not the logic that managers learn at business schools, and it would have been a hard pill for Kodak leaders to swallow." Business schools exist to teach management. They rarely cultivate transformational leadership.

In its simplest form, I define Transformational Leadership as the ability to metabolize constant change in the outside world into concrete value inside our organizations and communities through the products, processes, and people we transform. We are able to metabolize change not just once, but many times, as times change. I understand a "transformation" as a sustained and valuable change—that could not be predicted by extrapolating the past—that drives positive and exponential impact with problems that really matter in the world. By continuously leading and landing transformations, we ensure that whatever group, community, organization, or society we lead remains fitted to the rapidly changing environment.

We make sure that no mismatches exist long enough to make us, and our organization, fail. We are quick to recognize and act on signals of fading. We are always looking for "weak signals" of value sources of the future in the present. As a result, we retain our value in the world, as individuals and organizations. We maintain our right to continue to exist by generating value. In business, that means being paid to solve important pain points for customers that they cannot solve themselves. As the people are ever more empowered, then we continuously have to lead transformations that solve emerging pain points, not needs that they either no longer feel to be painful; or have found ways to resolve themselves.

Transformation is not violent rebellion or aggressive revolution that seeks to upend the existing order by attacking, denigrating, and diminishing it. Transformation is caring and compassionately critical: it carefully includes old patterns of order and organization—recognizing and honoring the value and role of each element that came before as adaptive to the moment in the past—yet courageously transcends these patterns to allow novelty to emerge that fits the world better. Transformation refigures and reshapes historical/legacy elements of value, in a product or policy, while allowing genuinely new ones to emerge that are sparked by deep insight into the needs, wants, and pain of current and emerging users.

Transformational leaders consciously seek to avoid the repetitive and damaging cycles of revolution-reaction, and blanket rejection of the old only to recapitulate outdated elements unconsciously. They must be strong, adaptive, and proactive, not defensive, brittle, and defiant. Transformation cannot be predicted by the past, but it honors it, includes it, and returns to it in order to free up the present for the future that is rushing headlong toward us. In the words of Lao Tzu, (probable) author of the *Tao Te Ching*: "the Way of heaven profits without destroying."

To be a transformational leader we have to take ownership of changes in the environment and transmute them with our creativity and insight into exponentially value-creating and transformational innovations; and then land these innovations through excellent execution in the markets and systems of which we're a part. These transformations—whether in business models, culture, or strategy (and usually all three)—then ensure that our enterprises, our employees, and the ecosystems we are part of thrive into the future—no matter what challenges we face and no matter how tough the environmental pressures get.

As a former medic, I use the word metabolize very specifically. Metabolization is the process by which the cells in our bodies take in nutrients and resources from the outside world in the form of food and converting the energy and the micronutrients within them into value in our body. This is what our billions of cells are doing, day in, day out, and it's the same for transformational leadership. We take changes out there that show up as pandemics, or climate change, or decking market share, into ourselves—into our consciousness, within the wetware of our brains and bodies—and apply our human brilliance to them. We turn problems into opportunities; customer pain points into user possibilities; employee frustrations into team freedom. This is the beauty inherent in each MetaMo.

The absolute key to transformational leadership is realizing that, in order to metabolize constant change into concrete value, we have to be ready to change *our own* beliefs and behaviors. We must be prepared to transform our own thoughts, our own assumptions, our own habits, our own reactions, our own activities, and our own emotions inside us: otherwise we will think and act the same while telling everyone else to change. If we remain static while hoping the world around us transforms—our team, our business partner, our organization, our community, our network, our system—we can change little about our organizations or system.

People, products, and processes only transform when someone leads and lands the change, becoming a different person himself/ herself in the process. Transformational leadership is about learning how to transform our world *from the inside out*: one transformation of our own habits of sensing, feeling, thinking, and acting at a time. We constantly move from outside in (external trends and drivers of change) to inside out (how I feel, think, and act around these environmental pressures); and back again. We ground each MetaMo in the center: in the organization within which we lead; and which must execute our transformational ideas in order to change anything concretely.

16

THE TRANSFORMATIONAL LEADER

The reactive leader/manager who cannot transform himself/herself lets things happen. Such leaders wait, hope, plan, predict. They deny reality, make excuses for failures, get pulled into melodrama, cover up signs of mismatches, and blame other people, competitors, or 'the market' for problems. The transformational leaders ensure that things happen because of them. They adapt, reflect, challenge their own assumptions, come up with creative responses, and act. They acknowledge reality, learn from failure, use mistakes for triple-loop learning, and see all problems as Transformational Challenges to be metabolized.

I don't believe it is very helpful to hero-worship any leader. Each has his/her strengths and failings. However, I will use the example of Nelson Mandela to demonstrate the role of self-transformation in transformational leadership (not because he is a saint or sage). Mandela, like all of us do, had many failures and foibles. Being a transformational leader is never about being perfect. It's about constantly developing, learning, and expanding our consciousness so we can be of more use in the world. Mandela provides an amazing example of someone whose individual transformation enabled him to enact profound transformation in his nation and possibly the global socioeconomic system.

As a young man, Nelson Mandela was understandably angry at, and frustrated by, the racist Apartheid system in South Africa. He attempted to solve this problem through angry activism and violent protest. As a result, he was incarcerated, not just for his political beliefs, but because of his actions as part of a violent resistance movement. But, while in prison, a fellow inmate reportedly smuggled in a book by the Stoic philosopher (and Roman Emperor) Marcus Aurelius. The book, *Meditations*, contains insights about how we can shift our consciousness around external events that we cannot control. Mandela said that a particular passage was transformational for him.

Marcus Aurelius, speaking to us from ancient times with remarkably contemporary vigor, states that we should: "keep this thought handy when you feel rage coming on—it isn't manly to be enraged. Rather, gentleness and civility are more human, and therefore manlier. A real person doesn't give way to anger and discontent. Such a person has strength, courage, and endurance—unlike the angry and complaining. The nearer a man comes to a calm mind, the closer he is to strength." Mandela reflected on this, and other transformational insights, for a long time years. He was in prison for twenty-seven years.

Soon after he was released, with tempers running high across the country, he spoke at an ANC rally inside a large stadium. Just before he went on stage, he was handed a note that said: "No peace. Do not talk about peace. We've had enough. Please Mr Mandela, no peace. Give us weapons. No peace." At least 300 people had been killed by the white security forces in that area during recent protests. Mandela spoke in front of a crowd of thousands, in a speech that transformed the country: "It is difficult for us to say when people are angry that they must be non-violent . . . But the solution is peace, it is reconciliation, it is political tolerance . . . We must accept that responsibility for ending violence is not just the government's, the police's, the army's. It is also our responsibility. . . . We should put our own house in order. If you have no discipline, you are not freedom fighters. If you are going to kill innocent people, you don't belong to the ANC. Your task is reconciliation."

The crowd reacted angrily to these words. Many jeered. Mandela continued: "Listen to me, listen to me . . . I am your leader. As long as I am your leader, I am going to give leadership." He went on to say many times, "as long as I am your leader, I will tell you where you are wrong." During this time, he appeared on national TV with the leader of the oppressive white minority, F.W. de Klerk.

Remember, Mandela's loved ones had died, his people had been traumatized and abused, and he himself had been jailed for most of his adult life by these people. Yet on primetime TV he reached out and held de Klerk's hand: he physically modeled peace and reconciliation to his supporters. He fully embodied the transformation he wanted to see.

Long after his release, and after being awarded the Nobel Peace Prize, he stated (on Oprah Winfrey's couch, no less) that, "If I had not been in prison, I would not have been able to achieve that most difficult task in life: changing yourself." Mandela emphatically claimed that the transformation of his own consciousness—of his own feelings, thoughts, and behaviors—was what enabled him to transform his country as a leader. He mastered himself in order to transform his system.

As he himself said: "for all people who have found themselves in the position of being in jail and trying to transform society, forgiveness is natural because you have no time to be retaliative." Thus, Mandela explicitly linked the transformation of his own personal consciousness with the transformation of the realities of his system. He saw the collective effort of societal change must start within: the locus of control or leverage point where we have most ownership and so capacity for change.

The transformation that Mandela led and landed was unprecedented. It could not have been predicted by extrapolating the past; either the past behavior of Mandela as an angry activist or that of the minority government as abusive masters. Mandela's inner peace allowed him to see and leverage a hugely transformative 'customer' insight: the white minority government was looking for a way out of Apartheid by the time that Mandela was released from prison.

The government had realized that the system it was shoring up was out of date and failing. It was buckling under evolutionary pressures: from within the country and from the international community. Mandela, the transformational leader, knew that to return to a cycle of abuser and victim would not lead to the outcome he wholeheartedly new was possible. So he harnessed a future-forward insight that arose within his open mind and heart—precisely because they were not defending assumptions and addictions—to generate exponential value with it.

Nelson Mandela is a very real example of how transforming ourselves can enable us to transform our systems. If Mandela had come out of prison with his old feelings, thoughts, beliefs, and behaviors, he would not have been able to create lasting, positive transformation. Although South Africa still has many problems, it transitioned from minority White rule to majority democratic governance with very little bloodshed when compared with other analogous societal shifts. Given how much collective trauma the people of the country had, South Africa enjoyed a remarkably peaceful transformation into a multiracial 'rainbow' nation. Transformational leadership. Exponential results.

The Transformational Leader: Invitation to Engage

Q. Where might you be wanting other people to change whilst hoping you can stay the same? Where might your comfort zone be holding you back?

Q. Where might you be blaming others—or complaining about customers/the market/politicians—rather than leading the change you want to see?

Q. Where might you be defending outdated assumptions that are blocking future-forward insights from arising within you?

PART 2
THE ANATOMY OF
TRANSFORMATIONAL LEADERSHIP

The time will come when intelligent students will have disregarded mechanistic and atomistic conceptions altogether in favor of viewing all the phenomena in terms of dynamic and chemical processes, thus making the divine life in nature more and more manifest.

Johan Wolfgang von Goethe, *Scientific Studies*, c.1795

To deny the truth of our own experience in the scientific study of ourselves is not only unsatisfactory, it is to render the scientific study of ourselves without a subject matter. But to suppose that science cannot contribute to an understanding of our experience may be to abandon, within the modern context, the task of self-understanding. Experience and scientific understanding are like two legs without which we cannot walk.

Francisco Varela & Humberto Maturana, *The Embodied Mind: Cognitive Science and Human Experience* c.1991

17

INTRODUCING BIO-TRANSFORMATION THEORY & PRACTICE

I have spent my life asking myself, in various ways and in various contexts: How do I transform my world? How do I transform myself in that world? And, once I was leading a start-up: How do I become, and remain, a transformational leader? I wanted to be able to change things in the leadership of my own life, the leadership of my wider family, the leadership of my kids, the leadership of my own enterprises, the leadership of my communities of practice (fellow innovation, leadership, and change facilitators), the leadership of our clients (for I have no vertical 'management' power with our clients, only soft 'leadership' power), and leadership of our global society. I started attempting to answer this perennial question at age 13, when I entered psychotherapy for the first time. Now, in my late 40s, I am still refining the answer.

In the intervening period, I studied, both professionally and as an amateur: human biology, medicine, psychology, psychoanalysis, Western and Eastern philosophy, systems thinking, and scenario planning. I also gain endless insights from advising large organizations how to innovate (a special case of transformation), adapt, and invent. I continue to study everything from the latest neuroscience of creativity to cutting-edge behavioral change studies; everything from the latest translations of ancient philosophical texts to emerging techniques in coaching and change management. The answer to the question—how do we human beings both lead and then land transformations in effective ways in ourselves and others—has become a much larger body of work than I first anticipated! In fact, it has become a theory, suite of processes, and a set of tools and practices of its own: Bio-Transformation Theory & Practice (BTTP).

In order to lead transformation, you must first have a theory of transformation. This is easier said than done as very few of us really stop to think about how change happens, and how best to accelerate it. To have a Theory of Transformation (ToT) about anything that involves human beings, as opposed to machines, the ToT has to be rooted in human biology: in *bios*, the Greek word for life. After all, for anyone to change his/her health or wealth, relationships and team, products and organization, and his/her system, then biologies—how brains fire and bodies—have to change first.

When it comes to change, we can't bypass biology. We can't lead change in our own lives, in our love lives and family lives, in our community groups and companies, and in our industries and systems, if we don't understand that change begins from within: in our biology. Yet, back in the 1990s, even after studying the medical sciences at one of the world's most august scientific institutions, I still had very little idea how *consciously* to change my own body and brain, let alone influence or inspire anyone else's to change, too.

Sparked by my own challenges as a leader, I began a deep dive into the available science—as well as the treasure-trove of human wisdom in our collective philosophies—to piece together a Theory of Transformation (ToT) that was robust enough to work in any domain of human endeavor. I soon realized that, while science provides us with amazing knowledge about the human brain and body, science is not enough to guide us to a mastery of transformation. Science of material nature needs alongside it a science of our inner reality—philosophy, wisdom, or what can be called the contemplative sciences—in order to provide a reasonably comprehensive and coherent ToT and philosophy of transformational leadership. As leaders, we have to jump from what the 'facts' are to how we want the world to look in the coming weeks, months, and years. To do this takes huge moral capability, skillful intuitive and insightful discernment, and great wisdom. I have written other books about the limits of science and how to marry reasons with wisdom; however to summarize, some of the reasons that science is not a complete knowledge system for the transformational leader are:

The funding for scientific studies, especially very expensive Randomized-Controlled Studies (the gold standard of scientific evidence about interventions in human systems), goes toward specific areas that scientific funders find valuable and that deliver political power, either in career advancement or in society. This means that entire swathes of human experience go unstudied. The scientific method was not developed to understand the vagaries of human consciousness and subjective experience, but to create 'hard' facts about the physical world of atoms and acceleration.

Many human science experiments have had as their subjects young Caucasian graduates as opposed to people of diverse color, ethnicity, and worldview, skewing the data and so knowledge. It has been a major challenge in the last decade to replicate many classic psychology experiments, casting their certainty in doubt. And, above all, science as a whole is a project that determines what *is* in nature not what *ought* to be in human organizations and societies. To harness user data and scientific studies to determine how you and your market 'should' be, especially when facing Transformational Challenges and crises, necessarily means leaping from scientific material into conscious wisdom.

Therefore, BTTP is informed by the three great rivers of human knowledge to make a coherent, cohesive, and compelling methodology of transformation. They are:

1. Human Sciences: Particularly the latest brain science (neurobiology); advances in behavioral, cognitive, and affective (emotional) psychology; and the sciences of complexity, networks, and chaos

2. Philosophy: Collective human insights and practices from rigorous meditation, introspection, and other contemplative sciences from both West and East (what Aristotle called *sophia)*

3. Practical Wisdom: Tools and ideas from coaching, entrepreneurship, growth hacking, mass marketing (changing behavior at the societal level), counseling, trauma therapy, and personal development (what Aristotle called *phronesis)*

These three great strands of human knowledge have been woven together with tireless rigor into BTTP. BTTP is a methodology that balances our heart-led intuitions to contribute to the world through care and compassion; with our scientific and materialist instincts to get stuff done (using evidence-based techniques that have been 'proven' to work).

Never one to pontificate from the sidelines, I've spent two decades putting all the ideas in BTTP to the test on the front lines of transformation in the business and personal spheres. I've honed and crafted the ideas and tools through helping senior leaders within ambitious organizations—from Microsoft and Intel to Unilever and HSBC to WWF and Oxfam—come up with breakthrough ideas that ensure they flourish; while supporting kick-ass starts-ups and amazing social entrepreneurs to fulfill their purpose at scale; and when training social workers, teachers, probation officers, doctors, unemployed youths, MBA students at places like Yale and Oxford, aid workers, to be empowered. I have also employed the methodology as a transformational coach on BBC TV, MTV, on radio, in lifestyle magazines and high-end newspapers, at festivals, and with celebs.

BTTP seems to work. And it appears to work each and every time, to solve massively varied problems, across radically different types of people, in a broad array of cultures and countries, and in organizations of every shape and hue.

As well as signifying 'life', the prefix *bio*-has two further and important meanings. To the Greeks, a *bios* was a life and leadership philosophy. I have always wanted a life and leadership philosophy that was practiced and consistent; and that could also nourish me, inform me, and guide me toward transforming myself sufficiently so that I could play a part in transforming the organizations and systems of which I am a leader. BTTP has within it a rigorous yet generative *bios* with which leaders can make good choices. It is a *bios* that allow us to thrive not despite the many personal and institutional challenges we face but *because* of them: because we can metabolize anything 'put upon us' into value.

Another reason for the *bio*- signifier is that BTTP is *biodynamic*, which means it is responsive to what is emerging *now*—in mind, body, relationships, team, organization, system, and environment—rather than being locked into what worked in the past (or what a facilitator, coach, therapist, or consultant assumes is 'right" way to do things). Biodynamic approaches, from healing to wine-making, are holistic: based on the whole interacting with its environment. BTTP is responsive to the actual lived experience, activity, energy, insight, and intuition of the individual leader or team to which it is being applied; as opposed to attempting to execute a fixed, predetermined strategy or plan about how things 'should' be that cannot change when circumstances demand it.

Rooted in our biologies, which are *alive*, BTTP allows us to adapt ourselves and our organizations in real time—responding creatively to new information and insight as it arises and emerges—to stay in step with the changing reality.

BTTP also has within it a process—pathway of transformation—that allows anyone to lead a team, company, or system to transform. This process, which follows a J-shaped curve that you will encounter in the final part of this book, allows us to marry up inner changes in our individual emotional and somatic bodies with changes in our collective beliefs, mindsets, and behaviors within a team.

Thus BTTP has grown past being just a life and leadership philosophy and Theory of Transformation to consist of a 6-phase transformational innovation process; an extensive transformational leadership curriculum and leadership model (covering conscious, purposeful, creative, inspirational, collaborative, and systemic leadership); 90+ proven and printable transformation tools; and 40+ brain-based transformation practices.

I will use the remainder of this book to outline some of the key elements of BTTP as they pertain to leadership; in particular, what we have come to call the 7 "gems" of BTTP. The 7 gems are:

1. The One Unified Self
2. The Two Modes of Consciousness

3. The Third Way of Creative Harmony
4. The Four Elements of Transformation in Self and Systems
5. The Five Stages of Transformational Development
6. The Six Spirals of Transformational Action
7. The Seven Steps of The Transformation Curve

Before I describe the gems in more detail, I want to locate them in context. We've looked at the outside world, using the 3D Futures Framework, to understand how it's changing; and we've looked at what these changes are demanding of leaders and their organizations with the Transformation Imperative (adapt or die); and the Leadership Invitation (adapt or fade). Now we are going to look at leadership from the inside out. We're going to look at what we can change within us to *respond* creatively to intense environmental stresses and adaptive pressures that challenge *all of us* to adapt at pace and with alacrity.

It is worth reminding ourselves of an important truism that is easy to forget when we are caught up in the illusions and delusions of proposals and plans: all transformations in *matter* originate with transformations in *mind*. Every new service idea, product innovation, stock-keeping unit (SKU), process, new line of code, new way of doing our family Christmas or Thanksgiving, or way of behaving with our kids *ultimately originates* with changes in how our nerves, most importantly our neural networks, fire.

We can't lead transformations of any kind if we don't know how to transform the very human beings—how they feel, how they think and how they act—who we need to innovate and execute transformations in our products, policies, and processes. Yet most of us have not been given even 10 hours of high-quality education on this critical topic. If, as Malcolm Gladwell has suggested, mastery of any skill takes over 10,000 hours of learning and practice, then to master transformation in ourselves and our systems will require we understand a lot more about what makes us tick; and to put in the time needed to master transformational leadership skills and practices.

However, my version of BTTP is just a map, a blueprint: one of many. No map is the territory itself. It is a model, system, method, approach designed to help us gain profound and valuable insight into how we act as leaders; and how our colleagues act as human beings; and, by understanding more about human emotion, cognition, and behavior, we can then lead people—and the organizations and systems that the people generate—to create a better and more adapted future than the one they are currently on course to deliver.

BTTP is an abstraction like any other. We can use it to gain a better understanding—and a more effective set of tools and practices—of a massively complex reality. But it is not The Truth; and it is not the ultimate and final map of human being. As a Theory of Transformation, a life and leadership philosophy— and a toolkit and practice-set—BTTP is itself alive and growing through the lived experience of those who employ it; and constantly emerging scientific evidence that improves it. Anything at all in it can be discarded if a more compelling and empowering insight or technique surfaces as time goes by.

However, I will be candid—and own my own contribution— and say that I do think BTTP is about as useful as any other maps out there. This is a result of rigorously weaving together the genius of so many giants.

I firmly believe that if you wholeheartedly leverage the principles, methodology, tools, and practices found within BTTP, you will be able to lead and execute value-creating, future-forging transformations in any area that you care about. Yet don't take my word for it. All leaders have to develop and fine-tune their own map for how to find inner peace within the storms of life and business; express their purpose fully in their projects; and lead their organizations into a regenerative future of possibility.

No one has ever lived your life before, and nobody else will. So follow the motto of the Royal Society, the British science institution: *nullius in verba*, or "take nobody's word for it." Siddhārtha Gautama, the historical Buddha, said something similar in the *Kalama Sutta* (or sutra): "Do not go with what you have acquired from repeated hearing, nor upon tradition, nor upon rumor, nor upon scripture." Try everything out for yourself.

I invite you to test out everything I share about BTTP and decide what works (or not) for you as a leader. However, bear in mind that some tools and techniques take more than one experiment to test as the first few times we try them out, we are unlikely to do so skillfully. So try things out more than a few times, take on board the feedback, and explore, over time, what delivers to you a transformational life; and transformational results as a leader.

18

BTTP GEM 1: THE ONE UNIFIED SELF

The first tenet of BTTP is that human beings are not fractured with a body and a mind that are separate, with one somehow generating or influencing the other. This dualistic view tends to lead people to privilege the intellect, and relegate the body to a lump of flesh that needs feeding and watering every few hours but is otherwise a prison for our mental genius. Taken to its extreme, dualism led to smart people wanting to be Masters of the Universe even as they are addicted, traumatized, mean, and avaricious in their emotional bodies (from Hitler to Gordon Gecko). It can also lead to religious leaders harming their bodies as the site of their corporal weakness; and athletes and elite soldier focusing on body-building over wisdom and intelligence.

We believe that our body, that senses and emotes and in doing so guides us forward, is just as amazing as our mind. In fact, the last two decades of human biology research have conclusively proven that we cannot think without our body. Eminent neuroscientist Antonio Damasio has shown that patients with damage to the emotion-processing areas of brain cannot make simple 'rational' judgments.[3] Even though we tend to think that reason is the supreme attribute of humankind, our conscious, rational minds are actually quite limited and utterly prone to making mistakes.

There are over a hundred scientifically-verified 'cognitive biases' that distort our understanding of reality to worrying degrees: they have us see things we want to see; that prove us right; or that discount facts so we feel safe. We can counter these biases—which lead us to fails all the time—with the wisdom of our bodies. We must ground our capacious and clever egos in the concrete somatic reality of the lived experience of having feelings in our guts; and sensations in our chest.

Thoughts in our mind are intimately related to feelings in our body, even if we are not conscious of so-called 'interoceptive' sensations. In fact, we go further than this and state that what appear to be psychological phenomena in our minds are the same entities or processes as physiological phenomena in our bodies. We just happen to have seen them through different cognitive lenses for a few millennia. Therefore, there is no mind separate from the body through which it thinks and feels.

There is just one entity, that has mental and somatic aspects, that we call the "bodymind." We use the term bodymind for the single combined entity that we all walk, sit, work, think, feel, love, cry, and decide in and through. Gazing internally into our own subjective experience, we see it as mind or consciousness. When we gaze externally at our arm, or looking at fMRI scans of our bodymind, we see it as matter or the body. The key is that this entity or series of processes is just one thing: a unified field of being and becoming, called the bodymind.

"Bodymind" can be an awkward term but it serves to remind us constantly that every physiological state has a psychological component; and every psychological state has a physiological component. Physiology and psychology are two aspects of one complete and whole system. There are two aspects to one thing. Distress in mind can generate dis-ease within the body. Diseases in the body often manifest as distress in the mind. Likewise, positive interventions to either what we think of as 'mind' or 'body' can bring us into to health and harmony. We are aware of some of these connections. Many we are not.

The more we choose to become more aware of them, as I urge you to do, the more mastery we have over this one bodymind: which is all you have to play with as a leader. All your potential for innovation, change, and transformation comes from having a resilient, creative, and powerful bodymind. Destabilization in either aspect of it, in 'mind' or 'body', will disintegrate and diminish our leadership capabilities. Positive nourishing of either realm can bring us into leadership power. We have to take care of both aspects at all times. This is self-care for leaders that want to be truly transformational—and stay that way.

This idea of a united bodymind challenges the default view in the West: that the mind and body are separate. From this artificial split comes two opposing beliefs that have defined modernity. One group believes that as we know nerves in the physical body are real, then the mind must just be an illusion that appears when brain cells are firing. Hardcore reductionist thinkers believe this. Some influential philosophers, like Daniel C. Dennett, appear to go so far as to claim that even their own conscious experiences (through which they have ideas and write the books that popularize them) are an illusion!

The problem with this belief is that it doesn't account for creative, innovative, or transformational thoughts; and removes all free will from the space. Free will is pretty important if we want to be leaders who freely choose a new path, and help others choose freely to change, too. Creativity and novel thoughts are also pretty important if we want do anything other than what we have done in the past. Reductionists state that our ideas and decisions are predetermined by the movements of molecules. Therefore, there can actually be *no leadership at all*; given that leadership exists when we exert our free will to shape an alternative path and forge a visionary future.

The other group, called idealists, believes that as thoughts and ideas are definitely real, then the body must be an illusion or "prison of the soul" (as Plato wrote). As everything we know— data, statistics, theories—is filtered through subjective experience, we cannot ever be sure that what we measure through our senses in scientific experiments is absolutely true. Proponents of this view, like Bishop George Berkeley, believe that not matter, but *consciousness*—in the form of human will, or universal spirit—is the ultimate foundation of all reality.

Many modern-day spiritual teachers teach that consciousness is more important than matter. This view sees the material world as a compelling experience that is ultimately an illusion. The illusion leads us to suffer, since we crave some material things and are averse to others. Such schools of philosophy teach people to reject the material world and renounce all worldly goods. The logical end point to this is to become a monk or spiritual mendicant, taking the path of the ascetic. This is in some ways life-denying. As leaders, we might neglect or ignore our body: becoming ill, wizened, and exhausted; and making a lot of mistakes as our body is vital to clear, insightful, and well-informed decision-making.

The philosopher Descartes helped create this enduring mind-body problem in Western thinking. The problem stems from the artificial separation he created between matter (neurons in the brain) and consciousness (our thoughts and feelings). This duality made some really important questions all but impossible to answer: How and why does "mind stuff" arise from "material stuff"? How do matter and mind interact? And, if consciousness is not the same as matter, then what the hell is consciousness?

So far, Western logic, based on assuming that matter is real and consciousness is just an illusion—or predominately Eastern thinking that is often interpreted as seeing consciousness as real and matter as an illusion—has failed to answer these questions in any coherent way. Descartes tried to solve it by stating that matter and consciousness interact in the pineal gland in the brain, to him the seat of the soul! However, this may not be as wild as it seems. World-famous physicist and philosopher Sir Roger Penrose and the iconoclastic medic Stuart Hameroff (who hosts a scientific conference, *The Science of Consciousness,* at which I have presented) have suggested that the dual aspects of our reality might be "entangled" in the microtubules in the brain.

Their hypothesis sees consciousness not being 'caused' by neurons firing in mechanical ways, but elemental to the nature of quantum processes within neurons. Consciousness is not *produced* by nerve activity, but is related to it, intrinsically linked to it, and co-arises with it. Consciousness, in this view, is no longer an illusion, but intrinsic to all matter. Fascinating research studies into quantum processes happening within photosynthesis and animal smell have shown that quantum decoherence, once thought to only happen in very cold and clinical laboratory conditions, can happen in the warm and wet biology of human beings.

Whatever the science says, in practice in BTTP we refuse to allow Cartesian mind-body dualism to underestimate the power of our consciousness. We need to be clear that our consciousness and physical changes in our body are one thing. Then we can optimize this one thing, our bodymind, to deliver concrete changes in matter.

In BTTP, we do not allow Western philosophical habit to split our inherent wholeness apart. We dissolve the mind-body problem away because we see mind and body as two aspects of the same unified bodymind.

We do not need to privilege or prefer either aspect. With a unified bodymind, we see all problems in human systems as both physiological and psychological. Pills, immunizations, surgery, and other interventions in our biology will quickly change the material aspect of our bodymind. And shifts in our *consciousness*—from interventions in our thoughts and feelings from meditation, introspection, or connection—will change how we physically feel.

We see mind and matter, consciousness and embodiment, as two sides of the same coin; a truly remarkable bodymind that is the most sophisticated organizing system in the universe as far as we know. BTTP sees that the materialist lens of indestructible matter and the idealist lens of pure consciousness are looking at the same thing, one thing, one bodymind, in different ways. Matter is immanent shape and form. Consciousness is transcendent awareness. As it states in the Buddhist *Heart Sutra*, emptiness is form and form is emptiness. Because they are two aspects of the same thing, all remains one.

We know that this unified bodymind has the capacity, once we understand how it works, to be fluid, flexible, and free; and creative, generative, and transformational. By experiencing ourselves a s a unified, non-reducible bodymind—and conceiving of others that we lead in the same way—we aim to live fully *embodied* lives as leaders, consciously choosing, with free will, to create awesome regenerative solutions to tough Transformational Challenges. Only by unifying our experience into one bodymind can we ensure—by free choice and through mastery of both aspects of our one being—that we live fully, love wholeheartedly, and lead transformationally.

19

THE BRAIN OF THE TRANSFORMATIONAL LEADER

Until recently, most people believed that what sets human beings apart from other species is our intelligence. Intelligence has been generally understood as an ability to focus on tasks without distraction; solve problems using good existing knowledge (like algebra, coding, historical insight, physiology, or engineering); make useful and rational predictions about the world; and take action to mitigate risks from those predictions. It is often suggested that the prefrontal cortex of the human being—the large part of our brain in our forehead area—is the seat of human reason.

This correlates to a network in the brain that scientists have called the Executive Control Network (ECN) or Cognitive Control Network. It lights up in brain scanners when we focus on a task. It was therefore assumed by scientists that when we are not focused on a task, controlling the world around us, our brains are more or less 'off.' But then a number of 'anomalies' started popping up in scientific experiments that have precipitated a veritable revolution of brain science that is crucial for leaders to be aware of.

In 2012, a research study co-led by scientists from the National Institute on Deafness and Other Communication Disorders

EXECUTIVE CONTROL NETWORK
Control & Task
Execution

FIGURE 1 *The Executive Control Network*

(NIDCD) at the National Institutes of Health (NIH), put rap musi-cians—who are brilliant improvisers and extremely creative human beings—into an fMRI scanner. They asked the rappers to do two things: first, perform lyrics they had already written to a specific few bars of background music.[4] Second, they were asked to improvise lyrics in the moment to the same bars of music. The research-ers scanned the blood flow to different parts of the artists' brains to understand what was different between performing tasks (akin to performance management) and improvising new, spontaneous, and creative solutions (akin to transformational leadership).

They discovered that the prefrontal cortex, the supposed site of human reason, was actually *less* aroused when the musicians were improvising as opposed to when we they were focused on a task. In other words, when we are creating, we are less in control, less focused, *and so less conventionally smart*! Further studies have shown that people with increased creative capabilities have *decreased* thickness in their higher cortex.[5]

In fact, it turns out that the rappers were using an entirely different brain network to improvise as opposed to the one they used to execute. Rather misleadingly, it was called the Default Mode Network (DMN). Researchers have repeated these fMRI findings with other creative types, like jazz musicians. Pioneering neuroscientist Frederik Ullen states that "the most experienced improvisers use much less executive control." In other words, adapting, creating, and improving brains are looser, more open, and more available to new thoughts. They are less ordered, more chaotic, more flexible, and freer.

At one point, scientists began to call the DMN the "daydreaming network" because we shift into a divergent, creative, improvisational but non-focused mode of thinking—the very opposite of how we were taught and trained to think in school. Researchers Mathias Bendek and Emanuel Juak write in *The Oxford Handbook of Spontaneous Thought*: "spontaneous thoughts that address unsolved problems can be viewed as a very adaptive, functional mechanism of our brain. More generally, mind-wandering can be seen as spontaneous mental simulations that build on previous experience to better prepare us for the future, which are relevant for personal planning and creativity."[6]

The DMN lights up when we create and improvise but quiets down when we are focused and in control. Then the ECN activates when we focus on a task to solve a problem we already have figured out. It is only when we are *not* focused on a task that the DMN becomes fully activated. If we are focused, using convergent thought or best practice to solve a familiar problem with a known

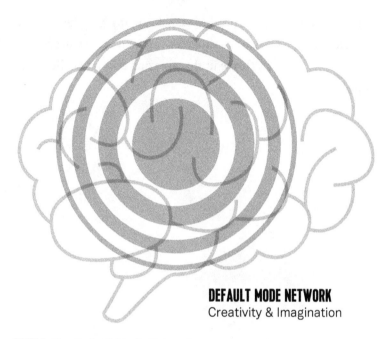

DEFAULT MODE NETWORK
Creativity & Imagination

FIGURE 2 *The Default Mode Network*

solution, the DMN—and its creative divergent thought style—*is disabled from switching on.* In other words, our neural networks have evolved to allow for two fundamentally different ways of seeing the world, processing information about it, a*nd then taking action.* They act as antagonist pairs, much like our biceps and triceps do.

One network allows us to complete tasks successfully with convergent thinking (the domain of management). The other allows us to create new solutions to emerging problems with divergent thinking (the domain of leadership). As one published research paper has it: "our neural architecture requires us to switch between two fundamentally different information-processing modes, which support different, yet complementary, ways of understanding the world."[7] All of us were born with *both* of these brain networks.

Therefore, everything we need to transform anything lies within us. Each brain network has a different function but we need *both of them* to survive and thrive in this amazing and yet challenging world.

20

BTTP GEM 2: THE TWO MODES OF CONSCIOUSNESS

Working from the emerging science of our two brain networks, but without being limited by what science has 'proven' from current research studies, in BTTP I propose that every human being, every leader, has two fundamental "modes of consciousness" within their one unified bodymind. Each mode delivers different evolutionary advantages, problem-solving benefits, and outcomes. Each mode is a good fit for specific moments. Each mode has a different neural architecture and biological pathways in the material body that underpins it. And each mode has a different set of qualitative and subjective experiences that manifest it in our minds. To be clear: we need strength in both modes in order to survive and thrive in a fast and furiously-changing world.

In BTTP, we call the task-oriented and focused mindset "Control & Protect Mode" (or C&P Mode). Its role is to control the craziness and chaos of life, parsing information/data with our intellect into frameworks where we can understand reality and predict what best to do next to survive; and to protect us from threats to our existence from predators, social challenges, and rotten food. C&P Mode is likely associated, or correlated, with the ECN in our brain. In C&P Mode we are highly focused and get stuff done, seek firm answers and drive toward certainty rapidly; play by the rules and technical expertise we have learned, measure success by metrics and goals achieved, act strategically and rigorously, and are risk-averse.

In C&P Mode, we think in straight lines, build algorithms, and deliver linear solutions. Conventional intelligence, 'smarts,' is a feature of C&P Mode: getting exam questions right, knowing the answer when our boss asks us, looking like we're in control so we feel safe, optimizing algorithms in business models and software, developing perfect plans and detailed spreadsheets, and delivering efficiency upgrades as managers. In C&P Mode we love to make continuous improvements to Business as Usual to deliver predictable outcomes that lead to fame, fortune, respect, and recognition. Most leaders have already optimized smart and logical C&P Mode to become managers and traditional leaders in existing hierarchies.

What we call "Create & Connect Mode" (or C&C Mode), on the other hand, is associated with the brain's DMN. Its role is to connect with other people, ourselves, and sentient beings to furnish collaboration and co-operative actions; and to create novel solutions to novel problems that we haven't encountered before. In C&C Mode, we are curious, creative, and empathic. We are more interested in better questions than firm answers, happy to challenge the rules, more interested in being interconnected rather than isolated, seek meaning and purpose over metrics, and prioritize possibility over stability and security. We think in non-linear systems, complex webs of relationships, and about dynamic processes more than fixed entities.

C&C Mode allows us to connect with others and empathize with their situation, ideas, and context; to appreciate and learn from cognitive and ethnic diversity; to listen to each other and gain future-forward insights from this empathic attention; to pause, slow down, and reflect on complex problems rather than rush to solve them; to cultivate safe spaces for innovation and change; to come into coherence and cohesion with others; and to co-create ideas with peers that we couldn't come up with alone.

In environments that are stable, familiar, predictable, and clear, C&P Mode is a very effective problem-solving mindset: it prevents us from having to exert the enormous emotional and cognitive effort needed to come up with fresh insights and create new ideas consciously. For crossing the road, ironing, doing our taxes, reciting our ABCs, doing everyday calculations, and tweaking an existing production line or algorithm, it is usually a good and efficient fit.

CONTROL & PROTECT MODE

Focused
Get stuff done
Convergent thinking
Rule-based
Self-contained
Metrics
Rigorous
Strategic
Risk-avoidant

CREATE & CONNECT MODE

Open
Explore possibilities
Divergent thinking
Rule-breaking
Interconnected
Meaning
Curious
Imaginative
Possibility-focused

FIGURE 3 *The Two Modes of Consciousness*

Yet in environments that are rapidly changing, like the VUCA reality we all must deal with, C&P Mode is not a great fit. Linear and task-oriented, it applies existing best practice—derived from technical expertise, historic experience, and (professional) training—to new, emergent, and Transformational Challenges that nobody has ever solved before. C&P Mode expects neat, incremental, linear, algorithmic tweaks to solve for complex, adaptive problems caused by the powerful evolutionary stressors and adaptive pressures of the digital, disrupted and damaged reality. This is a mismatch.

C&P Mode dooms many *smart* leaders to end up in failure, as we can see from high-level executives at Kodak and Nokia failing to adapt not just their execution but their entire business model. Smart leaders fail to spot and adapt to change because they lock into a mode that is a mismatch for the moment. C&P Mode did not evolve for empathy (with customers and employees), for listening, for reflecting, for collective sense-making, or for co-creativity.

C&P Mode flattens out potentially salient insights, intuitions and ideas; and drowns out the weak signals of future sources of value that always exist in the present. C&P mode is an epic mismatch for the situations in which we all find ourselves: dealing with epically complex and intense challenges as leaders, and existential risks to our species. When we need to lead the transformation of business models and operating models—as well as our outdated politico-economic system to resolve the four crises of modernity—C&P Mode cannot succeed alone.

Rather than bow down to the wisdom and generative power of C&C Mode though, C&P Mode tends to cling to old ideas as if they were eternal truths. It gets positional and conflictual. It becomes attached to our existing solutions and legacy beliefs, usually based on our successes to date in the workplace. It projects its existing meaning-making framework and organizing narrative onto the world to silence the variations, nuances, and anomalies that presage disruption and transformation. It simply was not evolved to spot the signs and symptoms of what is breaking down (because it is fading from fit); and what is breaking through (because it fits the future better). If we only see problems through C&P Mode, we will eventually become obsolete in our roles—and be disrupted from our market positions—because we only see technical problems to deal with; and not Transformational Challenges to rise to by leading adaptations and preadaptations that emerge within the adjacent possible—if, and only if, we can find our way there in C&C Mode.

Perhaps the greatest challenge for the aspiring transformational leader is that all through our education, management training, and the incentive systems, we have been taught to, and rewarded for, getting things right and getting stuff done in C&P Mode. This shift from creativity to control is an understandable and necessary process of maturity. In fact, recent work by Prof. Alison Gopnik, a developmental psychologist at Stanford University, suggests that all toddlers start out *without* much task-based, knowledge-led thinking.

Everything is a glorious and costly (in terms of cognitive energy) experiment to the young child. When we are young, we have a very 'plastic' brain that can change and adapt fast as it learns how to walk, talk, and get its needs met. Parents know that this playful creativity and endless experimentation causes many amusing and also frustrating mismatches for grown-ups. The child's brain is in a disordered state, akin to intense moments of C&C Mode. It has lots of connectivity in local areas, but it is not very efficient. Kids spend a lot of energy on experimentation with new ideas that often don't work. They are also very emotionally changeable and 'labile.' This creates, in the language of information theory, a lot of 'noise.'

As we grow up, nature has us reduce the amount of noise, experimentation, and creativity so we can focus and get stuff done. Our brains lose some of that local connectivity and neuroplasticity in favor of strong long-distance connections. We shift out of C&C Mode and become more able to spend long periods in C&P Mode: learning, doing tests, delivering answers. The brain becomes more stable and controlled, which helps us do important repetitive tasks—like eating, reading, and using the bathroom—quickly, efficiently, and safely.

The downside of this natural process of maturity is that we lose some of that creativity and agility. This is then exacerbated by an entire equation system that sees only the value of C&P Mode and appears to be ignorant of the importance of C&C Mode to our existence and evolution as a species. Society, schooling, and most training methods—as we will soon see, combined with the long-term impact of Adverse Childhood Events (ACE) and trauma—cause us to move too far into C&P Mode. We then get stuck thinking old thoughts, while Rome—and California and Australia—burn. The world around us is changing too rapidly and too intensely not to become masters at C&C Mode, too: yet our schools and MBA programs poorly develop us for this necessity. We have a lot of muscle in C&P Mode but little muscle in C&C Mode.

Nature is very successful in developing antagonistic pairings. Take our muscles, for example: on each arm we have a bicep and a tricep. But if we only had one or the other, we would move our arm once and never move again. Imagine if your quadriceps muscles were as strong as the young Arnold Schwarzenegger were back in his body-building heyday; but your hamstring muscles were as soft and buttery as a baby's. How adaptive, agile, and elegant would you be in moving around? Likewise, our two different brain networks work together to provide us with the capacity for transformational leadership.

A transformational leader knows which Mode to use in which moments. When crossing a busy road, you do not want to be in C&C Mode and have a radically-creative brainstorm in a middle of a freeway. You want to be in C&P Mode, using the rules and best practice you learned as a child to survive: look left, look right, look left again, walk! But if we are trying to solve the climate crises—or coming up with a transformational innovation that leverages Artificial Intelligence to scale positive impact to millions of people—then we want to be in C&C Mode, inventing new possibilities.

However, most strategists and senior leaders apply smart thinking C&P Mode to all Transformational Challenges. This is a mismatch, a lack of fit, and fails the future. We have already seen how hard it is for highly-paid smart managers to buck their decades of training to use C&P Mode for all problem-solving and the devastating impact this can have on business and our planet. If we do not consciously keep and rebuild muscle in C&C Mode, we end up as adults who typically spend very little energy on experimentation.

Instead, most of our time is spent on planning and winning at the 'game' of life (C&P Mode tends to see the world as a zero-sum game with winners and losers). We become optimized to win, compete, get stuff done, and perhaps even 'crush the competition'; yet, over time, lose access to our creative, imaginative selves. We are more emotionally stable and calm but no longer fecund and generative. We need to dare to daydream to be able to adapt to forge the future! I believe that the ideal place for a transformational leader to be is poised between the two Modes, able to use the right one for the challenges we face in any given moment.

Albert Einstein, who knew a thing or two about being a transformational leader, said, "logic will get you from A to B, but imagination will take you everywhere." At another point, Einstein said that "imagination is more important than knowledge. Knowledge is limited. Imagination encircles the world." In other words, knowledge-based C&P Mode will solve a linear, goal-orientated problem very well: one that has a right and a wrong answer. But it is imagination-driven C&C Mode that we need as leaders to imagine new thoughts, have innovative breakthroughs, and lead and land transformations. Einstein went on to say that, "I never came upon any of my discoveries by the process of rational thinking." Einstein used the divergent thinking and imagination of C&C Mode—like the thought experiment about what it would be like to ride at the speed of light, which allowed him to form the concept of relativity—to come up with transformational ideas that won him the Nobel Prize. He then went back to prove them in C&C Mode with math and scientific rigor. Importantly, C&C Mode has to innovate *before* C&P Mode evaluates; otherwise, the latter Mode will crush the breakthroughs before they take hold.

21

DARE TO DAYDREAM

It is essential that all leaders who want to be more transformational find ways, times, and spaces to get into C&C Mode. This will unlock divergent, daydreaming thought styles. We need to be less worried about having the 'right' answer in C&P Mode and more curious and possibility-focused in C&C Mode. We swap certainty for insightful and future-unfolding questions to inquire into. Rather than basing all our work beliefs and behaviors on existing rules and best practice, we develop the confidence and clarity necessary to break the rules and disrupt conventional thinking to develop next practice.

We can only develop future-forward ideas—driven by insights revealed by spotting what is breaking down and breaking through in culture and customer groups—by choosing, consciously, to switch on and enter C&C Mode when faced with Transformational Challenges. We have to do this proactively—I suggest scheduling it into your week—otherwise C&P Mode will see all problems as technical rather than adaptive (leading us to fail); and it will convince us that we don't have the time to reflect because we just need to get stuff done.

CONTROL & PROTECT MODE

CREATE & CONNECT MODE

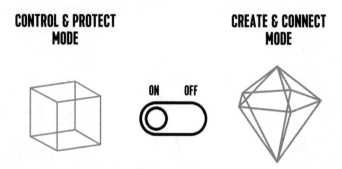

FIGURE 4 *Switching Between the Two Modes of Consciousness*

To be truly transformational, we must be *less* smart, less self-contained, and much more interested in being interconnected: empathizing with customers to find the insights we need for transformational innovation and engaging with our colleagues and team members to better glean their contribution and wisdom and also serve their needs. We want to be less interested in metrics and more interested in meaning. We should prioritize being present with each other over yet more productivity. We want to be inquisitive and imaginative and less worried about taking risks. We want a bias toward possibility not just for action. We want to daydream more.

In a recent biography of the incredible creative and disruptive writer Franz Kafka, *Kafka: The Decisive Years,* I read this: "Kafka often spent half the day in bed or on a sofa, languid, inaccessible, daydreaming." This transformative thinker, who wrote books like *Metamorphosis* over 100 years ago—about a boy becoming a giant insect, thus exploring how utterly alien the machine age can be to humankind—proactively chose to daydream for huge parts of his day. Rather than tap away at this typewriter obsessed with producing pages and "getting stuff done," he chose to give himself the time, space, and permission to get fully into C&C Mode to dream up his wild and influential ideas. He then spent time in C&P Mode, of course, translating his flights of fancy into concrete prose.

Therefore, the watchword of a transformational leader is to ensure that, as regularly as possible, we make time and space to "Connect & Reflect": to choose to enter C&C Mode for long enough periods that we explore pressing problems properly to find creative, insightful solutions. You have to give yourself full permission to do this and to see this time to connect (with customers, ourselves our colleagues) and reflect (on what is a Transformational Challenge and how to resolve it) is as important, if not more important, than delivery on KPIs. It helps if your boss understands this too, but you cannot afford to wait for anyone else to give you permission. You need to start this today.

Jack Welch apparently spent an hour of each day, as CEO of a Fortune 50 firm, in what he called "looking out of the window time." Such strategic daydreaming gives us time to reflect on what really needs attention; connect with people we want to serve as leaders; cultivate our curiosity for how the future might be; and gather up the inspiration needed to turn ideas into action. Put simply, we need space and time away from the everyday pressures and demands to even enter C&C Mode.

In a survey of 2,000 employees across 25 organizations by the Forward Institute, it discovered that: "Remarkably few respondents agreed with the statement: 'my organization allows me time to reflect.' Many organizations instinctively find a preference for noise and immediate action; valuing efficiency over effectiveness." We can get stuck into repetitive patterns, going faster and faster, using the same thinking and behaviors that got us into the problem in the first place, rather than taking time to process what's going on and shift consciously into a creative response.

In C&P mode we don't connect with others in authentic ways. We don't want to befriend an alligator or have a brainstorm on the 405 Freeway. Therefore, we relate to others with what philosopher Martin Buber called the I-It relationship: a disconnected and static transactional relationship between me and an inert and abstracted 'thing' like 'the consumer' or 'the competition.' Wise, open, and curious, C&C Mode prioritizes listening and contributing in genuine dialogue; sensing into our shared purpose and vision; and supporting what's seeking to emerge between us. We enter what Martin Buber called the I-Thou relationship: a respectful and dynamic 'relational field" between two living, sensing, sentient beings. We define a relational field as the conscious/emotional and material/physiological space that forms in the connection between two, or more, people.

C&P Mode is about convergent thinking to solve a problem *on our own*; whereas C&C Mode affords divergent thinking *in community*. But to be in C&C Mode, we have to be sufficiently relaxed, connected, purposeful, and trusting. Only then can we release the old habits of thought and action that are preventing transformation. This is biology and we can't bypass the biology. It is useful to remember this when we're on our way home, full of corporate vim and stressful vigor. Few lovers, parents, or kids enjoy us storming into the house with fierce energy to control the chaos of life and to protect ourselves from attack. In these moments, C&P Mode vacuums up intimacy and destroys connection.

We want to give ourselves space to Connect & Reflect *before* we get home – and before we run a creative workshop or team coaching session—to allow us to come into C&C Mode where we can actually connect with, and come into resonance with, those we care about. Yet we never want our daydreaming time to become bone idleness. We want it to be the wise, not just smart, way of working. Learning from this, we can see that every transformational leader needs to provide himself/herself with time and space for C&C Mode; to innovate for transformational, adaptive challenges with exponential ideas; and also to balance this with time and space to be in C&P Mode, to use our smart skills and know-how to solve technical problems and nail tasks. We want to go into C&C Mode to invent the future of our industry; and then go into C&P Mode to analyze it, criticize it, improve it, and deliver it.

Dare to Daydream: Invitation to Engage

Q. What meeting or activity can you drop for the next few weeks to give yourself 60 minutes a week for reflection time on where you are fading or failing?

Q. When might you want to get into C&C before a work event, meeting, or workshop in order to deliver more creative and empathic outcomes?

Q. When might you want to get into C&C before a social or family moment in order to boost a sense of community, intimacy, and trust?

22

THE TWO MODES IN CULTURE & SOCIETY

It seems that most societies either evolve a controlling, hierarchical mode of organizing; or a flatter, more connective mode. It seems likely that the hierarchical model emerges in societies that privilege C&P Mode—and train citizens to develop it (and downgrade C&C Mode). Such systems inevitably start to dominate those at the bottom with violence, oppression, and "tyranny from the top." I believe that the connective model emerges in societies that promote C&C Mode—and the regenerative relationships that thrive when citizens are in it. This model leads to more peaceful, sustainable, and collaborative societies—though they may not be as productive or efficient. They can also result in a forced flatness that leads to "tyranny from below."

Riane Eisler proposed, in her book *The Chalice and the Blade*, that—despite cultural narratives normalizing Western *dominative* hierarchies (there can be generative kinds)—we are not doomed to exist within systems of authority. We can reclaim and reinvent the relational model, which has deep roots in earlier forms of Western culture (such as the thriving society of Minoan Crete). This promise is supported by anthropological research, which has identified around 40 or so predominately peaceful cultures,[8] which have a fascinating similarity: people within them consider cooperation to be more important than competition. In fact, they see competition as dangerous because it breeds aggression. So adults teach kids to play to learn, not to win. Boys pretend to hunt together, collaboratively. Girls play together at creating a home. All swing on vines, jump through waterfalls, and create fantasy worlds—without a winner and a loser. In some of these societies, such as the Semai of Malaysia and the Zapotec in Mexico, no one can remember a single violent event ever having happened. People are peaceful because they have been trained to be collaborative in Create & Connect Mode rather than competitive in Control & Protect Mode. Survival of the fittest is not true in all cultures.

Contemporary sociology and social psychology have similarly posited that there is always a tension between control and create in societies. Every culture/country is somewhere on this spectrum: control, 'tightness', at one end; and creativity, 'looseness', at the other. University of Maryland psychologist Michele Gelfand studied 33 national cultures to explore how 'tight' (C&P Mode) or 'loose' (C&C Mode) they are. She found that how controlling versus how creative they are determined their capacity to change. Crucially, how loose or tight a culture becomes is in large part down to how much threat (natural or social) a society has faced; or perceives that it has faced. Past traumas and disasters linger long in culture.

Researchers Anne Pisor at Washington State University and Martin Surbeck at Harvard University suggest that, as a species, we have evolved the flexibility to be able to promote 'fission' (C&P Mode) and 'fusion' (C&C Mode), depending on the moment. We can be empathic and tolerant of outsiders when collaboration and cross-cultural exchange are valuable; and we can also be highly defensive and aggressive when under threat.[9]

Like many social animals—chimps, dolphins, elephants—we live in societies, and work in organizations, that allow for both fission and fusion. When food and mates are abundant, we will allow our boundaries to dissolve and become more porous. We will connect, collaborate, and co-create with those outside of our genetic family and even our tribe. But we can quickly get territorial and competitive when scarcity and threat levels rise: for example, during pandemics. Pisor and Surbeck suggest that we are uniquely tolerant among fission-fusion species. They think that this is due to our massive brains and the fact we birth few young that take a long time to mature. We have *had* to learn how to rely on other people/tribes during periods of scarcity and challenge. In fact, this capacity to merrily be in Create & Connect Mode may account for our successes as a species.

Science-driven moral philosophers Allen Buchanan at Duke and Russell Powell at Boston University have suggested in their book, *The Evolution of Moral Progress: A Biocultural Theory*, that this flexible morality has been key to our evolution. We can promote an 'exclusivist' morality (C&P Mode) or an 'inclusivist' morality (C&C Mode), depending on our situation. This gives us a fitness advantage over species that are capable of only being exclusivist: controlling and protective. (The authors also go on to say that we become more exclusivist when we have been subject to "demagogic manipulation" by "extremist political elites".)The fact that we can be tight, exclusivist, and focused on fission in C&P Mode—as well as loose, inclusivist, and focused on fusion in C&C Mode—is the key to the unbelievable spread of humankind.

Going deeper, the grandfather of modern psychology, William James, used his research into religious experiences, and other 'non-standard' states of awareness, to propose that human beings can be in 'normal' states of consciousness (dominated by C&P Mode);

as well as what he called states of 'cosmic consciousness': in which people sense themselves as somehow united with the universe itself.

In my experience developing many leaders—and running countless innovation and co-creation workshops—it is this form of consciousness that we are in when we are in the more intense states of C&C Mode. We experience intimate connections between ourselves and customers, which unleashes future-generating insights; and creative ideas burst forth in what can only be described as a mystical way. I believe that at this end of our spectrum of consciousness—a spectrum that spans create/loose/inclusivist/fusion and control/ tight/exclusivist/fission capabilities—we experience what I call "connective consciousness," where everything seems connected in some majestic way. On the other end of the spectrum, we experience what I call "analytical consciousness": everything is disconnected and separated; and so objects can be measured and figured out (to analyze means to 'break apart' in Greek).

Rex Jung, a professor of neurosurgery at the University of New Mexico, is one of the pioneers of creativity neuroscience and the neural basis of human intelligence and generativity. He has speculated that some people's brains seem to spend all, or most, of their time at one end of the spectrum: in connective consciousness. This is, of course, not adapted to every moment. Society calls these moments, that do not fit convention, 'psychoses'. Psychotic people often exhibit extreme creativity and describe having many connective experiences, like hearing voices.

Other brains mature to spend much time at the other end of the spectrum: extreme analytical consciousness. Society often calls such experiences 'autistic.' Jung proposes that people who spend most of their time in one brain network or the other, at the far edges of the normal distribution curve, are labeled psychotic (extreme creativity) or autistic (extreme control). He thinks that it is rather remarkable that roughly the same percentage of the population, around 3%, are on the autism spectrum; and also suffer from psychosis and so "lose touch with objective reality".[10]

Another Jung, the great psychologist Carl Gustav Jung, built on James' work with his theory of the 'collective unconscious,' holding that all humans share an unconscious well of wisdom. I believe that states of connective consciousness—C&C Mode—allow us to tap into Jung's collective unconscious to learn and grow as leaders. For example, we can gain access to the strengths, skills, and insights of archetypal leadership styles that we have yet to embody.

Unlike his contemporary Sigmund Freud, Carl Jung was a big fan of meditation, hypnotherapy, dream work, and creative imagination techniques because he saw that they enabled people to reached the connective consciousness of our C&C Mode. There we can harness wisdom not available through the rational thought of C&P Mode; and bring these insights and intuitions into our life and work to solve Transformational Challenges. While Freud focused on analyzing the psyche using logic—using C&P Mode to understand something beyond it—Jung wanted to get people out of their box and into C&C Mode. Jung saw the value in entering this mindset, in which we cannot control everything but can create anything. In C&C Mode, we can gain wisdom that can help us transform our world. Without this kind of creative and empathic thinking, transformation in life, love, and leadership cannot occur because we are biologically locked into old thoughts and outdated ideas.

23

BTTP GEM 3: THE THIRD WAY OF CREATIVE HARMONY

When in C&P Mode, it is easy to think: "OK then, I need to be in C&C Mode at work more often". However, the most recent neurobiological research has shown that we actually need to use *both* brain networks co-operatively, in the same stretch of time; even if not exactly at the same microsecond (the brain can cycle between being active and passive states up to 180 times a minute!). Highly innovative people are able rapidly and repeatedly to shift between convergent and divergent thinking. The complex process of imagining and executing high-value new ideas—whether everyday adaptation or long-range transformational innovation—involves a complex interplay between creative and controlled thinking. We need to have ideas with C&C Mode and then sort them, evaluate them, and prioritize them with C&P Mode.

According to an article called *Why Are Some People More Creative Than Others?* in *Scientific American*, the consumer magazine of the most prestigious science journal *Nature*, genuine innovation—the ability to improvise and create a new solution and then execute it as a transformation—"involves a complex interplay between spontaneous and controlled thinking—the ability to both spontaneously brainstorm ideas and deliberately evaluate them to determine whether they'll actually work."

C&P Mode and C&C Mode do not work against each so much as collaboratively; they are coupled together, partners-in-crime. As researchers state in *The Oxford Handbook of Spontaneous Thought*: "increased coupling of DMN and ECN has been observed for different creative domains, including creative idea generation, creative drawing, poetry composition, and musical improvisation. These findings show that creative cognition involves the activation and cooperation of brain networks linked to spontaneous thought and cognitive control."

In other words, the most innovative people can flex between *both* divergent *and* convergent thinking. They are masters at both. Although C&P Mode likes to see polar opposites—where we are *either* in Control Mode *or* Create Mode—really we need to be in *both* Control Mode *and* Create Mode. This means shifting from either/or 'dualistic' thinking to both/and 'dialogical' thinking. This

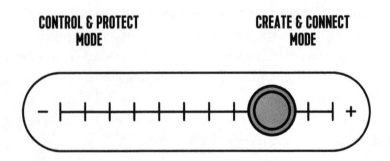

CONTROL & PROTECT MODE   **CREATE & CONNECT MODE**

Palintonic: A
creative tension

Both/and not
either/or

FIGURE 5 *The Third Way*

is the heart of the 3rd Gem of BTTP: to find the Third Way between seeming opposites within a creative tension or harmony.

As leaders, we are invited by the complexities of real life to move beyond easy and conflictual dualisms (self/other, mind/body, nature/nurture)—that see the world as either X or Y—and embrace dialogical thinking that sees that both X and Y can be true. As I discovered from reading *Embodied Being* by philosopher professor and bodywork practitioner Jeffrey Maitland, one of the earliest philosophers in the West, the pre-Socratic Greek writer Heraclitus, gave us a fragment of wisdom to embrace the seeming paradox of being both controlling/protective and creative/connective.

Heraclitus says, "they do not understand how, while differing from itself, it is in agreement with itself: stretched back and forth in harmony like that of the bow and lyre." A lyre is an ancient instrument. A guitar would be a modern-day equivalent. Imagine the tension, fertile with potential, that exists across the strings of a guitar between two poles, two opposites. Transformational leadership inhabits that creative tension, embodies that creative tension, and harnesses that creative tension to lead and land positive lasting change.

We embody the tension between *both* C&C Mode *and* C&P Mode; between *both* working productively alone *and* working co-creatively in a team; between *both* becoming an efficient manager *and* developing into an effective leader; between leading an enterprise that is *both* on purpose *and* profitable. We can and must bring seeming opposites together into a dynamic "palintonic harmonie," the term Heraclitus uses. We can still discern and distinguish opposites but we reconcile them together into a creative harmony: a Third Way that is the best of both polar opposites. The binary opposition of dualities so common in the West, centered on "either/or" logic, melts into the unity of an integrated bodymind. We can then embrace "both/and thinking," that still discerns important differences between two seeming opposites but understands how they can be brought together into a Third Way. When we lead transformation projects, there are many seeming paradoxes. We are invited as leaders to melt away dualistic polarities in the wisdom of our ever-expanding connective consciousness. Otherwise, we will become overwhelmed and confused by paradoxes; and so lose effectiveness. Genuine embodied wisdom dissolves dualities and divisions into palintonic harmonies.

Way back in ancient India, the Buddha also posited in his teachings the cubical importance of a Middle Way or Middle Path. He knew that human beings tend toward nihilism (nothing is important and nothing is real) and essentialism (thinking everything we do is significant and everything is real). Likewise, leaders tend toward becoming modern-day ascetics, denying pleasures and embracing endless self-criticism on the path to perfection (including a bit of self- and employee-flagellation); or we become hedonists, indulging in material pleasures like fame and fortune and not paying attention to our mind and the importance of ideas in consciousness.

Buddha says to us: "Everything exists: That is one extreme. Everything doesn't exist: That is a second extreme. Avoiding these two extremes, the [Buddha] teaches the Dharma [wisdom, path] via the middle."[11] This Third Way approach seems to be how the brain itself is organized. The complex process of imagining and executing high-value new ideas—whether everyday adaptation and agility or long-range transformational innovation—involves a complex palintonic and generative harmony between creative and controlled thinking. As Dr. Roger Beaty, from Penn State, puts it, "creative people are better able to co-activate brain networks that usually work separately."

Through developing our leadership consciousness so we can see creative tensions instead of polar opposites, we get to resolve the tensions we see in the world today: between dispassionate objective science and passionate subjective purpose; between Hayekian laissez-faire economics and Keynesian government-investing economics; and between conservative meritocracies and progressive liberal equalities. As transformational leaders, we have to learn how to tune the string between opposites as we walk a constant Third Way between a 'scientific' gaze outward at our projects and balance sheet; and a contemplative gaze inward at our own inner experience.

BTTP explicitly creates this Third Way creative harmony between the objective materialist lens that seeks proven, reliable, consistent information about profit/loss; and the subjective idealist lens that is inspired by reliable, consistent insight about the world through introspection, reflection, and contemplation. BTTP as a leadership philosophy unleashes us to harness *both* scientific material interventions (say more caffeine in the morning or more agile development processes) *and* consciousness interventions (say team meditations and psychological safety practices) to thrive as leaders.

With BTTP, we are in the game of mastering *both* the material *and* the conscious aspects of our single bodymind at all times. With empathy, imagination, and intuition from C&C Mode, coupled with accurate data and logic seen though C&P Mode, we learn how to metabolize pain points into opportunities for smart and wise solutions that resolve transformation challenges. The Third Way is about always finding the path that brings the best of all worlds, without descending into banal centrism.

Sometimes, when we try to stand between two stools, we fall between them. We end up in a Lowest Common Denominator

(LCD) compromise between two opposites. This low-energy beige-vanilla center has very little passion and vibrancy within it to lead sustained transformation. It relies on smart minds trying to find a middle-ground that pleases no one much. However, with wise hearts embracing the paradox as well as smart minds, transformational leaders can find a Highest Common Factor (HCF) creative harmony that brings the best of both worlds without reducing creativity and possibility.

We can see ourselves as *both* individuals looking out for ourselves *and* an elemental part of society that cares for one another (although not everyone will be able to be a billionaire and have everything their hearts desire; but don't need). We can *both* manage our teams to drive excellence and high-productivity *and* support them and coach them to unleash their potential for their own actualization. We can run a business model that delivers *both* profit for investors *and* genuine purposeful impact for staff and users (albeit we might deliver less profit than a purposeless business).

A Highest Common Factor creative harmony can help us find our way toward a more regenerative and responsible form of capitalism. Thus transformational leaders in businesses can choose to drive sustainability through their supply chains (airline Emirates is leading the way in a carbon-heavy industry); put purpose at the heart of their business (as companies like Patagonia and Unilever are doing); and even give up some equity to workers (as outdoor retailer REI, and electronics chain Richer Sounds, both do).

24

LEADING THIRD WAY ORGANIZATIONS

There is an important Third Way for transformational leaders between the seeming polar opposites of top-down management (hierarchy, central control, micro-management) and bottom-up empowerment (coal-face insights, self-management, distributed creativity). Transformational leaders give those in the center and 'at the top' responsibility for thinking systemically and strategically to ensure the long-term survival and thriving of the enterprise. They are paid to have the big ideas that are going to future-proof the organization and forge the future of the industry.

Often with years of experience and an intellectual bent, such leaders are expected to engage with long-range opportunities and threats; and marshal and allocate the resources necessary for success through continuous transformation and innovation. They engage with the 3D drivers of change: new exponential digital technologies, disruptive shifts in human societies, and the existential risks of a damaged planet. They provide bird's eye, top-down insights and intelligence—without tyranny from above.

At the same time, we also want those at the edges—at the coalface—to find and act on future-forward insights about hyper-local problems with agility and entrepreneurial zest. We want our people at all levels to be responsive, in real-time, to the reality on the ground to which only they have access. We want to ensure they feel enabled and supported to think on their feet, connect in heartfelt ways with the customers they serve, and feed back fresh insights from the edges to the center so those at the core can act on the weak signals that they spot. We must always be humbled by the capacity for all individuals in our teams and systems—often living on low or minimum wages, and struggling with the four crises—to contribute to collective intelligence, crowd-driven creativity, and distributed wisdom that exceeds our own.

There is no master-slave dualistic dichotomy in this Third Way. Both those at the core and those at the edge are equals serving the common purpose: the collective intention of serving society in some real and truthful way. Both are valued the same as individuals, as human beings. Those with more business responsibility can be paid more for their extra effort, commitment, and investment. Yet we never make the mistake of thinking senior managers and leaders are any better than the colleagues and employees who do a lot of the actual work.

Such Third Way organizing, strategizing, and executing is key for solving the Transformational Challenges we all face. We want great systemic thinkers who are *both* humble and openhearted *and* courageous and confident to develop strategic innovation to ensure the long-term success of the complex adaptive system that is their organization. And we all want empowered, well-rewarded people executing on the ground who are both ready to listen to the systemic thinkers at the core/top; and also be able to think creatively and execute brilliantly. We also must avoid a desire for consensus at the edges leading to a tyranny from the bottom.

This set-up, "middle-out" leadership, is mirrored in how our bodymind works. Our brain is constantly integrating top-down cognitive genius from the 'upper brain'—that is predicting what might happen in the future—with bottom-up visceral information about what is happening in the present from the brainstem and the entire viscera (the 'lower brain'). This middle-out structure has evolved because it is the best way of blending cognitive and embodied genius together in a creative harmony.

The brain fuses, without effacing distinctions, predictions about how the world *should be* with information from the senses about how it actually *is*. According to a leading expert in emotions, Prof.

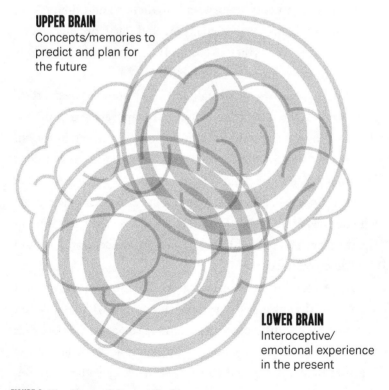

UPPER BRAIN
Concepts/memories to predict and plan for the future

LOWER BRAIN
Interoceptive/ emotional experience in the present

FIGURE 6 *The Upper & Lower Brains*

Lisa Feldman Barrett, dissonance between top-down predictions and bottom-up sensibilities creates much of our emotional sense that things are in some way 'right' or 'wrong.'

Unsurprisingly, recent advances in Artificial Intelligence have been predicted on deep learning through neural networks that mirror this Third Way, middle-out cognitive strategy. They take in information from the bottom up and compare it with hypotheses generated at the top.

In cutting-edge AI, General Adversarial Networks generate predictions about how reality should look (e.g., the shape of a cat) and then examine incoming data to see if it fits these expectations. The AI learns about the world through a middle-out process of creativity (hypotheses, theory, and prediction) and then taking in inputs from how things actually are and "fact checking" them, updating the theory as they go (control). This is also similar to how the scientific method works in practice.

When a society gets the palintonic harmony between create and control right, innovation blooms. This appears to account for the huge flowering of civic and cultural innovation seen in ancient Athens that has so influenced our modern world. As Stanford historian Josiah Ober points out in his book *The Rise and Fall of Classical Greece*, in centralized control systems rulers "determine who does what in the production of goods and who gets what in the distribution . . . wealth and power are concentrated at, and distributed by, the center."

In contrast, what he calls the 'Greek miracle' was in part a result of decentralized creative cooperation with innovation and investment distributed throughout society. Ober believes that the greatest achievement of Athens was to bring people together in a cohesive and coherent Third Way without erasing the important differences between central control and local creativity. Wise Greek leaders were leading a Third Way millennia ago.

Recently, researchers have attempted to understand what works best when trying to change systems and societies. There are some clear lessons from organizations as diverse as Mothers Against Drunk Driving and the National Rifle Association. What works best to transform complex systems is to have an organization that operates in a creative harmony with *both* a strategic, generative hierarchy at the core (with top-down accountability and people leading the change) *and* hyper-local and empowered 'chapters' activating citizens in towns, villages, and cities to support the movement (and be the change.).

It appears that the key reason that both the Arab Spring and the Occupy Wall Street movements failed to land lasting transformation is that they suffered from too much distributed leadership and agility; and did not have enough systemic hierarchy for stability. C&P Mode and C&C Mode need to be poised in a Third Way creative harmony for the best results.

25

LEADERSHIP INCLUDES YET TRANSCENDS MANAGEMENT

In every moment, you can be predominately in C&P Mode or C&C Mode: the former optimized to manage continuous improvements and deliver predictable returns on investment within your existing business model efficiently; the latter optimized for leading continuous transformations that effectively work to adapt your organization to the rapidly changing world.

With C&P Mode driving management consciousness, we are highly interested in efficiencies, productivities, performance, output, profit, metrics, data, strategy, success, rules, and growth. With C&C Mode inspiring our leadership consciousness, we are much more interested in empowerment, purpose, influence, reflection, vision, innovation, safety, intuition, transformation, vulnerability, principles, and creativity.

Ultimately, we must be able to switch between modes rapidly, sometimes in the same conversation. With mastery, in every moment we consciously choose which Mode we are in: is this a moment for a management conversation, for efficient best practice; or is this a moment for leadership conversation to lead transformation and adapt to the changing world?

The Third Way gem ensures that we fully realize that both modes are vital. We have to develop our capacities for Industrial Age management; a technical skill within the hierarchy of an organization. We also must build the capacity for Digital Age leadership; which is a human skill that can occur anywhere in the conventional hierarchy but that takes a great deal of commitment and awareness to master. Our biological bodymind is geared to favor survival predictably over possible thriving, so we have a tendency to overuse transactional management skills instead of deploying transformational leadership skills.

As individuals, we must master our biology so we can calibrate ourselves and our cultures to lead transformation; thus avoiding the failures of 'good management.' This is why our transformation enterprise is called *Switch On*: because we have to choose to switch on from the everyday comfort zone of C&P Mode into C&C Mode. Failure to switch on causes us to fade from relevance, become unfitted to the world around us, and so become obsolete.

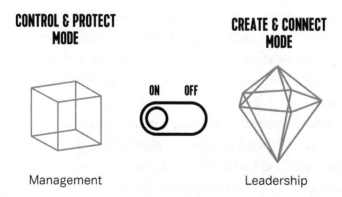

CONTROL & PROTECT MODE

ON   OFF

CREATE & CONNECT MODE

Management   Leadership

FIGURE 7 *Switching Between Management & Leadership*

I suggest that having a clear distinction between a C&P Mode "management conversation" (change yourself for the me/company) and a C&C Mode "coaching conversation" (change yourself for you) is critical. Yet the truly transformational leader understands the power of helping team members find a Third Way blend: that if they change their own mindset and behavior to adapt, it can benefit *both* themselves *and* the organization.

In fact, every team member's adaptation and conscious expansion has the potential to deliver three benefits, a win-win-win or "Triple Win". There can always be a Triple Win for every transformation: a benefit for them, a benefit for you/the enterprise, and a benefit for the world. The transformational leader seeks to find Triple Wins at all times, whether internally or in external collaborations. We transformational leaders understand that we must help others to give up what they crave in order to have what they will be of most sustainable value (like a world that works for all).

Triple Wins are much easier to find in groups that share a compelling purpose. People are much happier to give up being competitive—having what they desire and being right—when they have common cause: a genuine collective vision for a regenerative world. Triple Wins are also far easier to presence for others when we ourselves are embodying our own leadership purpose. It is only when we are congruent, authentic, ethical, and have tamed/befriended our own inner demons that we can help others do the same.

When managing and leading transformational teams, we have to get people poised in a creative tension between Getting Stuff Done (GSD) and having the time and space for reflection, insight, and adaptation. This is a fundamental challenge to Business as Usual for two reasons: first, the fresh insights and ideas that come when teams Connect & Reflect often challenges existing management plans and strategies.

Second, giving people the time they need to get into C&C Mode, introspect, become aware of mismatches, be curious about them, authentically engage with users, come up with new ideas, and test those ideas—enacting Triple Loop Learning all the time—can derail aggressive timing plans and the meeting of ambitious conventional (as opposed to transformational) KPIs.

Somehow, we have to manage performance, ensuring team members get stuff done to time, budget, and quality; while ensuring that we guide them to adapt where necessary and innovate where possible—without overwhelming people with change programs and innovation initiatives that burn them out. This is part of the art and craft of transformational leadership.

As we practice shifting out of C&P Mode dominated management and into C&C Mode dominated leadership, it can feel uncomfortable, strange, and confusing. We are moving from old, established, and comfortable patterns of behavior—inside our comfort zone or "the box"—into new emergent ways of acting that may or may not work well first time. This kind of shift can feel disorienting, and even destabilizing. Our comfort zone is comfortable for a reason. But it is not adaptive to fast-changing environments. It is not our friend when we need to solve mismatches and fit better.

As we leave our management comfort zone, we can experience very physical feelings of confusion, disorientation, even dizziness. The classical management mindset does not tend to like being out of the box like this. It has been trained and optimized to know the answer, to know more than its reports, to be certain, and to be fast. As we switch on and enter C&C Mode, we are suddenly vulnerable, empathically connected to people rather than bossing them around, coming up with creative ideas that might be rubbish, and forced to be honest about not knowing everything.

Genuine leadership therefore includes confident and clear management but transcends it to become so much more: masters at the profoundly challenging, complex, and yet rewarding process of transformation. We learn that this sense of discomfort with the world, outside of our box, is our ally in fast-changing times. The poet John Keats called this capacity to not know the answer 'negative capability': it is the ability to think through a Transformational Challenge without trying to find a single 'right' answer with C&P Mode as fast as possible. Keats wrote this paragraph in a letter: "It struck me what quality went to form a man of achievement . . . I mean negative capacity, that is when man is capable of being in uncertainties, mysteries, doubts, without any irritable reaching after fact and reason."

C&P Mode always tries to shut down openness and curiosity in favor of clarity and certainty. There is a fitting time for this. However, C&C Mode must be utilized to explore challenges that technical know-how cannot solve fully. For this, we need to be able to stay in uncertainty and not knowing. Zen Buddhists call this essential transformational leadership mindset *shoshin*, or 'Beginner's Mind.' Whereas 'good' management requires and rewards technical expertise—having the right answer right away—transformational leadership benefits from cultivating *shoshin*. This means being able to regularly inhabit the mind of a beginner to a subject: curious, open, humble, eager, with nothing to lose—and without a bunch of assumptions about what the 'right' way is that lock us into obsolescence.

26

THE ROLE OF EMOTIONS

If only transformational leadership were as simple as finding time and space to Connect & Reflect (with our customers, team members, and stakeholders)—and then solve problems from within the appropriate Mode! It would seem simple and obvious to learn to use one Mode in moments where best practice is required; and the other Mode when next practice is required. But . . . there is a complication to this story that generates the fundamental barrier to transformation, but also shows us how to hurdle and hack to accelerate transformation. We cannot rationally *control* which Mode we are in (although we can learn to guide ourselves to an appropriate Mode) because of a third important brain network that determines, to a large degree, which Mode we are in: the Salience Network.

This Salience Network is richly connected to the emotion-processing parts of our brain in the limbic system, such as our amygdala. It is, to all intents and purposes, an emotion-driven system. Scientists use the term 'salience' as this important brain network helps us attend to what is salient, or important, in the moment. It shifts our attention onto urgent and salient matters for us to deal with. Is it a moment to control the chaos with the 'right' answer, or is it a moment to create more chaos (i.e., variety or innovation)? Is it a moment to protect ourselves from threats, or is it a moment to connect with others? What makes this mechanic so evolutionarily brilliant is that our Mode switches before we're even aware of it: our emotions activate conscious shifts up to 0.5 of a second before our cognition is aware of it. Rational thought takes time. Emotions are so fast they ensure we survive long enough to have rational thought.

Our emotions are designed to be an immediate and direct guiding system that ensure we survive . . . and also allow us to thrive when we are safe. In my experience in boardrooms across the land, there is still a lot of cynicism about the elemental role of emotions in leadership. Yet leading Harvard psychology professor Steven Pinker says, in the book *How the Mind Works*, that "the emotions are

SALIANCE NETWORK
Attention

FIGURE 8 *The Salience Network*

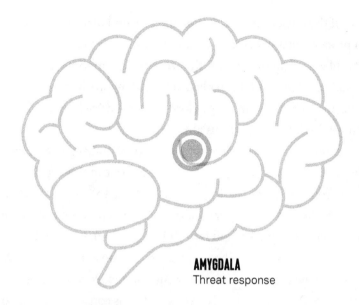

AMYGDALA
Threat response

FIGURE 9 *The Amygdala*

mechanisms that set the brain's highest-level goals" not the lowest. Emotions are not our basest form of consciousness, but actually the most radiant. Emotions evolved because they are hard to fake: they are clear and present guidance that this moment is a good fit to Control & Protect or Create & Connect. The neuroscience is clear: if we don't have emotions to guide us, we can't make even logical decisions.

Emotions drive thoughts and actions. They are the royal road to transformation. Emotions are a vital signal to our brains and bodies to act in a certain way. They aren't corruptible by a lot of noise; they remain a clear and strong indicator of what to do next. When we sense threats—existential, social, or imagined—we act to control the crazy world, and protect ourselves, before we've even had a thought about a threat. I discovered the power of this system a few years back when walking in very rural China. My legs suddenly turned me off the track to the left. It took me a second to look to my right to process what my eyes could see but I had yet to become aware of a black snake turning off the track in the opposite direction. Emotions of fear and danger had activated my stress response, our crucial survival system, way before I was cognitively aware of the danger. This system keeps us alive.

Although we call feelings of fear, anxiety, and anger 'negative,' they actually play a crucial and very positive role in either getting us away from danger or gearing us up to fight it. This is the so-called 'fight or flight' stress response; although many now include freeze (stopped in our tracks) and fawn (please people), too, as adaptive responses to danger. When our stress response is triggered by powerful 'negative' emotions, our Autonomic Nervous System is activated. Our Autonomic Nervous System is constantly acting to keep us alive without us ever being aware of it. It has a sympathetic chain that can elevate us; and a parasympathetic chain that can calm us down.

Under stress, the Sympathetic Nervous System fires up the hypothalamus and pituitary gland to release adrenaline; and then cortisol. These two chemicals increase our heartbeat, increase our blood pressure, and send blood to our limbs so that we can fight, flee, or fawn. If that doesn't work, we freeze or faint. Our visual field is massively reduced. It is more adaptive to focus only a very small area containing the potential threat than having big-picture thinking. We get tunnel vision, but also tunnel thinking and tunnel memory: we can only think about, and remember, similar threats in the past. This is extreme C&P Mode. C&P often kicks in when we, as leaders, or our teams, feel disempowered, forced, uncertain, exhausted, anxious, threatened, alienated, overwhelmed, stressed out, confused, inadequate, pressured, fearful of losing power, status, money, or our reputation.

SYMPATHETIC NERVOUS SYSTEM
Stress response and protection

PARSYMPATHETIC NERVOUS SYSTEM
Relaxation response and connection

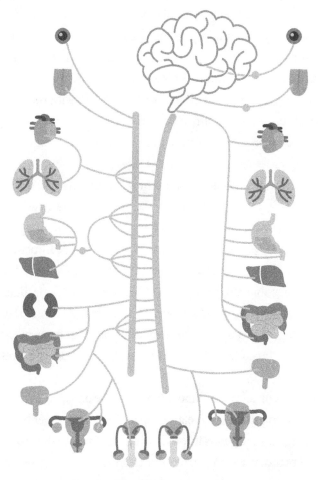

FIGURE 10 *The Autonomic Nervous System*

On the other hand, there are the so-called 'positive' emotions, such as feeling purposeful, cared for, safe, and loved. These co-activate with the other major strand of our Autonomic Nervous System, the Parasympathetic Nervous System (PSN). This chain of nerves acts as an antagonistic pair to the sympathetic chain. We become relaxed and calm, with hormones like oxytocin and acetylcholine flooding our body. Leading psychologist Barbara Fredrickson has suggested this is a 'broaden and build' function as opposed to fight and flight. We can build connections and see broadly. We can then use our fresh insight to build on the work of others, with others.[12] A number of studies have confirmed that 'positive' emotions drive creativity, inventiveness, big-picture thinking; and build resilience, motivation, persistence, and a sense of humor.

Our positive emotions are the biological drivers for agility and adaptability, exactly the skills and qualities we need for transformation. We can have new thoughts and solve complex problems because we can create; and we can collaborate, co-operate, and empathize because we can connect. We are in C&C Mode. We have a higher possibility of being in C&C Mode when we, as leaders, and our teams, are feeling: passionate, purposeful, empowered, in service, courageous, curious, connected, belonging, trusting or trusted, excited, loved, cared for, meaningful, united, loving, and safe.

In moments of calm, our 'upper brain' can be engaged with all its higher-level cognitive and creative capabilities. This upper brain plans for the future and sends its predictions and ideas to the 'lower brain' to be blended with information from the viscera. We use high-level cognitive functions like concepts, memories, narratives, ideas, and memes to think. Meanwhile, the main job of our lower brain is to sense what's happening in the present moment: to keep us breathing, eating, digesting, metabolizing, and scanning for threats.

Most of the time our upper brain dampens down the urges and emergencies of our lower brain. This allows us to stay stable, thoughtful, and responsive (even if we might be controlling). However, in moments of fear, when threats are sensed, we become *destabilized* emotionally. The upper brain no longer dampens down the lower brain and we lose access to those higher-order cognitive functions like reason, insight, and sense-making. Our upper brain cannot deliver the wisdom and insight we need in moments of great challenge.

The great Tragicomedy of Humankind is that just as we need to grapple with intense challenges like being disrupted by AI and nimble upstarts, or dealing with pandemics, climate change, and inequality, we usually shift into C&P Mode. Through emotional dysregulation, we lose our (wise) minds just as we need them most. Emotions felt in our Salience Network disconnect our higher cortex networks and we retreat into old patterns of protection and control. The scale of the problems, perceived threats to ourselves and our children, narratives we tell ourselves of disaster and doom, and intense interpersonal anxieties *all* tend toward flipping us into C&P Mode. We have to find ways to hurdle this huge barrier and hack our own consciousness or we are condemned to forever use the wrong Mode for the moment.

This survival system worked well on the savannas of Africa where we evolved—and perhaps still late at night in downtown Savannah, Georgia, to avoid cars and aggressive bouncers—but it is a mismatch for most of the threats we face today. Our stress response is rarely activated by actual snakes and fast-moving vehicles: physical threats to our biological existence. It is, however, activated regularly by *social* threats to our reputation and sense of being in a group. Perceived threats to our power, status, standing in society, and self-esteem activate our survival system, just like a tiger would. We have the same intense fear, the same awful-feeling anxiety, and the same knee-jerk reactivity. Our fight/flight/freeze/fawn reaction does not know the difference between physical and social threats.

Fear and anxiety, even when people consciously choose to disregard them, interfere with performance. In the stress response, people become wary of threats and become hyper-vigilant. They are primed to see attacks and to react rapidly with emotions. A few decades of research has shown that when people become emotionally dysregulated like this—even if there are no visible signs of fear because they learned how to have their emotions on lockdown (say, to be safe in a corporate world)—productivity falls and decision quality drops.

Neuroscientist Matthew Lieberman at UCLA has shown that when the neural circuits for reactive stress are triggered: people lose the capacity for paying attention, planning, and problem solving. When we become dysregulated like this, we 'flip our lid,' with our lower brain becoming primary and our upper brain going offline. Our emotions are no longer containable so we react with ancient drives to fight, flight, freeze, or fawn. With such emotional dysregulation—when intense feelings like fear, alienation, and rage arise—we switch off and lose creativity and connection; as well as even our capacities for control and analysis. We enter what we might call "Extreme Protect." We no longer have the intelligence of Control. Instead, we are consumed by pure survival instincts.

The grand challenge is that our in-built fear of pain or loss—especially social loss, like losing our reputation or standing—is usually much greater than our excitement about the potential gains from innovation and transformation. We are slightly more biologically conservative (C&P Mode) than we are progressive (C&C Mode) even though we can, of course, be both. We tend toward holding onto old thoughts, habits, and moods, even when they are sabotaging us.

We become rigid and fixated just when we want to be fluid and flexible. This rigidity—and the *emotional* fear of loss that drives it—can permeate through organizations, both formal and informal networks, in minutes. It reinforces negative power dynamics, which shut people down from being curious about challenges; and stops them from challenging authority just at the moments when we need to adapt thinking. This is what happened at Nokia.

As leaders, we then find ourselves activated into a fear-driven reaction in situations where we actually want to be open, sensitive, and creative. Then we have a mismatch between how our biology works—with its sensitive trigger to threats, perceived or actual—and what the actual environment demands: courageous transformational leadership. We get a lot of 'false positives' whereby we are activated into fight-or-flight mode but we are not actually being threatened. We take things personally, get reactive, and use an old defensive pattern to ward off the social 'threat.' We jerk into C&P Mode.

C&P Mode evolved to push dangers away and fight threats. It can help us *avoid* what we are scared of: like a lack of money, recognition, or power. Yet only C&C Mode can give us what our hearts truly yearn: safety, adaptation, meaning, connection, a sense of belonging, a sense of being valued, creative flow, and collaboration. C&P Mode, when we are dysregulated, blocks transformation. Therefore a key job skill for the transformational leader to cultivate is an emotional state that allows us to switch into the right Mode to respond effectively to the situation at hand.

27

PROTECTIVE PATTERNS:
THE BLOCKERS OF TRANSFORMATION

When we feel threatened by anything, our emotional guidance system will switch us into hard C&P Mode. At this point, we use *predictable* habits, learned over a lifetime, to escape the threat. We rely on what I call "protective patterns" to *control* the chaotic world and *protect* us from the threats. These protective patterns are the ways we learned to deal with life reliably; and to get our needs met (more or less) in our formative years. Over time, they have become burnished into our nervous system as habits of emotion, thought, and behavior. Nerves that fire together, wire together: so by the time we have learned to protect ourselves by being quiet, 'nice', aloof, arrogant, or angry over a decade or more, we have recruited millions of nerves into a neural signature that is triggered whenever our bodymind senses a threat. Different threats become coupled with specific protective patterns.

In essence, our protective patterns become our default way of operating within life. Protective patterns form 'the box' we need to think outside of if we are going to lead transformation. As we are just one person, protective patterns tend to show up everywhere in our life, although we may have found socially acceptable ways to enact them in 'polite' company. If you have a pattern in your personal life, chances are it manifests in your professional life as well (perhaps in a slightly different form). And vice versa.

For example, a few years ago I was cooking a soup with one of my sons. He was only three or four at the time and I was teaching him how to cut vegetables safely. I was in C&P Mode, teaching him a protective pattern to avoid cutting off his finger with a knife. Then I was switching into C&C Mode to create a soup without a recipe. After the chopping was done, we put all the vegetables in the pot to sauté. I turned away from my son for a few moments to get something from the fridge. When I returned to the pot, I saw that my son has put all of the peelings of the vegetables into the pot— the skin of the onion and the garlic, the carrot tops, the dry bits of celery. This was his creative child's brain generating 'noise.' It was an experiment!

However, part of me must have found his creativity threatening as a protective pattern popped up and I was suddenly upset with him. I judged his ideas as 'bad,' rejected his experiment, and ruptured the relational field between us. I popped out of C&C Mode and into C&P Mode. It was near-instant. Liking to eat my own dog food/caviar (you, dear reader, decide), I went online that night and found a recipe for 'Vegetable Peel Soup.' I did this to remind myself that I do not have the ultimate, right way of making soup. Just *a* way.

Today, I still have that same protective pattern available to me, of course, when actually threatened. But I am always practicing how to be more polite, calm, and appreciative when engaging in ideas that challenge my own. This example demonstrates how effortlessly and easily a protective pattern can arise within us—and how much they tend to block connection and creativity.

Protective patterns can seem innocuous. Others appear 'good' and 'right.' Some appear 'bad' and 'evil.' But it matters not whether society approves of our protective patterns or not: they were *always* invented by a less wise version of ourselves—often through mimicking our caregivers—so they are *always* historic and therefore usually out-of-date. Almost invariably, patterns are a learned reaction to a past threat, so a mismatch for this present moment . . . right here, right now.

We could easily sweep such protective patterns away, or ignore them altogether. It is *so* tempting. Even more juicy is to blame them on other people, the system, or something like 'God.' When in a protective pattern, our empathy usually drops and we often start to blame, shame, and complain about other people, our bosses, our customers, or our competitors (rather than taking responsibility for ourselves). In fact, whenever we hear ourselves blame, shame, and complain, it is usually a sign that we are in pattern.

Our protective patterns often show up as the hard-won strengths that got us through life. They are us being funny, charming, smart, sexy, intellectual, pretty, problem-solving, rigorous, focused, silly, committed, perfect, shy, arrogant, and pretty much any other way we have found that reliably gets our needs met. As we grow up and engage in new environments with new challenges, these strengths now hamper our growth. But as they are so heavily etched into our neural architecture, we tend keep using the patterns—overusing the strengths—to get our needs met, even when they no longer quite do.

Patterns *approximate* need satisfaction—*kind of* getting us attention, safety, connection—and that seems to be enough until we become conscious of just how sub-par they are at serving us. In fact, until we switch on, we really do believe our needs are being met fully by our strengths. In the moment we realize we are in pattern, the transformational leader must own it. Identifying and owning a protective pattern is the key to leading genuine transformation. If we don't transform ourselves, it is highly unlikely that we can transform others, and the systems of which we are a part.

It is easy to assume that we *are*, in some essential way, our patterns: that our strengths and habits are simply our identity; just "who we are." In fact, we often grow rather fond of them: dear friends that have stood with us through bullying, being bossed around, and being scared in the schoolyard. Our elemental patterns become the 'personality' by which we know ourselves, and through which others relate to us. We believe nothing can change them. However, BTTP holds that just as our protective patterns were learned at some point in time, and then conditioned into our nervous system with practice, so too can they be unlearned and new ones put in place that are more adaptive.

Our protective patterns are not who we actually are but just *who we became* to control the crazy world and protect ourselves through our formative years. I stake my reputation on the

CONTROL & PROTECT
MODE

Protective Pattern:
Predictable reaction
to deliver safety
and order

CREATE & CONNECT
MODE

Transformational
Breakthrough:
Creative response
to deliver invention
and relationship

FIGURE 11 *Predictable Reactions & Creative Responses*

knowledge that *every* protective pattern can be transformed. I don't say this lightly. I know it can take many years, if not decades to fully transform strong protective patterns. But I do know it is possible because I am living proof of this fact.

This insight is crucial because, as our patterns are 'the box' that blocks our transformation and so the transformation of the organizations and systems we lead, we need to dissolve *our* patterns if we want to lead transformation. But because the box has a vital function to protect us and help order a chaotic world, we cannot just ignore its protective role and magically 'get out of the box.'

We have to find ways to make the box/pattern no longer needed as a defense mechanism. Otherwise, the trigger-pattern reaction to threats will lock us into behaviors that fundamentally diminish our capacity to lead: our perspective shrinks, our actions are less generative, and our thoughts are more righteous. We lose our capacity for flexible, fluid, and appropriate responses.

We may consciously *want* to change the pattern. We may try really hard to do so. We might even have some counselling or coaching. But if we do not find a way to shift the emotional state that anchors the pattern in, then we will keep having to cognitively *remember* to change, rather than be genuinely transformed.

It is only by truly transforming a protective pattern—which only happens when it is no longer needed—that we can become the leader that we were always meant to be. Protective patterns are a prison that enchain possibility. They suck creativity from the space. We act in ways that diminish ourselves and others. Hurt leaders go on to hurt colleagues. Protective patterns may have served us well in the past to protect us from the scary world and to control the inherent chaos of life with structure and order. But then those self-same patterns start to *sabotage* our potential as transformational leaders.

Until we learn how to transform our patterns, we cannot become more adapted versions of ourselves. We are stuck repeating what worked in the past to forge the future. This is what philosophers call a 'category error.' It can only ever bring about an epic fail, whether a dramatic bankruptcy or divorce; or a subtle, but no less devastating, decline into maladapted behaviors. These could be social withdrawal and isolation or an obsession with money or power. They can be people pleasing, by saying what people want to hear; or a damaging addiction to social media or being at work.

28

ARCHETYPAL LEADERSHIP PATTERNS

I've worked with perhaps 70,000 leaders over the last 25 years to support their journey to become truly transformational; and so be able to change their organizations and systems at will. During this period, I have seen common protective patterns that show up regularly. We've grouped these into twelve leadership archetypes. I've cross-referenced and improved these using the work of Carl Jung and his intellectual heirs; as well as explored other popular 'personality typing' products on the market to find a fit.

The way we use these archetypes at *Switch On* is crucial and it differs markedly from the way most organizations use personality tests and models. Instead of identifying people by their patterns—which risks reinforcing any beliefs that these patterns are who they really are—we make it abundantly clear that each personality pattern, or archetype, is simply a box that each person has developed and conditioned into his/her nervous system. In reality, we all have the capacity to inhabit and harness *any* of the archetypes. It is vital that we don't use any typology to lock ourselves further into any pattern. Remember, patterns are never all we are. They are simply who we have become to cope. They can all be loosened, expanded, and developed by conscious choice. The archetypes we use are:

The Rigorous Perfecter
The Compassionate Carer
The Intellectual Authority
The Passionate Connector
The Wise Mentor
The Playful Rebel
The Imaginative Maverick
The Resolute Warrior
The High-Tech Magician
The Skillful Artisan
The Visionary Explorer
The Charismatic Leader

Each archetypal pattern has a number of strengths which help the embodier to succeed (in a conventional sense of pay grade, profit, and status). Identifying the archetypes that we regularly inhabit allows us fully to acknowledge these strengths (usually in Getting Stuff Done and being accepted socially). We don't want to judge ourselves harshly for the patterns we copied, invented, and practiced to defend us from threats and have our needs met. Such inner criticism—the Voice Of Doom we can call it—generates angst, which threatens us so we retreat further into C&P Mode.

That said, we definitely *do* want to be able to discern, acknowledge, and own the patterns that limit us; and then compassionately apply our critical thinking capacities to understand why we might have embodied this archetype. As each archetype is a box, no matter how shiny the box is, each locks us out of adaptive and inspired responses to novel challenges. By conscious choice, we can 'try on' the attributes of other archetypes to discover new strengths and ideas; and so expand our palette of responses to life and leadership challenges.

With the same attitude, we can also understand the value of the protective patterns that people around us have developed; and the archetypes they inhabit most frequently. This helps us empathize, validate, and value their patterns—and so them. This is especially important when their patterns frustrate or trigger us. With insight into the value and role of every pattern and archetype, we give ourselves space for compassion and care to blossom. We can then find ways to help others break their patterns; and try out fresh archetypes.

Remember, *all* fixed protective patterns were designed to help us deal with life but, in doing so, they shut us off from capabilities that we might need to be a transformational leader. Each has areas of weakness where we lose power: power to create and transform, not power over others. This loss of power leaves us unable to be responsive and transformative in the moment. When we overuse strengths, we sabotage our potential to be transformational leaders.

Instead, we want to broaden our range of archetypes, of responses, to the VUCA world. One way to do this is to identify a key growth area, the human equivalent of a plant's 'growing tip.' This is what I call our "Leadership Edge". Our Leadership Edge is the place where we are at the furthest edges of our capabilities, and so have the most potential to develop as leaders the most. We can choose to push ourselves to our Leadership Edge (but not over the edge!) every day. Here, we restlessly and eagerly seek our own growth by expanding our consciousness to include new responses and archetypes that are not yet strong in our bodyminds.

To keep this book agile, I have outlined—for the first two of the archetypes only—some key strengths, possible areas of self-sabotage; and potential areas for conscious expansion. This should demonstrate that *every* archetype has amazing benefits, some blind spots, and specific areas to focus on for leadership development that will allow more responsive and creative ways of being to emerge. (We harness the full list of 12 in our leadership programs.)

Archetypal Pattern: The Rigorous Perfecter

Strengths: A detailed commitment to best practices which avoids (known) mistakes and careless errors. Pushes people to go one step further to deliver extraordinary results. Turns 'good enough' into truly great. Restlessly seeks perfection in products and processes. Spots problems in strategies and plans before they go to market. Pushes projects forward on time and on budget to deliver a high-quality outcome which meets user/stakeholder expectations; and builds brand and business loyalty. Keeps colleagues feeling safe and stable with a clear process and set of expectations. Brings order to chaos. Provides reassuring structure.

Potential Sabotage: Can block the vital serendipity, improvisation, and creativity needed when engaging in Transformational Challenges where solutions are not established and there is no best practice. Over-emphasis on a known process or solution reduces the chance that important insights and ideas emerge from the 'unknown unknown.' Driving everyone to deliver perfection every time can exhaust and demoralize; particularly when perfection can never be attained with fast-moving adaptations. Can diminish the energy needed for creative activities as so much effort is going into perfection. An addiction to excellence can prevent curious experimentation and prototyping; which limits learning from useful mistakes as possible solutions to Transformational Challenges are tried out. Can stymie motivation and inspiration as people feel nothing they ever do is good enough. Limits shared accountability for quality as people rely on this archetype to find the faults and fix issues.

Leadership Edge: Practice making low-risk spontaneous decisions and testing out creative ideas in low-cost ways with what I call "smart experimentation." Explore how it feels to launch projects in 'continuous beta,' before they are perfect. Encourage yourself and others to prototype many possible solutions for a problem quickly and cheaply to get rapid learning.

Model to others how you can make mistakes, learn, and grow from them. Dwell in the idea that insights and ideas always emerge from a group that is committed to specific inquiry without always having a clear process. Join innovation and design projects to experience well-facilitated and well-designed creative workshops and experiences—so you can become comfortable not knowing what happens next.

Become more comfortable with not knowing what is going to happen next by taking the team out or going out for leisure time with no or minimal plans (ensuring this is still safe). Invite colleagues (and friends!) to responsibly and politely challenge your process expertise and project rigor when they sense it is shutting possibility down.

Ask people for updates on projects early, before they could possibly be perfect. Then demonstrate your appreciation for the work in progress without telling people where they are wrong. Store your fixes for other peoples' projects until they have had time to find them themselves. Coach people to find their own optimizations rather than always pointing them out or solving issues for them.

Archetypal Pattern: The Compassionate Carer

Strengths: Consistent and continued compassion for whomever is in pain or struggling ensures that team members feel safe, soothed, cared for, and appreciated. This builds loyalty so that people will often go the extra mile when asked to. Caring also generates reciprocity, which is key for community health; and authentic relationships, which allow possibility spaces to arise. When people feel safe, seen, and heard, they open up—and feel free to express bold ideas which might challenge received wisdom and the assumptions of senior managers.

This archetype generates psychological safety that builds team trust, the lubricant for all transformation and innovation. Trust encourages users, customers, and consumers to share their needs and insights; and allows the organization to act on them together to optimize sales, marketing, and innovation. Strength in authentic caring can lead to great sales, negotiation, and business development skills; and can drive 'rain-making' activities.

Potential Sabotage: Can focus on caring and emotional support at the expense of getting stuff done and driving forward execution. When over-used, can allow team members to dwell in their emotions, bring inappropriate content into the workplace, and suck energy with constant 'letting off steam' (also known as complaining and blaming). Can quickly disable team members from developing their own emotional resilience and courage; and prevent them from learning how to 'self-soothe' themselves in the many challenging moments on the journey of transformation.

For the leader, it can quickly become a pattern that is focused on being liked and being needed rather than genuine compassion. This reduces a leader's capability to make tough decisions that often won't be liked by all. The desire for everyone to feel good all the time reduces the discord and discomfort that is natural and crucial within transformation and innovation journeys. Without chaos, which often does feel good immediately, creativity cannot emerge; and without passionate debate, ideas cannot be winnowed and optimized before launching them into the world. Inauthentic connection often leads to manipulative sales and marketing; and coercive management styles.

Leadership Edge: Become increasingly aware of any desire to be liked, to be respected, and to be needed that sit at the core of any acts of care and compassion. Expose yourself to more moments of discord and discomfort in innovation projects and adaptation projects. Find ways to be at peace with others feeling unsafe, unappreciated, and confused—and watch the desire to swoop in and fix their pain for them.

Coach others to become more able to regulate their own emotions, soothe their own fears, and find their own ways to comfort themselves. Experiment with making tough and unpopular decisions and delivering them in kind yet quick, straight, and direct ways. Explore spending less time with people in the caring mode and instead spending more time on your own transformation projects.

Try out new ways to allow people ways to vent their feelings in appropriate, time-bound, and generative ways—without them needing lots of attention or distracting from the challenges ahead. Become fascinated with the power in maintaining strong but semi-permeable boundaries that allow in insights but do not suck the energy you need to lead transformation.

29

THE BODY OF THE TRANSFORMATIONAL LEADER

When we feel strong 'negative' emotions, we can quickly become dysregulated in our nervous system(s) and disabled in our minds. We then react with well-established protective patterns to shut down the chaos and defend against perceived threats. In the last decade, large amounts of exciting research have begun to paint a picture of our cognitive and emotional world that challenges the old view that we think clean, clear rational thoughts with our mind (that is somehow driven by our cerebral cortex). This new picture that is emerging is much more complex. Hundreds of research studies have shown that we are *not* rational brains that are irritatingly tethered to skin-covered bodies; bodies that are weak, get tired, and stop us from being machines of productivity.

Scientists are now realizing that we actually think through the *feelings and the sensations* of our entire bodymind. For example, a study was conducted where subjects were given mugs of coffee or tea. Some mugs were hot, some were not. Those who were given the mugs of the *hot* physical drink felt more *warmly* about new people they met. Further research has shown that physical sensations of hunger, tiredness, and fear impact rational decisions. Judges who are asked to sentence convicted criminals just before lunch, when they are hungry, hand out tougher sentences than when they are full after a nice lunch.[13] We are not disembodied creatures of pure reason. We are fully embodied beings that live, think, and act as much through our bodies as we do through our minds. As William James wrote back in the 1880s: "A purely disembodied human emotion is a nonentity." Emotions are our body aspect guiding and directing our mind aspect.

The tissues and organs in our viscera are constantly sending what is called 'interoceptive' information to our brain, particularly an area called the insular cortex. When we make decisions, we do so with the input of somatic information: breathing rate, blood pressure, cardiac signals, temperature, digestion, elimination (poop and pee) sensations, thirst and hunger, sexual arousal, touch, itches, pleasure, and pain. This information travels up strands of our vagus nerve. The insular cortex integrates these bottom-up signals from the body with top-down thinking from the cerebral cortex, such as predictions of what is about to happen; and sense-making narratives of what it all means.

The insular cortex processes all this information; and we make a decision or take an action. The vagus nerve, which wanders from the brain to all the internal organs, has long been known to transmit instructions from the brain to organs like the heart, lungs, and stomach. However, it's only lately that medics have found that 90% of the fibers that run through the vagus nerve run *upward*, taking information from the core of the body to the brain and not vice versa. The vagus controls the parasympathetic nervous system, which works to rein in our stressed-out sympathetic nervous system, and seems to drive the repair of brain tissue and neurons.[14]

At school, we were all taught that we have five senses. A new and vital sense has recently been added to our sensational universe:

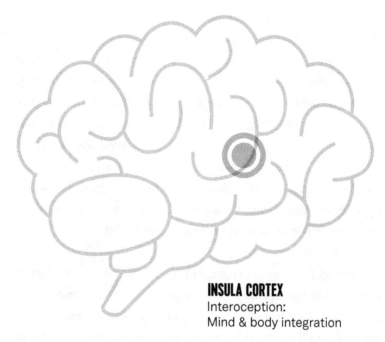

INSULA CORTEX
Interoception:
Mind & body integration

FIGURE 12 *The Insula Cortex*

interoception, which is the sensations we have of the *inside* of our body that provides us, consciously or unconsciously, with information about our physical condition and underlying mood or emotional state. Research into interoception is expanding rapidly and has recently revealed that experienced athletes and elite soldiers in the battlefield have a highly developed insular cortex, and a heightened ability to sense what's going on in their bodies at any one time. US Navy Special Forces personnel show increased activation of their insular cortex at the moment they anticipate a change in their interoceptive state.[15] Athletes and soldiers are keenly attuned to what's happening in their entire bodymind. This helps them stay in peak condition during moments of stress on the battlefield or running track, and helps them make the right call in tough conditions.

Brain research into our emotions, called affective neuroscience, shows that many of our feelings are altered or exacerbated by our physiological state: like whether we are hungry, tired, excited, or repulsed. Prof. Lisa Feldman Barrett, at Northeastern University, suggests in her book *How Emotions Are Made* that our biology only has very basic purely interoceptive signals: toward or away from something; and heightened or reduced activation. All our other interoceptive and emotional sensations are co-created between our physiological state and the ideas and narratives we have within our upper brain. This means we can learn how to master our emotions by consciously transforming how we label, and perceive, everything from fear to frustration.

Indeed, fresh research is showing that people who have a higher interoceptive intelligence—that is, a greater ability to monitor their own internal states and make sense of them—have a more stable sense of a unified self. This allows them to be more grounded and emotionally regulated, which allows them to have more empathy for others. They exhibit clearer boundaries between self and others, and so have fewer boundary issues like co-dependency and taking things personally that do not need to be. This means leaders with interoceptive intelligence are far less reactive, upset, and stressed out.

However, when we are unaware of our interoceptive sensations and do not take ownership of the emotions that arise within us, we often confuse our state of emotion and activation with the state that others are in. If we cannot process our emotions and interoceptive signals well, we blur how we feel with how the world feels. We might then project our mental map and sense of emotional regulation onto other people. For example, we might feel fear and label something a catastrophe; and then we will catastrophize the situation further (a situation that may not be worrying for most people). The archetypal leadership pattern of the crisis hero does this. They need a catastrophe in order to save the day. As psychology professor Manos Tsakiris, at the University of London, says, "interoceptive processing acts to stabilize the model of our self," so we can "attribute emotional and mental states to the self or to others without blurring the distinction between self and other."[16]

Leaders must develop interoceptive intelligence, what we call "embodied wisdom," if they want to be transformational. If you want to make better leadership decisions, without being destabilized by fear and other strong emotions; and have more useful leadership insights, without blurring the boundaries between yourself and your colleagues and customers, a constantly deepening embodied wisdom is crucial. Interoceptive intelligence begins when we choose to become much more aware of the 'somatic markers' that arise across our day and week.

In leadership development and transformation lingo, this is known as being aware of our "felt sense." It is vital that, whatever situation we encounter, we learn to explore what we *feel* about it as much as what we think about it. This is important because our feelings will often guide the thoughts and behaviors that come after. Therefore, mastery of our embodied experience—in the hot, wet flesh of our biology—becomes mastery of leadership.

30

PERSISTENT & PERNICIOUS PROTECTIVE PATTERNS

Persistent physiological feeling-states in the body influence *all* our decisions as leaders, regardless of whether we understand them or experience them consciously. The neuroscientist Antonio Damasio has called them "somatic markers." What psychologists and biologists are now realizing is that painful memories from our past lodge themselves as somatic markers in our nervous system—that we feel as familiar sensations like a tightness in our throat or butterflies in our pelvic floor. These then get triggered in present-moment meetings, stressful situations, or difficult conversations—and so influence our state of mind and our decisions—without us even knowing it. We become dysregulated and destabilized inside even while we look to others like we have everything in control on the outside.

Somatic markers that have their origins in past emotional pain make deep imprints in our bodymind, causing us to repeat protective patterns over and over again even though the patterns themselves are now hurting us and diminishing our potential (and that of those we lead). We get stuck in "looping patterns," attempting to get our needs met over and over again with remarkably sub-optimal habits.

We loop around over and over as we try to get what we think we need (respect, safety, connection), yet all the while our effectiveness as leaders decreases with every sabotaging act. We cognitively *want* to change, maybe even get coaching on it, and try so hard to change; but because we are *emotionally* hooked into somatic markers of old emotional and social wounds, we simply cannot let go of the old protective patterns to embrace new ones. The old patterns will continue as long as C&P Mode believes that the habit is needed to protect us; and control the inherent crazy of modern life.

So even though most of us are doing our best as leaders, we will all have a bunch of protective patterns that do not seem to be transformable. We may have tried a bunch of interventions, from New Year's resolutions to therapy, and the protective patterns have not shifted. These persistent protective patterns can often become quite pernicious: they not only start to sabotage our potential as leaders but lead us into ever-decreasing circles of performance and potential where, one by one, we corrode or fully break every important relationship in our lives. It is these patterns, both persistent and pernicious, that become most important to transform if we are going to be able to play *any* part, let alone our full part, in future-proofing our organization and in bringing about a more regenerative world that we all yearn for.

This is what we call doing "inner work." Like outer work— running projects, reporting performance, writing books—inner work takes time and attention. However, it is not focused out there in our material world but in here in our conscious world. Doing inner work allows our outer work to be creative, responsive, and fitting. Inner work means proactively, and with maximum self-awareness and wisdom, exploring the persistent patterns that are blocking our transformation; understanding the emotional and interoceptive markers of them, and doing whatever we can to resolve the issues that are anchoring these patterns in place. Inner work is what happens when we metabolize a Transformational Challenge within us by first accepting that our reactive and protective patterns—always created at some earlier time to ward of danger and then conditioned into our nervous system by repeated usage—need to transform before we can transform our enterprise or system. All patterns are from the past: so almost all are a mismatch for the present at some point (and possibly always).

The Germans have a (long) world for this: *Vergangenheitsbewältigung*. It means to overcome or master the past. This, of course, is a constant process: we all have a lot of past! Inner work is never finished. There are always more patterns to transform and possibilities to unlock. We all have so many foibles that we are never a finished product! We are in continuous beta ourselves, always becoming a more transformational leader. Every time we notice that we are reacting with a pattern, no matter how innocuous, we make a date to do some inner work around it. We sift regularly, daily, for mismatches in our behaviors and beliefs that show there are hidden nuggets of gold: sources of future value in the present, both in ourselves and our world.

The point is not to be a finished item: the point is to constantly do the work of becoming our truly transformational selves. The alternative to doing the inner work to transform each persistent protective pattern is an inevitable retreat into ever-decreasing circles that come from repetitive mismatches. We may be rich, powerful, and famous; but if we haven't done our inner work, we will likely be lonely and purposeless, and suffer, too. We might also not have a hospitable planet in which to spend all that money.

Inner work requires time and permission to Connect & Reflect. It also can be accelerated with transformation tools and practices that help us. Practices help us do our own inner work and also engage in co-creative interpersonal inner work with others. This means we can become our 'best leadership self' in relationship to others in the team. Transformation practices and tools help us track and transcend interoceptive jitters in our viscera, understand and flatten out emotional roller-coasters and mood traps in our feelings, explore and adjust narrative distortions and self-talk in our minds, and spot and transform addictive habits in our behaviors.

If we choose to transform emotional and interoceptive remnants of past issues within our bodymind, we become more transformational as leaders. We are able to keep a stable connection to ourselves, others, and the world around us even as stressors emerge. We are less reactive to our peers, our colleagues, and the highly pressured sectors in which we all operate.

How persistent and pernicious our protective patterns are appears to be largely dependent on the quality and strength of our initial relationships with our parents (and other loved ones). One of the key tenets of modern-day psychology, brought to the fore John Bowlby, is that the connections we form (or don't) with our caregivers create templates with which we then approach all relationships later in life. Our patterns are forged one relationship— one connection and one conversation—at a time during our formative years.

Our childhood experiences, particularly those in which our sense of love, trust, and safety are first generated, set the tone and tenor for every subsequent interaction. As Feldman Barrett puts it in an online essay in *Aeon* magazine, "early attachments prime us for a lifetime, and we keep seeking echoes of early experiences in later relationships . . . mammals learn to manage hardship through relationships, and bonding is their key mechanism for stress reduction."

Our ability to soothe ourselves and regulate our emotions as adults is influenced from a very early age, when we rely on our caregivers to help us because we don't know how to soothe ourselves. People who made secure and safe attachments to their caregivers tend to have a better ability to regulate their emotions, and to have greater interoceptive intelligence. As children, any ruptures in attachment with our caregivers—and thereby to our sense of safety and security—can remain as ruptures in our ability to sense our inner life and make sense of our emotional life.

If our early relationships don't leave us feeling safe, secure, and sure that we are seen—and studies suggest that few do, which is unsurprising given our cultural histories of trauma, abuse, industrial alienation, and fractured communities—it is harder (though still absolutely possible) for us to build openhearted and secure relationships as adults.

In fact, doing my best to summarize some of the key research on attachment theory: the quality of our early interactions with caregivers dramatically impacts our beliefs about ourselves and our world; our expectations of bosses and co-workers; the way we make sense of challenging situations; how we parse new information and insight; how well we cope with stress; and how well we regulate our emotions without doing inner work. In other words, our early relationship templates inform much of how we act as leaders… until we take ownership of our relationships—the ones we have with parts of ourself as well as those we have with others—and develop richer and more secure ones through our inner work. That is to say, our templates do not dictate our future *if* we are prepared to transform them. Our bodymind is malleable and our neurons are plastic.

Positive and consistent early 'attachments'—with caregivers who were attuned to our needs and reliably delivered on them—provide a lasting imprint of security in our relationships for the rest of our lives. If our relational fields are based on a blueprint of feeling safe, seen, and heard, we will likely have fewer persistent and pernicious patterns that block important aspects of relationship: actively listening, taking risks, being authentic, being vulnerable. Our boundaries will be neither overly defensive and rigid nor overly weak and permeable. We will find it easier to 'contain' our emotions; and stay stable and self-regulated. Lots of researchers have confirmed this: when compared to those with insecure attachments, those with secure attachments have a greater sense of autonomy, have higher self-esteem, are more comfortable with uncertainty, and are more able to update their beliefs in the light of new data. These are precisely the qualities we want as transformational leaders of a world in crisis.

Distortions in the relational fields that arise in our formative years can show up years later as difficulties in our relationships with our bosses, colleagues, employees, investors, and collaborators. If we have some kind of disrupted or damaged attachment—because our early caregivers could not give us the love and safety we needed in the way we wanted it, even if they did their very best given their circumstances—we tend to have more challenging relationships with others.

Imprints from less stable and secure attachments can have us activate protective patterns when we are not actually under threat. We take things personally when they are not personal. This can be extreme. Seniority provides no immunity to this. In fact, it can make it more problematic. In *Boarding School Syndrome: The Psychological Trauma of the 'Privileged' Child*, Joy Schaverien suggests that those who go to prep/private schools often show 'emotional blindness' with very limited emotional 'range' (a rich and wide spectrum of emotions). Such leaders have real challenges forming close and trusted bonds and struggle to be vulnerable with co-workers.

We need to be vulnerable and emotionally present to lead the collaboration and collective innovation activities needed in such challenging times. If we are a leader with significant relational field challenges, we may well be forced to rely on hierarchical power, manipulation, command, and force to get what we want done rather than leading people to change with care, inspiration, story, and ethical influencing. Research has shown that power, used as a proxy for inner strength, causes leaders to treat their colleagues as a means to an end.[17]

People with disrupted relational fields often have low self-esteem, but they may not always show up like they do. They may have learned to cover their emotional wounds with protective patterns that give an air of success and confidence. Some will tend to rely more on the *fight* response (what we call "outies"): with overly weak boundaries, they find it hard to contain strong emotions and so splurge them onto others. They try to get their needs met with anger, outrage, and drama. They might expect employees to perform well for them as a proxy for the love they didn't get. They might exaggerate threats and transmute everyday situations into catastrophes, making people run around fighting fires that may not exist.

Another group of people tend to rely on the *flight* response (what we call "innies"): they quickly become overly boundrified, numb, dissociative, and withdrawn. They may look cool and collected in meetings, but they are actually afraid within. As they flee the scene, they become emotionally and intellectually absent, which means they cannot contribute to innovation and transformation projects wholeheartedly. They may not let anyone get close and may struggle to let their true selves out. While every human can develop innie and outtie patterns, we all tend to rely on one defensive play; until we choose to master ourselves and do the inner work.

Outties tend to get a lot of critical feedback for their protective patterns of anger and upset from an early age. Innies can hide under the radar and seem 'nice' and 'calm'; and therefore 'good.' Let me be clear: no protective pattern is 'good' or 'bad'; or 'better' or 'worse' than any other. They all developed to get needs met in the past; therefore they are all likely to be a mismatch for many vital moments of leadership, love, and life in the present. *Every* pattern, no matter what it is, reduces our creative responsivity as much as it protects us and keeps us safe and in control. That is the very point of it. The task is not to blame ourselves or others for our protective patterns; but to own them and metabolize them into potentials and possibilities that serve us better. A clue that we are 'in pattern' is when we become rigid and 'right.' Time to do some inner work!

Bear in mind, that we all do our best as leaders given our own relationship templates. I know I do. And I mess up regularly. Life is inherently chaotic. As children, we all had to cope with intense fears, from: necessary separation/individuation; scary dreams; the behaviors of other kids and adults; and inevitable uncertainty and change.

This also means that when it comes to being parents ourselves— and one could see parenting as a special case of leadership (and vice versa!)—no matter how securing and present we are, our kids will develop protective patterns. This is natural. However, we can do our best to set them up—and our team members—to be more resilient and resourceful around stress and chaos. We can all do our best—through ownership and inner work—to pass on as few diminishing patterns as we can… without ever crucifying ourselves for our foibles as parents or leaders. To err is human. To forgive (ourselves and others) is divine.

31
STRESS & TRAUMA

Whenever we are under stress—which is a lot of the time for leaders until we switch on and step up to take charge of change—we will likely touch into an old attachment imprint and fire up an ancient somatic marker. Then we will react with a protective pattern that keeps threats at bay depending on whether we are an innie or outtie. Not all stress is bad, though. There are two types. The first is eustress (Greek 'eu,' meaning good). Good stress activates us, it gets us moving, gets us performing. It arouses us emotionally and gets us to move toward challenges with confidence and courage. If we are doing a keynote, leading an important meeting, or going on a date, eustress elevates our bodily functions. Without stress like this, we wouldn't be alive to read a book, let alone act as high-performing leaders of transformation.

However, there is also distress, which leads to elevated levels of cortisol, increased inflammation, the degeneration of our neurons, sleep issues, anxiety, and poor memory. When prolonged distress becomes 'toxic', it is as dangerous as smoking in terms of cardiovascular risk; and the likelihood of having heart disease, or a heart attack. It is estimated that 60-80% of primary care visits to doctors are related to distress.

When we are distressed, C&P Mode activates much quicker than it does when we are rested, relaxed, and rejuvenated. It immediately shuts off our ability to empathize with customers and colleagues. Empathy and connection are the keys to both innovation and transformation, but we evolved to cut them off when under threat because we don't want to befriend the saber-tooth tiger or tribal warrior who is attacking us. Without empathy we don't have trust. Without empathy there is no insight; and without creativity there are no ideas. So protective patterns that reduce insight and ideation, that were developed in our relationships with carers and loved ones during our formative years, can really tank our capacity to lead transformation.

What makes this ironic is that the VUCA (volatile, uncertain, complex, and ambiguous) environment itself is stressful. VUCA triggers pain and fear in the same parts of the brain that are triggered by physical pain. Research suggests that we actually feel emotional and physical pain in the same area of the brain, and with the same intensity.[18] Sticks and stones may break our bones, but words equally hurt us! As we experience both uncertainty and change as pain, the VUCA reality (and constant change programs!) drive us into a distress response which causes us to enact old pernicious and persistent protective patterns pretty much all the time.

As a result, unless we pay attention, our ever more digital, disrupted, damaged world will lead us to react with old, outdated protective patterns rather than new, creative responses. Just as we need to be most transformational, we become more of a dinosaur. Distress will trigger persistent and pernicious C&P Mode protective patterns to repeat over and over: whether balling out a co-worker, avoiding conflicts, or being right in meetings.

The most persistent and pernicious protective patterns we have—those which most sabotage our potential as transformational leaders—evolved to deal with difficult experiences in our childhood and early adulthood. Which means no matter how much we try to change our beliefs and behaviors, only a shift in how we sense and feel will allow the pattern to become redundant. Adverse experiences in our formative years can drive persistent and pernicious patterns indefinitely until we find a way to unlock ourselves from being stuck. This is trauma.

Trauma acts like a leaden anchor, with a light and often invisible titanium chain, that holds back our potential by locking in protective patterns that make adaptation and agility impossible. The world today is so fast that even the speed of change itself can be profoundly traumatizing to us, throwing us into endless cycles of distress reactions to the constant threats of modern life. The relentless need to manage school drop offs, monthly KPIs, hundreds of emails, and scores of meetings a week can be traumatic.

'Trauma' is often assumed to mean dramatic and horrible negative events. An ongoing revolution in psychology and neuroscience is shifting this perception. Trauma is actually *any* experience that was too much for us to process at the time it occurred. Dutch psychiatrist and pioneering PTSD researcher Bessel van der Kolk says in his book, *The Body Keeps the Score: Brain, Mind, and Body in the Healing of Trauma*, trauma is what happens when an intense (and usually threatening) experience overwhelms our capacity to deal with it effectively in the moment.

The result of this failure to process the "shock" of intense experiences in the moment is that the traumatic events stick around in our bodymind. They become somatic markers that get activated in our viscera, nerves, and brain whenever we see a threat that bears a resemblance to the original trauma. Trauma also alters the way we process and recall memories, so we start to see many events as traumatic, and understand ourselves to be right about it. This keeps us repeating patterns to defend ourselves against anything that looks like it might traumatize us again. We will do anything we can to avoid a recurrence of pain, even if it means sabotaging our careers and marriages in the process.

Many of us had traumatic experiences that have been encoded within our cells, which then trigger patterns with us. We can pass these patterns, and possibly even the trauma, down to the next generation. We also pick up traumatic wounding, and protective patterns, from our caregivers. This happens in our genes through 'epigenetic' changes due to stress. For centuries, scientific dogma held that we could inherit genes but not behaviors from our parents. Now that is being reconsidered.

Recent studies have shown that stress-driven changes can be passed down to descendants. We don't just mimic patterns of our parents, we inherit them directly in our cells. Early research on humans has shown that growing up in a stressful environment frays the ends of our chromosomes. These protective 'caps' are 20% shorter in children from poor and unstable families compared to those from more nurturing homes.[19] Children from grandparents who were subject to traumatic events, like the Holocaust or intense famines, have been shown to have stress response systems that remain on high alert.

Any event can be traumatic if it overwhelms our capacities to make sense of it; or if it was not controllable at the time. Most of us have had such traumatic experiences, even if we have been lucky enough not to suffer what professionals would label 'abuse' or 'neglect.' There will have been many moments where we just couldn't work out what was underway, it didn't feel safe or good, and we didn't know how to change it. These traumatic experiences can stay with us for a lifetime, affecting our emotional states, our mental states, and our behaviors as leaders and team-members. Complicating matters even more is that traumatic and stressful experiences during critical periods of brain development can actually transform the functioning of specific circuits in our brain as adults.

As 70% of people—so 7 out of 10 leaders—have had at least one Adverse Childhood Experience (ACE), that means many of us are walking around with brains that are geared to be in distress and reactivity. Every ACE we have impacts our emotional functioning as well as our longterm health. For example, for every traumatic *psychological* experience someone has in his/her earlier life, the risk of *physiological* death due to HIV+ infection goes up by 17%. If someone had 3 ACEs, the risk of death through developing full-blown AIDS increased by a staggering 83%. It is likely this has been playing a part in how people respond to the coronavirus.

If trauma is an intense emotional experience we cannot process fully at the time, and so we store it up in our bodymind as a source of stress and disorder, then we will become more traumatized as leaders if we don't find time each day, and certainly each week, to process fully all the disappointments, overwhelms, upsets, and shameful moments that are abundant in today's world. The shock caused by every conflictual email, missed KPI, project gone south, costly invoice, exhausting flight, endless commute, rupture in our relationships, frosty reception of our ideas, violent Netflix show, anxiety-inducing news headline, hurtful comment from a loved one, snarky comment from a boss, snide look from a co-worker, harsh feedback from the Board, dismissive response from a user, or moment that we are underestimated can wind up our hearts ever tighter.

Without processing our week fully, with regular inner work, everyday shocks stored in our nervous system act like silt that blocks the flow of transformational creativity and purposeful strategy in our leadership activities. 'Negative' emotions that are unprocessed remain within us, making us more likely to become emotionally destabilized and dysregulated in the future. It is a feedback loop —full of looping patterns—that continues until we switch on.

Inner work is always in a tension with outer work. If we do too much inner work, then we will spend so long daydreaming, reflecting, healing, creating, and transforming that we will have little time for outer work. Nothing will get done on our projects and transformation in our enterprises and systems will grind to a halt. But if we do too much outer work, and give ourselves too little time to process our emotions, adjust our narratives, and transform our habits, we will get locked into ever-decreasing circles of dysfunction, distress, and discord. The ideal is a creative harmony between inner work and outer work.

In order to step up as powerful leaders of positive and lasting change, we must be able to transform how we emotionally relate to ourselves, others, and the VUCA reality. This requires a lot of inner work, probably over many years. Wonderfully, we can use our everyday interactions with colleagues to heal ruptures and tears in all our relational fields (just as we can heal our relationships at home which will help us at work). We can metabolize relationship challenges at work to repair rents in our connection with our loved ones, both alive and dead; and the natural world that we are all intrinsically a part of.

Everyone has such tears and gashes in their relational field. The transformational leader knows it is an elemental part of their job to repair them consciously and consistently. If we haven't been taught how to repair relational fields—and most of us haven't been as society tends to avoid or repress conflict rather than acknowledge relational ruptures and repair them consciously and sagaciously—then damaged relationships corrode the trust we need to make transformation happen successfully and without violence. Sediment from ruptured relational fields, miscommunications, misunderstandings, snubs, and sensitivities block collective creativity.

When triggered into C&P Mode, protective patterns within our personality enter power struggles with the patterns of others. Each pattern fights to win. Each person believes that they are 'right' and 'justified.' But in such a power struggle—whether a fiery feud between two outies or a passive aggressive scuffle between two innies—there can be no winning. There can just be protection and defense. This merry, and exhausting, dance comes at a massive cost to collective innovation and organizational transformation. Such power struggles show up in what renowned quantum physicist David Bohm called 'discussions.' There is not a lot of connection or creativity in a discussion. The word, which has a similar end to the words 'concussion' and 'percussion', derives from the Latin for 'shaking apart'. In discussions, we are just trying to win other people around to our existing beliefs.

If we can find our way back to C&C Mode, rather than saying, or implying, "I am right about this . . .," we might instead say or imply, "I know I am wrong . . . I just don't know how wrong!" We listen to others to grok what they say and work *with them* to find better solutions. As we find our way out of C&P Mode and into C&C Mode, we can consciously relinquish long-established, but utterly outdated protective patterns that we usually enact to maintain power and control. Then we enter into *co-creative* conversations, what David Bohm called 'dialogues.' It is only in such generative dialogues that we can find transformational solutions to a Transformational Challenge *together*. We find the truth 'dialogically,' as literary critic Mikhail Bakhtin said.

32

PROTECTIVE PATTERNS IN ORGANIZATIONS & SYSTEMS

One of the great challenges of leading transformation in organizations and in systems (markets, industries, ecosystems, communities) is that we are not just dealing with creating sustained transformation in our patterns, comfort zone, or 'box': we are dealing with transforming many! Most employees in most organizations have been recruited precisely because they have the same protective patterns—and so the same view on reality—as everyone else in the organization. Organizations hire for specific boxes that they then ask everyone to think outside of.

Each new hire is further trained in the existing culture by comments, criticisms, and feedback from colleagues; by the training and development programs on offer; by the design of processes and procedures, like manufacturing processes, budget planning, expense procedures, and performance assessments; and by the explicit (bonuses, promotions, share options) and implicit reward mechanisms that build the culture by design (or by default). What remains is an organizational system that primes *everyone* to deal with technical problems in a consistent and efficient way; but also to react to Transformational Challenges with the same outdated and mismatching assumptions and habits.

Organizational patterns attempt to stop the comfort zone/box of the corporate culture from being challenged. The organization's patterns were designed (or, more likely, evolved over time, to fight fires and deal with failures) to deliver predictable returns on investment with as little risk as possible. They were premised on the organization existing in a stable environment, within which long-range plans work well to continuously improve best practices; and so deliver on performance, productivity, and profit targets.

In such historic (and perhaps even mythic) environments, organizations did not need to innovate or transform their products, processes, and people much, or at all, as the legacy ways of doing things worked just fine. All managers needed to do was tweak the existing algorithm/manufacturing line/marketing message from time to time to deliver small gains in efficiencies, all of which deliver reliable growth in results. So organizational patterns did not need to be transformed; and so, leaders never needed to master tools and methods for transforming them.

Pretty much every organization I have worked with in the last 25 odd years has great muscle, developed over decades, for executing established C&P Mode patterns (aside from a few super-creative yet chaotic start-ups). People often don't realize that institutions were actually created to do exactly this. The institution is there for a reason: to produce, manufacture, market, and deliver products/policies/processes as efficiently as possible with minimal transaction costs.

This means that muscle in C&C Mode—in creativity, innovation, empathy, and transformation—is usually inchoate at best. People are often disempowered and lacking in creativity and empathy after years of training people to obey the rules/boss. This is why internal innovation teams, or external consultancies, can *invent* innovations like smartphones and digital cameras—as Nokia and Kodak did respectively—but still watch the organization's protective patterns crush the ideas before they can be implemented in transformational business models.

When leaders cannot get into C&C Mode long enough to listen to diverse voices, unlike their own; empathize with emerging customer needs; and be curious about a future that is not like the past (in which they excelled) . . . then all attempts at transformational innovation in products and processes will fail. This is nobody's fault. It is how our biologies work; and when those biologies have all been tuned to feel, think, and act similarly for years, this becomes a prodigious force with which to grapple. This is why the metaphor of an institutional immune system is so powerful. Just like our own immunity, it fights with everything that it has to destroy biological material that seems foreign and 'wrong.'

Whenever you hear people (and yourself) in an organization say things like, 'this is the way we do things around here,' 'this is the right way,' 'we're not in the business of,' 'did you think it through properly,' 'we've tried that and it didn't work,' or 'they tried that and it didn't work!', organizational patterning is exerting itself and attempting to corral divergent thinking to protect its collective box.

I have discovered over the years that C&P Mode mindsets are so strong in most organizations—given they are usually operated through hierarchies that are designed by people in C&P Mode to perpetuate and replicate C&P Mode—that the organization will attempt to crush any sniff of C&C Mode activities as soon as they arise. C&P Mode will do it politely (usually). But it will do it. That means rigidly resisting seeing Transformational Challenges as anything other than technical problems, blaming 'the market' rather than taking responsibility for metabolizing change into value, shooting the messenger (consultants or internal agents of change), and sidelining mavericks. If that all fails, C&P-driven managers might commission another report.

The organization is akin to a living organism that attempts to survive by controlling complexity and protecting itself from threats. It uses a mass C&P Mode to diminish the "noise," creativity, experimentation, and chaos that could potentially damage its longterm viability. This is the design of C&P Mode for an individual; and it is the same when maxed up to the scale of an entire organization. C&P Mode is fractal: similar to itself at every level of magnification.

The box of C&P Mode tends toward killing innovation, blocking change, and resisting transformation even as everyone speaks about the need to do these things to stay competitive. This diminishes motivation, engagement, enthusiasm, and excitement. Leaders and managers at every level are rarely *consciously* seeking to stop change and transformation from occurring. They are just following the dictates of good management.

Underlying this is powerful and fearful emotions warning against danger and loss. Most people are anxious that the future—and the transformations needed to forge it—is going to cause them to lose something: reputation, power, influence, safety, livelihood. To feel safe, to control and protect, they will resist and block activities of transformation, even while believing they cognitively understand the need for change; and saying that they support it.

Even if we manage to transform our own protective patterning around a challenge or problem, often the 'groupthink' that exists within the organization will resist our insights. Groupthink exists because it is a survival advantage to bond with a group; and be protected by membership of a tribe. As Professor Feldman Barrett beautifully writes: "Recent evidence, including studies that film crowds from helicopters and use machine-learning algorithms, shows that humans have 'herding' tendencies; they synchronize their walking in large streets, match movements while waiting in long lines, and coordinate running in big marathons." Unfortunately, this desire to join a crowd—and the resultant mob behavior which often results—also scales organizational blind spots and blinkers. Then nobody can even see new insights or ideas as useful or valuable.

Again, this is just biology. There is an apocryphal story that because Polynesian people had never seen or conceived of a Western-style boat (like HMS Endeavour), they did not even see the ships in which Captain Cook sailed to their islands. Therefore, it is to be expected that colleagues will dismiss anomalies in data, weak signals that keep repeating, or even major fails as one-offs, inconsequential, or just plain wrong. C&P Mode does not like to engage in single-loop, let alone double-loop or triple-loop learning. It was rewarded for being right. Being right felt safe at school, and at home. It is a protective pattern, a habit, to crave being right even at the cost of losing the business.

The emotional attachment human beings have to being right about their existing mental maps, narratives, and beliefs makes them enact what psychologists call the 'backfire effect.' When presented with evidence and logical arguments as to why we are wrong, we actually resist the information and double-down on our original beliefs. This happens in labs when people are presented with policies from the political party they don't emotionally support (even if they were originally written by members of their own political party); and it happens when people who emotionally do not believe in science or climate change are shown incontrovertible 'facts.'

The more people push on our box when we are in C&P Mode, the more we resist: and we make up stories in real time that dismiss and diminish both the message and the messenger. In this way, the institutional "immune system" neutralizes the virus of new thinking, new ideas, and new possibilities.

It is natural for us as human to be 'groupthinkers'. Our brains tend to light up in similar ways to our friends and colleagues because we are geared toward thinking and feeling like those around us. We are social beings and we have social brains and bodies. We evolved our large brains in order to manage complex social environments and the co-operation needed to survive and thrive. A primary purpose of such a big brain is social thinking: to predict what is going to happen next in the group so that we survive.

We are fundamentally relational creatures. Our brains are shaped within, and wired by, our relationships with others. We literally develop our patterns in relational fields with others. We think within, and through, our relationships. Research shows that close relationships—more than money or fame—are what people yearn for most, and what keeps them happiest throughout their lives. The effect is so powerful that, by the age of 50, our level of satisfaction with our relationships is a better prediction of our physical health than our cholesterol levels.[20]

To fit within a group and bond with our people, we have evolved a very powerful hormone: oxytocin. It helps us bond to our genetic offspring and also to others 'like us.' But it also promotes a rejection of others outside the group. Much of human conflict and organizational dysfunction (among silos, departments, and teams) comes from this in/out distinction. As Prof. Feldman Barrett puts it in her *Aeon* essay: "synchrony of large crowds, underpinned by the molecule that glues us together [oxytocin], is comforting; it cements our sense of belonging to humankind, a race whose legs are stuck in dirt but with heads that can reach the stars . . .'" but "the very system that sustains parental care, pair-bonds, group sharing, and consoling behavior also became intensely sensitive to danger.

Oxytocin protects against danger by immediately differentiating 'friend' from 'foe.'"

To join a group and be safe, we must think like everyone in the group. This is why individual IQ actually goes *down* in social groups.[21] As we align our thinking with the group, outdated assumptions—the kind that underpin business models and that, if not adapted as times change, lead to organizational irrelevance and obsolescence—are not challenged but actually become stronger in what is called the 'cascade effect.' Everyone within the in-group is incentivized by the fear of social rejection and pariah-like status to reinforce old assumptions rather than focusing on the anomalous new ideas or insights that are breaking through. This is exacerbated by the lack of diversity often found in organizational groups. This means ethnic diversity and gender diversity; and also a diversity of thinking and feeling styles too.

At all times, remember what a huge step it is for ourselves as leaders, and our colleagues and co-workers, to break out of socialized conditioning to think (and feel) differently from the group. This phenomenon is powerful even in supposedly rational and data-driven science. Research published by the sociology of science journal *Scientometrics* shows that out of 24 Nobel Prize winners studied, all 24 of them encountered resistance to their breakthrough ideas.[22] The papers that they wrote to put forth their revolutionary thinking—and which won them Nobels—were rejected and criticized by the editors of the scientific journals that eventually published their papers.

Even brilliant gatekeepers of knowledge within the scientific community resist the transformational thinking that drives paradigm shifts in science. This is why one of the innovators of quantum theory, Nils Bohr, said that "science progresses one funeral at a time." In organizations, this shows up in experts—both those inside an organization and externally with market analysts and consultants—fundamentally underestimating the disruptive forces at play in the world. This is what had McKinsey dismiss cellphone adaptation and Bloomberg dismiss the iPhone. If we want transformation, industry experts are the last people we should ask . . . unless they can get out of C&P Mode and into C&C Mode.

33

BTTP GEM 4: THE FOUR ELEMENTS OF TRANSFORMATION IN SELF AND SYSTEMS

Being able to break through our protective patterns at every scale (from self to system) to then build more effective, adaptive, and fitting patterns is the key to transformation. Therefore, the more we can spot, understand, hack, shift, break through, and remake patterns, the more agile, adaptable, and transformational we will be. At the core of BTTP there is a framework for identifying and discerning an individual or organizational pattern so that we can then transform it. At every moment, we can discern and distinguish 4 elements within every pattern. Every element is operating at the same time, although one may appear to dominate in any given moment.

Once identified and understood, we can then explore different interventions that attempt to deliberately shift a specific element within ourselves, our teams, and the organizations and systems we want to change. Without this deep human insight, most transformation interventions will, and do, fail. The framework is not 'true' *per se*, as where we draw the line among the four elements is a little arbitrary: research has shown that our bodily sensations shape our emotions; and thoughts can change our emotions and sensations.

But by artificially pulling them apart to analyze and understand them, we have a better chance at transforming them. We use a part of the bodymind to signify each element, which aids with remembering them and communicating them: hands, head, heart, and *hara* (a term borrowed from Zen Buddhism and martial arts denoting the physical and energetic guts, stomach, and abdomen area). At the individual, personal level, each protective pattern is made up of the four elements:

Hands: Our behaviors, actions, and habits
Head: Our beliefs, assumptions, stories, and mental maps
Heart: Our feelings and emotions
Hara: Our felt sense and somatic sensations within interoceptive awareness

At the organizational and systemic level, each pattern is made up of:

Hands: Organizational/systemic behaviors, processes, and structures
Head: Organizational/systemic beliefs, narratives, maps, and models
Heart: Organizational/systemic cultures and values
Hara: The momentary felt sense, 'mood', or 'music' of the organization/system

It is a mistake to think of these as separate elements. They are, of course, fully enmeshed, blended together, and interconnected in the wetware of our biologies. What we are doing is gaining

FIGURE 13 *The Four Elements of Transformation In Self and Systems*

transformational potential by artificially distinguishing these four elements so we can become aware of, track, and alter our physiologies and psychologies within; and become aware of, track, and alter different parts of the enormously complex web of parts that make up any organization or system.

To lead transformation, we must be able to become aware of, and so consciously change, each of the four elements of every pattern in ourselves; help others in our teams to shift their patterning; and design interventions for an entire enterprise or system that consciously seeks to alter all four in effective ways, at the level of: processes and structures, shared narratives and mental models, culture and values, and the intangible 'mood' of the system.

Biology has shown us that our most established protective patterns as individual leaders are *anchored* in place by powerful emotions, unprocessed 'somatic markers', and traumatic memories (research has shown that painful and intense memories are stored much nearer the fear-centers of the amygdala than 'normal' biographical and procedural memories).[23] The same is true of organizations. As the saying goes, culture (shared values, feelings, and ways of being) eats strategy for breakfast.

You can invent the smartphone like Nokia did, or the digital camera like Kodak did, and not have the culture needed to transform the assumptions and behaviors that underpin outdated business models. Therefore attempting to transform individuals and systems with what, for linearity-loving C&P Mode, seem to be efficient and easy-to-measure behavioral **hand** changes—like new regulations and procedures, agile processes, rewards and incentives, or 'nudges'—tend to fail long-term if we don't also shift the emotional and traumatized **heart**, and edit the **head** memories, beliefs, and 'projections' (the way we view the world through distorted lenses) that anchor defensive and controlling behaviors in place.

In organizations and systems, byzantine procedures, policies that assume staff are avaricious or dumb, and overcomplicated processes for sign off in the organization's **hands** all block transformation. Suspicion of new ideas, arrogance about being a market leader, commitment to a business model that is failing, assumptions that the enterprise is in the same business it was in a century ago, a belief that marketing alone can solve declining sales in the organization's **head** all block transformation.

A perfection culture, cynicism about 'academic' learning, mocking people for making mistakes, or a rejection of transformational leadership in favor of heroic leadership and the cult of the individual in the organization's **heart** all block transformation. A non-conscious sense of being alienated, dehumanized, in danger, suppressed, or suffocated by an organization's **hara** all block transformation.

C&P Mode, of course, likes to focus on coarse behavioral interventions—like high-profile carrots and palpable sticks—rather than the messy, unpredictable, hard to see, and decidedly challenging work of transforming narratives, cultural feelings, and opaque moods. Yet the royal road to leading and lasting transformation is always to prioritize the 'lower' levels of **hara** and **heart**. We need to shift these before people can even engage with, recognize, and embrace breakthrough strategies and ideas in their **head** and transformational processes and products in their **hands**.

As my colleagues at McKinsey state: "employees are what they think, feel, and believe in. As managers attempt to drive performance by changing the way employees behave, they all too often neglect the thoughts, feelings, and beliefs that, in turn, drive behavior."[24] Even beneath our feelings are the felt senses in our **hara**. Because nobody has told us about these, many leaders start off totally ignorant of the sensations in their body. As we switch

FIGURE 14 *Every Protective Pattern Has Four Elements*

191

CONTROL & PROTECT MODE

CREATE & CONNECT MODE

Habits that we unconsciously reinforce: protection/addiction Habits that we consciously rewire

Meaning-making concepts that we unconsciously believe Meaning-making concepts that we consciously challenge

Emotions we unconsciously react with Emotions we consciously reshape and anchor in

Sensations we ignore/or are ignorant of Sensations we consciously explore

FIGURE 15 *The Four Elements of Transformation In Self and Systems In The 2 Modes of Consciousness*

on our somatic awareness, we become more conscious as leaders and we become aware of, and able to change, our felt sensations.

Without a shift in the **hara** and **heart** elements, our colleagues and customers will usually resist positive, lasting change no matter how beneficial it might be. As you have seen, people do not act as disembodied, rational brains wandering around doing the math on the positives and negatives of change. Humans do not think in logical costs/benefit analyses. They might do such a sum but most of the choice has already been made within their **heart** and **hara**.

People engage with things viscerally, in the felt sense and the hot and cold of their guts. Their sensational and emotional relationship to change determines, to a large degree, whether they embrace transformation or not. This does not mean that updating and upgrading **head** (beliefs/stories) and **hands** (behaviors/habits) is not crucial. It totally is. It just means that we cannot even start to rewire beliefs and behaviors until we have dealt with emotional and cultural blockers first. Once feeling states in our sensory and emotional layers of **heart** and **hara** are transformed, then we can set about editing stories and updating assumptions (such as the potential of smartphones or digital imaging) in **head**; and breaking and making habits of **hands**.

In other words, in order to change habits and addictions that disable us, we have to change the stories, beliefs, and self-talk that disempowers us in our mind. When we change our stories, we change ourselves, and the world around us. But if we have negative stories about ourselves or dangerous assumptions about the future of our industry, often they don't respond to purely cognitive story editing. When our stories are being held in place by powerful emotions and memories, we find it very hard to change them by positive thinking or rational rewriting alone. Strong emotions will keep our negative stories and our destructive self-talk in place until we transform the emotions that lock them in.

In an influential book by John Paul Kotter, Emeritus Professor of Leadership at Harvard Business School, and consultant Dan Cohen, called *The Heart of Change*, the authors state: "the core of the matter is always about changing the behavior of people, and behavior change happens in highly successful situations mostly by speaking to people's feelings." Safe, positive, purposeful, exciting feelings dissolve the assumptions and habits that block change; and so allow leaders to transform individual selves in teams and customer segments; and thus complex human systems.

PART 3
THE PATHWAY OF TRANSFORMATIONAL LEADERSHIP

Yesterday I was smart, so I wanted to change the world.

Today I am wise, so I have begun to transform myself.

Jalalu'ddin Rumi, The Mathnawi

Give yourself to the Way

and you'll be at home on the Way

Lao Tzu, *Tao Te Ching* (Translated by Ursula Le Guin)

34

SELF-MASTERY IN TRANSFORMATIONAL LEADERSHIP

The transformational leader can only lead transformations in their teams, organizations, and the systems they are part of when they have mastered themselves. This means we must all commit to developing mastery of: our unified bodymind and the state it is in, in any given moment; the two modes of consciousness and shifting between them to be in the right mode for the moment; how to find a Third Way creative tension between two seeming opposites; how to change the four elements of human and organizational patterns.

This is about mastering how to change our inner game to reach behavioral, cognitive, affective, and interoceptive *congruence* across all four elements within; and how to spread and scale that into the outer game of an organization to form behavioral, cognitive, affective, and interoceptive *coherence* at scale. This is how to break protective patterns in individuals, teams, organizations, and systems that are a mismatch for the emerging future; and craft new ones that do not just fit the future as it emerges; but play a part in forging the future we want to see.

The way to transform persistent and pernicious protective patterns is to transform each of the four elements that constitute them within **hands, head, heart,** and **hara**. We ensure that first we, and then our colleagues and collaborators, feel safe and connected enough in **heart** and **hara** to give up outdated assumptions and reactive habits in **head** and **hands**. Different interventions within each element can be used to generate transformations. The more interventions with which we experiment and become skillful in, the more mastery we have over ourselves and our enterprises.

Self-mastery, virtuosity, is not 'self-control'. Control is about suppressing and managing as opposed to understanding and leading. Mastery, not control, is the starting point of transformational leadership. We master the inner self of our consciousness in order to master how to change the external, material world. As psychologist Roy F. Baumeister wrote in *Scientific American*: "Mastery is another name for changing ourselves. It's by far the most critical way we have of adapting to our environment."[25]

Self-mastery—and only self-mastery—allows us to adapt to a changing environment. Therefore it affords us to the most fitting and adaptive life. The research on self-mastery is extraordinary. People who have high levels of self-mastery live longer, are happier and wealthier, are better at relationships, are more popular and trusted, and are less likely to be addicted or arrested. In the workplace, those who are masters of themselves earn more than other employees, give better customer service, adjust better to new assignments, and earn 50% to 150% more income. A study of over 270,000 students from kindergarten to year 12 found that those who were given training in social and emotional skills had an 11% gain in their academic achievement rates, as well as a reduction in poor behavior by 10%.[26] A good place to start our journey of self-mastery is becoming better able to recognize and read the felt sensations within **hara.** Then we can match visceral sensations with the emotions, thoughts, and habits that tend to accompany them in a protective pattern. When we feel emptiness in the gut or tension in our solar plexus, what kind of protective pattern are we likely in? What about when we feel a sense of spaciousness in our throat or energy rising in our spine? Over time, we develop perceptive interoceptive-affective awareness and can "track" our felt senses: the 'somatic markers' within us that lock in old habits and beliefs; and those that bring us into wholeness, fullness, and adaptability.

We can then explore the emotions that are arising in our **hearts**. Rather than being hooked by them and acting them out, we can explore why they might be arising and what they tell us about our past, present, and future. We can then identify what we are saying to ourselves in our **heads**, and whether these beliefs, assumptions, and stories are useful and accurate; or disempowering and limiting. Finally, we can see how this all plays out in the habits we enact in the moment with our **hands**.

By using the 4 elements (Bio-Transformation Gem 4), we can identify the four facets that make up every pattern . . . and then work out ways to transform them. However, a major challenge for our own wellbeing, and the adaptive capacity of our organizations, is that modern life has engineered out many of the moments where we might stop, take stock (allowing us to work through traumatizing experiences and shocking events), reflect, switch on, and stabilize our emotions.

Pausing, reflecting, and wondering are all seen as wastes of time and inefficiencies reducing profit and performance. It takes a concerted effort to develop our capacity as transformational leaders. We must invest time and energy in "processing" emotions, "sitting with" what is occurring, and "feeling into" what it all means. It takes practice to learn how to "contain" strong emotions without reacting or repressing; and investigating why they are there as well as how to release them.

Such emotional regulation is a core component of transformation and adaptation. Therefore it impacts not just our leadership capability but our health and wellbeing too. In a study of over 5,000 middle-aged people, those with the highest capacity to regulate their emotions were over 50 times more likely to be alive and without chronic disease 15 years later, than those with the lowest levels of emotional self-regulation. In another study of 1,200 people who were already at a risk of poor health, those who had learned to alter unhealthy emotional attitudes through self-regulation training were over 4 times more likely to be alive 13 years later than an equal-sized control group.

If we choose to develop interoceptive and emotional intelligence, we become increasingly wise about our sensations and emotions. We no longer mix all our emotions up into 'feeling good' or 'feeling upset' but start to notice nuances among feeling states. Research has shown that people who have the ability to name different nuances of emotion, known as 'emotional granularity,' actually go to the doctor and use medication less frequently, and spend fewer days hospitalized for illness.[27]

Leaders who develop protective patterns that hide their lack of emotional regulation and emotional granularity often show up as powerful, charismatic, and confident. They make up for their loss of emotional nuance, regulation, and courage by developing habits that get them power and control. But all power over people/things, rather than power to support and regenerate, comes at a price. They are often less able to transform their emotional relationships to external events beyond their control; so they are less able to adapt and transform their organizations.

Our emotional relationship to change, uncertainty, crisis, and challenge will determine our capacity to lead transformation. As we become more interoceptively and emotionally wise, we can shift our emotional relationship to crises and challenges, allowing us to be more adaptive and agile in our thoughts and actions. We no longer see any emotion simplistically as 'negative' or 'positive'. Instead we see each as a sign that there is valuable insight into ourselves to discover, name, explore, unearth, and defuse.

As we amplify self-insight, we learn how to regulate our emotions whenever they are dysregulated by stress, anxiety, and fear (when trauma is triggered). With increasing embodied wisdom, we become able to return to a sense of stillness and poise ever more quickly when we are triggered: when strong emotions within us destabilize us and pull us into reactive patterns. We become adept at healing intense emotions that are locking us into sabotaging patterns.

As we learn to regulate our sensations and emotions in our **hara** and **heart**, we then find it easier to edit our stories and update our assumptions about our business and industry in our **head**; and ultimately to change our behaviors in our **hands**. Any lack of agility, strength, and capacity in any of the 4 elements diminishes our capacity for transformational leadership. Each incapacity is like a dent in a pipe that blocks the flow of connective consciousness: and so empathy, insight, intuition, and creativity. Some of the main blockers of transformational leadership are:

Hands: Addictions that disable us, behaviors that sabotage us, and habits that diminish the humanity of others. E.g. always fighting to 'win' an argument; interrupting people; workaholism; never speaking our truth; always speaking our truth; or constantly ensuring we have a higher status than others with each speech act; constantly engaging in political machinations etc.

Head: Limiting beliefs, self-talk, narratives, policies, strategies, and traumatic memories that disempower us. E.g. wanting to be right; being judgmental; being closed-minded; being intellectually defensive; being cynical; never questioning our assumptions; always questioning everything; believing the "Man' is always out to get us; never challenging received wisdom or ideology etc.

Heart: Uncontained and unregulated emotions that destabilize us, disconnect us from others, and leave us emotionally labile and reactive. E.g. anger, frustration, distrust, fear, confusion, dissociation, freaking out etc.

Hara: Physiological sensations and traumatic somatic markers that distress us and drive looping maladapted patterns. E.g. hunger, tiredness, exhaustion, a sense of overwhelm, sore muscles, trauma-driven distress, and chronic pain (like backache, migraines, etc.)

As we become more aware of our patterns—and experiment with how to transform them—we mature as adults and leaders. There are specific stages of adult maturity and development that afford us varying levels of power and possibility as transformational leaders. That is to say, scientists have studied the development of our capabilities as we evolve from childhood into adulthood and it appears that there are key stages of development within our consciousness—across the 4 elements of sensation, feeling, thinking, and acting—that allow us different capabilities in generating change in the external world.

We are not trapped by our biologies: we can play a co-active role in our own leadership development. We can be participants in our own maturity to move to ever more transformative stages of leadership capability. The key, as always, is committed inner work to develop self-mastery that makes our outer work more effective and more adaptive.

35

THE DEVELOPMENTAL JOURNEY OF A TRANSFORMATIONAL LEADER

It appears that there is a natural order of transformational development that unfolds as we consciously mature as adults. Our self-mastery increases throughout this developmental journey. The child psychologist Jean Piaget was the first to carry out seminal studies into understanding the stages of development that we go through as we move from children (with plastic, creative brains) to adults (with strategic, focused brains).

More recently, research psychologists Lawrence Kohlberg (the six stages of his Theory of Moral Development), Carol Gilligan (3 stages in her Ethics of Care theory), Abraham Maslow (the Hierarchy of Needs), Clare Graves (Spiral Dynamics), Michael Lamport Commons (the Model of Hierarchical Complexity), and Erik Erikson (eight stages of psychosocial development) have all suggested that we progress through various identifiable and archetypal developmental stages to achieve higher levels of thinking capacity. Philosophers like Sri Aurobindo and Ken Wilbur have also contributed markedly to emergent adult development theories.

I find the insights from stage-based theories of adult development both powerful and persuasive. However, *caveat emptor*. Each developmental stage (as with archetypes) is idealized to provide insight. They are not to be taken literally. Every person has within them inconsistencies and tensions. As Walt Whitman said, we are large and we contradict ourselves. We are all on a spectrum rather than fully inhabiting a discrete stage; and we may exhibit thoughts and behaviors typical of a certain stage in one area of our life and those from a different stage in another sphere. That said, I use developmental stage theories as lenses to help me understand crises and potentials within people, organizations, and systems; and to inspire and empower myself, and those I work with, to push 'onwards and upwards'; continuously upgrading our consciousness so we can land more positive impact. I never use stage theories to be prescriptive or normative; or to judge or criticize others. Few of us need more criticism; or to be placed in yet another box.

I think of increasing cognitive capacity as the development of "Cognitive-Behavioral Complexity," or C-BC. A simpler term is "insightful action." It is the capacity we have to generate solutions to ever more complex problems in our **head**; and then implementing those solutions in ever more complex systems with our **hands.** Amoeba have very low levels of Cognitive-Behavioral Complexity. This fits their very simple environment: move towards food. Move away from danger. That's about it.

Transformational leaders, like Nelson Mandela, have very high levels of Cognitive-Behavioral Complexity: they can understand how a national system of various tribes and ethnicities interacts with a global system of nations and worldviews; and how to intervene in the various systems to realize their transformational vision (from private conversations with specific individuals to speeches that are shared across global media).

As we mature, assuming we choose consciously to develop our Cognitive-Behavioral Complexity, we are more and more able to understand not just how to follow rules but how to break and shape rules; how to lead people along the non-linear process of transformation; and how to intervene in complex living, adaptive systems. Clearly, a transformational leader wants to develop Cognitive-Behavioral Complexity so he/she can engage with, and then solve, complex Transformational Challenges in often-chaotic, stressed, and interdependent systems. This is what I call the *vertical* direction of intentional consciousness expansion.

Organizational theorists Herb Koplowitz and Elliott Jaques have suggested that as long as managers are one or more developmental stage higher than those they manage, then they will be making more nuanced choices that fit the level of complexity outside the organization. In other words, as long as we have higher levels of Cognitive-Behavioral Complexity at the top of the leadership ladder than at the bottom, then our organization will be well placed for adaptive, agile, and transformative strategies that can keep us surviving and thriving in the VUCA world.

However, many experiences at the front lines of disruption have shown me that this is anything but true. Many senior leaders are actually less able to think systemically and paradoxically than some of their more junior counterparts. Research shows that whereas IQ—a proxy for Cognitive-Behavioral Complexity—is a good predictor for the overall pay grade one reaches in an organization (brown-, blue-, white-collar etc.), it is actually emotional intelligence that is a better predictor of the level reached *once we achieve a leadership position*. In fact, the further up the organization we get, the more important emotional/interoceptive intelligence becomes. Over 50 years of research has shown that emotional intelligence is two hundred percent better at predicting leadership *effectiveness* than is IQ.[28]

I discovered this inalienable and unalloyed truth the hard way. My first start-up, which I co-founded when I was 24, quickly grew a reputation as an innovation powerhouse with dazzling C-BC tools and techniques for driving disruptive and systemic innovations into complex markets. Yet, without much wisdom, we also grew a reputation for having a revolving door. We hired the wrong kinds of people (going for IQ over Emotional Intelligence, or EQ) and, I for one, managed our people poorly. We ended up with a brilliant business that was making lots of money doing very prestigious consulting projects. But the company was doing innovation that was not guided by a genuine purpose (a matter of the **heart** not **head**); and had a fast-paced creative and empowering culture… that was also missing some relaxedness, compassion, and vulnerability.

As business psychologist Tomas Chamorro-Premuzic, a lecturer at UCL and Columbia, makes clear in his book *Why Do So Many Incompetent Men Become Leaders?*, emotionally-stunted people (mostly men) still rise up the leadership ladder. This is because many companies are still part of an old world order that rewards power, smarts, and confidence over creativity, wisdom, and connection. 'Toxic' masculine values and habits are still dominant, whether in the 'strong man' culture of mainstream corporations and nations, or in the 'tech bro' culture of Silicon Valley.

This has been compounded by the reality that trauma, Adverse Childhood Experiences (ACE), outdated moral and social conventions, and a failing education system all interrupt the progression of emotional intelligence, locking people in power in ever-decreasing circles of effectiveness. They may be productive and profitable, but their reliance on power over people in a hierarchy— rather than power to enable and enlighten people to be creative in a network—massively reduces their capability for transformation. Because of the VUCA reality and massive adaptive pressures for all, the writing is on the wall for this kind of leadership. A flourishing future of work requires us leaders to recalibrate the workplace away from 'toxic masculinity' to be more aligned with what some consider to be the 'feminine': relational, holistic, vulnerable, insightful.

While Cognitive-Behavioral Complexity matches well to the level of education and managerial position achieved by a leader, one could argue that in our technocratic, metrics-obsessed, extractive modern societies, emotional intelligence is often *inversely* related to conventional achievement levels. That is to say, my kids are often better at trust, intimacy, listening, compassion, and even co-creative ideation than many of those in positions of great power. Such differences between generations is stark: many Millenials and Gen Z grew up in a culture where vulnerability, transparency, spirituality, and embodiment practices have been elemental parts of life. They are often wiser, in an embodied sense, than their boss' bosses are.

We cannot *permanently* reach the highest levels of Cognitive-Behavioral Complexity without matching our smarts with an expansion of emotional intelligence within our bodymind. We can peek into the awesome transformational capabilities that arise in the highest stages of C-BC; but we will not be able to land truly transformational projects that regenerate systems without real embodied wisdom. If we lack it, we will likely end up injecting into our organizations/systems what Carl Jung called our 'shadow': unacknowledged and disembodied parts of ourselves (both conventionally 'good' and 'bad'). This often shows up as what people call 'toxic masculinity' (narcissism, obsessive meritocracy/competitiveness, arrogance, bullying, heartlessness, and tyranny from above) and 'toxic femininity' (victimhood, passivity, artificial niceness, obsessive flatness/consensus, and tyranny from below).

36

INTEGRATING EMBODIED WISDOM WITH COGNITIVE-BEHAVIORAL COMPLEXITY

Possibly because most of the developmental stage thinkers were, and are, people working in a rationalist paradigm within academia, the focus of most of the developmental models has been how we think and act—the **head** and **hands** of our 4H model—rather than how we feel and sense in our **heart** and **hara**. I believe it is crucial to include in any developmental model the reality that we can, and must, consciously develop our *emotional* and *interoceptive* intelligence as we go through life. We want to become ever more wise, not just smart.

We call this wisdom "Interoceptive-Affective Complexity" or I-AC. A simpler term is "embodied wisdom". I think of this as the *horizontal* development of conscious expansion. Interoceptive-Affective Complexity is less showy than Cognitive-Behavioral Complexity. But perhaps it is more important. Interoceptive-Affective Complexity contains, yet expands profoundly upon, traditional notions of emotional intelligence.

On this horizontal axis of development, we aim for mastery of: our senses so we can transmute suffering in the systems we touch; the ability to repair ruptured relational fields with speed and elegance; the capacity to innovate anything to adapt it to the changing world; and becoming ever more stable, compassionate, and forgiving leaders, no matter how loud and stormy the headwinds of change are.

Interoceptive-Affective Complexity, embodied wisdom, includes skills and qualities like: speed and alacrity in owning our own protective patterns; a rapidity of both forgiving and apologizing; humility in balance with hubris; a sense of spaciousness in the body and around us; regulation of our emotions; making consistent 'progress' in healing our traumas and wounding within; awareness within our sensory self; integrity and trust in our relationships; maintaining clear and strong yet compassionate and semi-permeable boundaries; a preference for participation as much as control; cultivating reciprocity and co-creativity within our networks; 'feeling the room' and 'sensing the music in the system'; being present and truly listening to others; openheartedness, compassion, and kindness even when we don't like someone; a disinterest in being 'cool' or being recognized for one's genius; a nobility of intent whether in a factory or festival; treating everyone as an equal in worth as a citizen, whether plumber or Nobel Prize winner; 'holding space' and creating safe spaces for transformation; deep listening, attuning, and mirroring; nurturing weak ties without manipulation; sensing weak signals that presage major change.

Following BTTP Gem 3, the principle of The Third Way, as transformational leaders we want to be developing *both* vertical Cognitive-Behavioral Complexity *and* horizontal Interoceptive-Affective Complexity. We want our wisdom to melt the seeming dualistic polarities of cognitive brilliance and emotional openness into a dialogical Highest Common Factor that affords us full transformational potency.

In my experience, the VUCA world is demanding that we do this. The VUCA reality and the 3D Future demand that we have a sharp **head** and skillful **hands** to simplify systemic complexity, solve really complex problems creatively, make sense of emergent realities rapidly, and make smart decisions that affect concrete change. But we also need an open **heart** and relaxed **hara** to make sensitive and wise choices in increasingly challenging times. We need a whole, or at least healing, bodymind with which to connect, hold, and make safe those we want to transform.

Will, intention, ambition, and even vast amounts of funding are never enough to deliver organizational or system transformation. However, when we have developed high degrees of embodied wisdom as well as insightful action, we can more easily and reliably handle the fear, chaos, and confusion inherent in the VUCA world without becoming reactive or righteously locking onto old ideologies and becoming fixated. Then we can sense into emerging customer needs and generate bold ideas to serve them; and deliver transformation into our organization by engaging and supporting scared and resistant people to be the change we want to see.

Ideally, the stage of Cognitive-Behavioral Complexity we are at is softened and tempered by matching increases in Interoceptive-Affective Complexity. This allows us to transform the shadow, or dark side, of every developmental stage—and prevent our egos running amok, which they are wont to do without wisdom holding them back. We learn to ease the protective urges of C&P Mode to always be smarter and in control by amplifying the connective inspirations of C&C Mode. We soften smartness with wisdom. Ideally, we are always progressing and expanding vertically

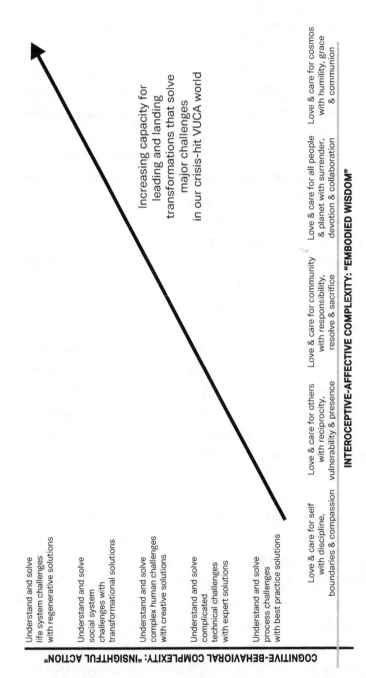

COGNITIVE-BEHAVIORAL COMPLEXITY: "INSIGHTFUL ACTION"

Understand and solve
life system challenges
with regenerative solutions

Understand and solve
social system
challenges with
transformational solutions

Understand and solve
complex human challenges
with creative solutions

Understand and solve
complicated
technical challenges
with expert solutions

Understand and solve
process challenges
with best practice solutions

Increasing capacity for
leading and landing
transformations that solve
major challenges
in our crisis-hit VUCA world

INTEROCEPTIVE-AFFECTIVE COMPLEXITY: "EMBODIED WISDOM"

Love & care for self
with discipline,
boundaries & compassion

Love & care for others
with reciprocity,
vulnerability & presence

Love & care for community
with responsibility,
resolve & sacrifice

Love & care for all people
& planet with surrender,
devotion & collaboration

Love & care for cosmos
with humility, grace
& communion

FIGURE 16 *The Two Axes Of Transformational Developmental*

and horizontally at the same time. We want our emotional and interoceptive intelligence to be in step with our cognitive-behavioral intelligence. I see them as a double helix, spiraling ever more widely and expansively as we age with style and grace.

The key to expanding our leadership consciousness *consciously* is to be biodynamic: responsive to both large and small changes in the environment (customers' needs, team vibes, market conditions, planetary warnings); and in our own "invironment" (changes in intuition, instinct, intelligence, and insight within). As we distinguish small or large changes within or without, we willingly metabolize them into ideas that realize our potential for truly transformational leadership.

The bigger and more gnarly the problems are of which we take ownership, the quicker we grow, stretch, and expand on our Leadership Edge. If we process everything as it occurs, the double helix of C-BC and I-AC unfolds without fixations or frustrations thwarting the emergence of order as we engage fully with the world around us (and the world within us). Although we must take time and space to connect and reflect, we can go right back to our Leadership Edge come Monday morning: pushing ourselves into challenging situations and experimenting with adaptive responses.

The danger of embracing C-BC without doing the inner work of self-healing (seemingly endless) trauma in I-AC is that we end up in philosophical cul-de-sacs and practical dead ends. Without developing an expanded and healing heart to match our expanding mind, we become systemic genii with stellar thoughts but never think to ask anyone about their experiences or feelings; cognitively brilliant gurus (in technology or spirituality) who sleep with their employees and/or abuse their power; famous philosophers with luminous thoughts who are also addicted and aggressive; financing wizards who are alienated from the human impacts of their deals;

or disruptive innovators who think nothing of crushing every competitor in their path of world domination.

There can be no genuine transformational solutions without interoceptive-affective resolutions. But many prefer the false illusions of intellectual profundity rather than risk the embodied vulnerability that is needed to genuinely transform unruly human systems. There are no shortcuts; though there are accelerants and hacks to the unfolding of transformational leadership development.

Please dear reader, be clear: developing mastery of both our Cognitive-Behavioral and Interoceptive-Affective Complexity is a conscious choice—and a life's work. It is unlikely we will ever reach the most transformative stages of leadership development by chance and a following wind. We have to *choose* to go deeper within to expand wider, and wiser, without. We may not make it where we think we want to get to; but we will have an enormously generative and exhilarating leadership journey—and so life!

If we retreat into arrogance, victimhood, or nihilism, we simply cannot progress far on this developmental journey. But if we do take inside us all the gnarly problems we see in our teams, in our organizations, and in the systems we rely on for life—and find ways to metabolize these problems into breakthroughs—we will develop more maturity and step into next-level leadership.

Such self-transformation only occurs though with committed inner work: the heavy lifting we do as we reflect on our problems, spot the patterns that we have used to deal with them in the past, and transform them into new habits that serves us and our organization better. Doing this inner work—on our Leadership Edge—is the daily 'yoga' of transformational leadership.

37
BTTP GEM 5: THE 5 KEY STAGES OF ADULT LEADERSHIP DEVELOPMENT

I have spent a couple of decades building on the incredible shoulders of developmental giants to fit these powerful theories to how we actually witness leaders entering, and stabilizing themselves within, expanding developmental stages. The basis of the BTTP approach to developmental stage theory is the work of Harvard educational psychologists Robert Kegan and Lisa Lahey. Over a couple of decades, they have traced out their very influential five-stage adult development model: Constructive Development Theory. It is premised, in part, upon what each person's ego-driven personality is constructed around; and so, the source of our sense of selfhood.[29]

The stages in their model progress in increasing levels of Cognitive-Behavioral Complexity, but also include many elements of deepening embodied wisdom. In my understanding, each adult development stage they proposed is reached by transforming how we construct our selfhood; what we feel we need to deliver to succeed in life; and how we relate to people and objects in the world around us. Each stage appears to alternate between a focus on solving for the values and needs of C&P Mode (like separation from others, analyzing problems and solutions, clear boundaries, and individual autonomy), and the values and need of C&C Mode (like trusted relationships, generativity, belonging, and connection).

In the five developmental stages of BTTP, I draw heavily on their evidence-based work yet include fresh insights from our own experiences of working with tens of thousands of adults on empowerment, healing, and leadership; and bring in some of the breakthrough thinking from Erikson, Gilligan, Maslow, Commons, and those working in affective-interoceptive neuroscience.

The 5 stages we use skip the childhood stages that most developmental theories postulate—as our focus is how the early adult can become truly transformational as they play their full part in their own evolution and maturity. I also posit an additional stage to Kegan and Lahey: an 'end of life' stage where we become a regenerative elder in our community. In essence, I seek to nuance and build upon the work of the masters of this field; and apply their rigorous thinking to our aims of leading and landing tangible transformation in the material world through conscious expansion.

Remember this: as philosopher Ken Wilbur states, the key to most adult development theories is that each stage *includes* the stage before—we bring with us the skills, qualities, and mindsets we mastered at the earlier stage—and then *transcends* it with new thinking and feeling, so dissolving away the challenges and crises of the previous stage. Things we used to find challenging no longer are. We have built new strengths within our embodied consciousness that allow us to seek more challenging and complex problems to solve. We keep raising our consciousness to match the challenges we face as they become more tricky; and so demand more from us.

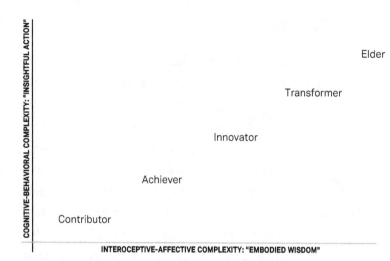

FIGURE 17 *The Five Stages of Transformational Development*

We cannot move effectively into a later stage *until we have fully embodied, stabilized, and integrated the one before.* To attempt to move into the higher stages of transformational power without nailing the core capabilities of the stage before leads to many of the issues we see today: narcissists running powerful nations and enormous companies; the application of Industrial Age solutions to systemic Networked Age problems; overconfidence in existing market rules and best practices; systemic leaders unable to show up on time and land projects; powerful people abusing their underlings; unsustainable business models and supply chains devastating our planet; a failure to understand the systemic impacts of every enterprise; lack of genuine purpose in organizations; poor emotional intelligence; and high levels of emotional reactivity at the top.

Stage 1: Contributors

Our first stage occurs in early adulthood, as we become an individuated person, separated from our parents. We can help make things happen in our groups, teams, and communities by following the rules: parents' rules, school rules, societal rules, and, most importantly, the rules of our peers. We are Contributors.

We understand how to follow best practice to generate desired outcomes; and so we can contribute to the aims of the group. This means we can be trained in the essentials of a profession or craft; on the production line; and in customer service. We can also achieve our own goals; and learn new skills that contribute to society. Extrinsic motivations like pocket money, pay bumps, and educational awards/badges are often effective to drive us forward.

Relationships tend to be transactional in this stage, as we are focused on getting our own needs met. Yet, paradoxically, we are dependent on those same relationships for our safety and nourishment. This can breed resentment, as we want to be fully independent but actually need a lot of hand-holding (both physical and emotional) until we develop the self-discipline, loving boundaries, and self-love we need to fully individuate. When we don't have our needs met, we can quickly become victims. This is the shadow of the Contributor. We can turn those we support, like parents, bosses, and teachers, into persecutors that we get to blame for all our ills.

To become a Contributor means we have been able to form a stable sense of identity based on our perceived needs, wants, and desires. As Kegan makes clear, this is a great developmental success. We have been able to move beyond the early *childhood* stages of development when individual needs are much less clear. Remember, *we must all fully inhabit and embody* this stage before we can move to 'higher' stages: otherwise we will always be confused about our needs, identity, and boundaries.

We have to develop a strong and loved psychological self in this stage otherwise if/when we transcend it, there is nothing at the core of ourselves. Then our boundaries will be too porous and leaky. Most people reach this stage around adolescence. Some never leave it. It has been estimated by studies of Kegan's comparable stage of the 'imperial mind' that at least 6% of adults *stay* in the Contributor mindset for good. I believe that *all* of us can regress here when we are interoceptively-stressed (e.g., exhausted, hungry, horny) and/or emotionally-destabilized (freaked out, fearful, furious).

The Contributor has an affinity for—and could even be considered a product of—Tribal O.S.: the Contributor stage necessitates both chiefs; and people under them that have to follow their rules.

Stage 2: Achievers

The vast majority of adults progress through the Contributor stage to inhabit the next stage. Here we no longer merely follow the manager's rules to get by, but actually take on those rules as our own and deliver on them so that we can be a respected and rewarded member of the group. Hence, I call this stage the Achiever. We have what Kegan and Lahey call a 'socialized' mind. Studies show around 58% of people remain here for life, which means the overwhelming majority of people in the workplace are Achievers.

To become an Achiever, we have to have worked out how to fit in, and belong to, the (in)crowd. To stay validated and so safe, we want to keep up with the Smiths or Singhs in terms of lifestyle, income, fashion, and job. To do this, we become great at playing various recognizable social roles—smart, funny, nice, inspiring, sexy, demure, etc., etc.—so the crowd gives us its approval. This is the source of many of the twelve archetypal patterns of leadership. Because we often rely on the approval of others for our own sense of self-worth, we often take things very personally. Therefore, we can be challenging to empower or coach.

As Achievers, we organize our work and personal lives to fit the dominant social values and codes in the system. We have learned how to compromise and also co-operate in order to move forward the needs of the group (above our own needs). This is a great developmental success as now we can play 'nice' with others. In fact, to succeed in our career, as Achievers we have had to internalize the ideologies of a system—whether dogmatic religion, glossy magazine ideals, laissez-faire capitalism, 'break things fast' Silicon Valley culture, or what the Board says is right—and then construct an identity around this doctrine or ideology.

Therefore, as Achievers, we have to suppress our own authentic nature, moral intuitions, and ideals of the future in order to fit in with the groupthink of the family, enterprise, or society. Instead, we become technical experts in our field, and can be relied upon to solve technical problems with best-practice solutions that deliver great results. The shadow of the Achiever is micro-management and control freakery. We enjoy the power that our (technical) accomplishments have brought and use it inappropriately to feel safe and in control.

The Achiever has an affinity for—and could even be considered a product of—Institution O.S.: the Achiever stage necessitates institutional ideologies that are encoded in laws (like best practice) and overseen by the authorities at the top.

Stage 3: Innovators

To step beyond Stage 2, we need to give up craving the respect and recognition of our peers to follow our own ideas and ideals and forge (a little of) the future. Around 35% of the general population makes it here, presumably meaning many senior managers and leaders. This stage sees us become fully *independent*, challenging, and often rejecting the ideologies that gripped us in the past. We have the cognitive and emotional freedom to strike out and determine our own path as innovators of our own lives, and possibly innovators in our industry. Extrinsic motivators, like reputation, reward, and peer approval, fade from significance and inner motivations, like cracking a challenging problem or starting up our own project, become driving forces.

We develop and hone truly critical thinking capacities and can author our own ideas and ideals about all work and play. We can hold competing frameworks and viewpoints without needing to decide immediately what is right. As freethinkers who are not attached to the views of others for our sense of self-worth, we *own* our own errors in projects, relationships, and conversations with alacrity rather than reluctance.

As Innovators, we develop our own meaning-making and sense-making frameworks, which is key for landing changes that disrupt the status quo. We move beyond excelling at best practice and actually envision and innovate next practice: inventing and implementing genuine value-creating innovations in products, services, processes, and even business models. We no longer fixate on getting kudos through solving technical problems; instead, we seek out Transformational Challenges that can only be solved by giving up conventional expertise. We have mastered the existing rules and can now challenge them maturely and break them wisely.

We are able to confidently conceive of, manage, drive forward, and complete projects of our own creation without relying on the approval of others to make it feel good.

We can contain multiple emotional states (like fear and excitement about change) at the same time. We don't feel the need to resolve the complexity and chaos of the VUCA world and have for both emotional and cognitive empathy: we can sense the moods and fears of others as well as understand what might be causing them (that is not necessarily to do with us). The shadow side of the Innovator is becoming a dominator of people and planet as seen in the hubris of science that tries to predict all of nature; the 'break everything quick' mindset of Silicon Valley; and the algorithmic domination of the market in hedge fund management.

The Innovator has an affinity for—and could even be considered a product of—Enterprise O.S.: the Innovator stage requires individual critical and creative thinking to challenge aristocratic/institutional ideologies; and be rewarded for it.

Stage 4: Transformers

In this stage, we fully perceive the complex driving forces and interactive human dynamics of the industries, systems, and societies we are part of and lead. We have understood our own patterns and the pain locking them in. We have realized that transformation in any human system is fractal: it starts with self-transformation, moves to relationship and team transformation, then to innovation and business transformation at the enterprise level, which ideally becomes positive transformation in the system. We have reached what Kegan and Lahey call the 'self-transforming mind,' which studies show only a handful, between 1% and 8%, of people reach.

However, this mindset is *critical* to reach for truly transformational leadership. I will expand on this stage of development in the next chapter.

The Transformer has an affinity for—and could even be considered a product of—Network O.S.: the Transformer stage requires collaborations of co-creative equals focused on a common purpose (and empowered by digital technologies).

Stage 5: Elders

This stage is conjectural in ways that the other stages are not because, first, the others are based on the scientific research of Kegan and others and, second, I have not lived through this stage personally. However, I believe that there might be a 'final' stage of leadership development where we have wisdom to share and a generative baton to pass on. This is the Elder: grateful to exchange youthful energy and entrepreneurial power for deep wisdom, a playful *joie de vivre*, and the capacity to recharge, renew, and rejuvenate systems *just by being part of them*. They don't need to *try* to regenerate people and places: they just do with a wise smile, a compelling anecdote, or a healing hug.

As Elders, I speculate that we move past Kegan's seminal work and embrace not just a self-transforming mind but actually a "self-transcending mind." We move past the need to self-actualize and fulfill our own potential and embrace genuine transcendence of the self without grand ambitions and transformational agendas. This is not about *giving up* on our needs or *compromising* our authentic self but about sacrificing our ambition to find higher-order regenerative solutions that take care of ourselves and those we care about: grandkids, citizens, flora and fauna, planet, and the cosmos. The final act of regeneration is to give back the nutrients of our cells to the soil, as we die. Perhaps Elders belong to an Operating System that is yet to emerge; if it ever does.

38

THE TRANSFORMER STAGE OF LEADERSHIP DEVELOPMENT

To be explicit, my sense is that we cannot be truly transformational leaders until we enter the adult development stage of the Transformer; and stabilize ourselves within it as much as possible. As Transformers, we have Cognitive-Behavioral Complexity that allows us not just to choose our own ideology, narrative, and leadership philosophy, but to go beyond a single meaning-making framework to hold *multiple* frameworks at the same time: challenging each, questioning each, exploring each, and using elements of each to be effective as leaders of change in the world. Fierce independence and ambitious innovation no longer constitute the reason for our existence, which allows us to relax and recognize the inherent limitations of *every* ideology, including our own. We become truly fluid, flexible, and free, but also highly effective, creative, and transformational.

Transformers can map and make meaning out of complex systems, resolving complexity into simplicity in order to galvanize the action of others (without reducing topographically rich and intense landscapes into a flatland). We know *both* simplicity *and* complexity are important, and can dial up and down specifics depending on the phase we are in within a project, and the audience we are connecting with in the moment. We use our understanding of vast webs of life, matter, and consciousness to find emerging Transformational Challenges that only truly *transformational* (systemic and regenerative) innovations can solve.

Rather than see everything through the single lens of our technical or industrial expertise, which leads to linear innovations owned by one company or institution, we seek to find how our products, services, and business models at the level of our enterprise can be leveraged to bring about shared systemic transformation at the global level. As developmental psychologist Lawrence Kohlberg proposed, we move from a *socialized* concept of morality to being able to critique and interpret *all* moral codes and to parse the value each.[30]

We understand that how we treat our workers in a factory or office in Illinois or Indonesia impacts their family, the entire community, and the societies of which we are intrinsically part. By the time we develop the self-transforming mind of the Transformer, we have fully metabolized the external moral codes found in conventional society and culture and can interpret and apply ideals of justice and rights dynamically, in the moment, rather than follow them blindly. We have refined our thinking into a very personal, yet paradoxically generalizable, moral compass that guides our everyday decisions. We are totally at peace with such paradoxes.

Feminist Carol Gilligan expanded Kohlberg's moral development theory to include the vital importance of more feminine aspects of morality, like *care,* not just concepts of rights and justice.[31] Gilligan posited that in the most developed stages of humankind, we develop an abiding sense of care for people and planet. This unalloyed and inalienable *love* for others, and the system as a whole, turns into concrete action through our "purpose." We have tempered our desire to do 'good' and be 'righteous' with a purpose that emanates from a healed heart. Our cognitive morality resolves into a fully embodied purpose. We then harness it to transform our business models to become ever more regenerative, minimizing negative footprints and maximizing positive impact.

In terms of embodied wisdom, Transformers have moved beyond the dependence on others of the Contributor, the co-dependence of the Achiever, and the craving for independence of the Innovator to settle in a profound sense of *interdependence* with all. We can surrender our egoic cravings and aversions for more richness in our relationships and projects. We have found ways to transform and make redundant our lower-stage needs (for example, for social esteem); and to meet other needs with transformation practices like meditation and nature connection.

Seeing ourselves as just one more node in the great web of life, we seek not to judge anyone else in the system for their human failings and instead bring great empathy and compassion for their situation. We forgive freely (even if we do not forget). We cultivate mutual respect in all communities. We understand the profound wisdom of non-violence—promoted by Mohandas Gandhi who used the term *ahimsa*—in *all* interactions. We seek dignity and justice for birds, bees, plants, and trees, as well as all human beings.

Transformers do not just collaborate with other leaders and enterprises to fulfill their own ambitions. They can actually *co-create* with others in trusted clusters of creativity without having a clear goal or set of success measures. We are prepared to always seek the Triple Win (success for my enterprise, your enterprise, and the world) even if it requires us to give up sacred cows, competitive edges, or defensive boundaries. We welcome feedback from across (collaborators, peers), below (employees, citizens), and above (shareholders/investors) and can engage in criticism without taking it personally; or as 'the truth.'

We are relentlessly curious about how others perceive us and can find the gold in every bit of information we receive, sieving through market and human feedback to find the insights that we can metabolize into value. We seek constant unalloyed feedback because we are totally committed to continuous transformations in ourselves as leaders in order to play our best part in transforming the systems of which we are part.

However, if our embodied wisdom is not as advanced as our insightful action, we can slip into the shadow of being righteous and right: convinced we have 'the answer' to all the ills of the world. We might believe that we have the truth about how to make The Good for all, which can lead us to hurt many in order to manifest our vision of what is best. Hitler, Stalin, and to some extent innovators like Steve Jobs were happy for some to suffer in order for their dream to be manifest. A Transformer must first seek to reduce suffering in systems before increasing thriving.

However, we must watch out for a fall into the trap of rationalistic utilitarianism, obsessed with counting the metrics of a social mission as opposed to feeling the embodied caring of a business purpose. When people 'don't get it,' we can find ourselves blaming systemic change failures on 'resistors'; and judging people as 'dinosaurs' or 'abusers' when they aren't meeting our expectations. We can slip into a Jesus Complex, prioritizing our social mission even above the needs of our loved ones. We might leave a string of purpose-orphans and purpose-widowers in our trail as we strive to change the world while remaining stubbornly unchanged ourselves.

When we have integrated the insightful action of C-BC and the embodied wisdom of I-AC, our decision-making apparatus as Transformers seamlessly blends all four major "invironmental guidance systems": protective *instincts* and predictive *intelligence* that arise within C&P Mode; and wise *intuitions* and creative *insights* that arise within C&C Mode.

We can then weave this invironmental data with environmental data to sense-make and decision-make on the fly. Even when there are multiple tensions and paradoxes—and there usually are—we come to a decision about what to do next and act with boldness and courage. We also know the value of not acting, not deciding, if we still sense that our guidances have yet to resolve into clarity from complexity.

Rather than endlessly deferring decisions to minimize the risk that we are wrong, we know that we must act even if we are wrong. However, we are confident enough to put off a decision, even when we are under enormous pressure from others, to allow us to reflect, discern our intuitions from our instincts, and come to a fully embodied choice. We are constantly listening in to our connective consciousness as well as our analytical consciousness without our separate, desiring, fearful ego forcing or striving. This is 'doing-not-doing' (*wu wei* or *wei wu wei*): it is at the core of the Taoist approach to leadership.

History may prove us wrong with our choices, yet we avoid guilt and shame even if our decisions turn out not to deliver what we hoped. This is because we understand that *any and every* action in a system is impacted by the Law of Unexpected Returns. As long as we genuinely sit with a moral dilemma—and give it our full cognitive and affective attention—we know in our core bodymind that we have done the best we can do with always imperfect knowledge and fallible wisdom.

Our sense of self is not tied to a specific worldview but constantly evolves through the insights we gain from our interactions with the people we lead, and the systems we touch. Contradiction, chaos,

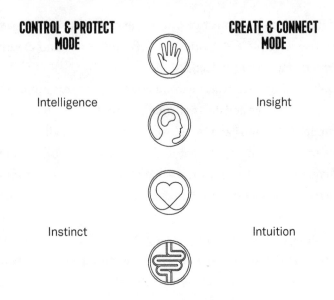

CONTROL & PROTECT MODE		CREATE & CONNECT MODE
Intelligence		Insight
Instinct		Intuition

FIGURE 18 *The 4 Guidances*

and conflict become not only tolerable, but actually nourishing as they afford continuous transformation. No longer avoiding chaos or conflict, we can lead ourselves relentlessly through transformation after transformation as we fulfill our potential. As our reward, we receive the greatest gift of life: a near-continuous sense of eudaemonic thriving not *despite* the many challenges we face as transformational leaders but actually *because* of them.

As Transformers, embedding and embodying the full power of transformational leadership, we embrace the three forces of radical change—the digital, disrupted, and damaged worlds—and find in them constant opportunities for self and systemic transformation. We consciously choose to transform our own minds as we discover new insights about the human experience through the act of leading and landing transformation with others. We readily own and metabolize any Transformational Challenge, yet have the wisdom to focus on those that are really ours to solve.

As our wisdom expands, we become less attached to dualities and polarities: whether a business is *either* for profit *or* for purposeful; or whether a project is *either* pleasurable *or* is painful. Instead, we lead through the Third Way: embodying paradoxes and weaving together dualities into one fabric. We are both a single, powerful, responsible leader where the buck stops; and one of many in the system who, at best, can guide and inspire but never change anything. We are 'special' and also a 'nobody'. We are endlessly humble but also have enormous *chutzpah* to think we can change the world. We are totally tapped into our purpose and present in the moment with people; while being totally agile with our decisions and getting massive amounts of stuff done.

39
BTTP GEM 6: THE SIX SPIRALS OF TRANSFORMATIONAL ACTION

Stabilized within the Transformer stage of leadership development, we now turn ourselves to resolving the Transformational Challenges we are facing: naturally thrown up by mismatches between our organization and the fast- and dramatically-changing world. With each Transformational Challenge we encounter as a transformational leader, I have identified six loops or "spirals" of sensing-feeling-thinking-acting that occur as we move from a focus on how we are showing up as an individual self . . . right to how we can use each unique moment positively to impact the system of which we are part.

Each of the six loops or spirals act as a specific sense-making and decision-making lens to see the challenge through. Each lens helps us to focus on a specific aspect of every Transformational Challenge *in an effective sequence*. Each helps us focus our limited cognitive and emotional attention within our **hara**, **heart**, **head**, and **hands** on the most salient features of a challenge. As we cycle through each spiral, we spot mismatches and maladaptations in protective patterns within ourselves, our teams, our organization, and our system. We metabolize each 'problem' within every spiral into value-creating ideas.

The six spirals start in the very core of our conscious being and end in the great web of systems that characterize metamodern life. We start by looking through a lens that draws our attention to our own felt sense within our emotional state of regulation, the self-talk and stories running in our mind, and the habits we are using to deal with things as they are. We then progress through ever expanding circles of action until we reach the system: the flows of money, information, goods, services, and carbon that constitute our industry or the global system as whole.

We start by transforming our *selves*; and progress smoothly, eventually in minutes and even seconds, to the *system*. On the way from self to system we focus attention on: how we act in the world with integrity and purpose; how to align our team members around our purpose and ambition; how to ensure our organization innovates to fit our purposeful ambitions; and how to engage, inspire, and influence others to change to deliver those innovations in the system . . . before returning back to the self again, tweaking how we show up in the next moment. It becomes one seamless loop of inquiry and action.

The six spirals act as a short-term 'heuristic,' or rule-of-thumb, that guides us in each moment with how to approach a Transformational Challenge. We ask and answer specific questions in each spiral. The rules of thumb ensure we don't forget pertinent principles and inquiries, which often happens when we are ruled by a rigid pattern. C&P Mode protective patterns are expert at eliding important details and ignoring crucial moments of reflection and insight in their rush to solve a problem quickly and safely.

The six spirals also act as a model for how to develop ourselves as transformational leaders long term. Each spiral can be used to find areas of underdevelopment that can form our Leadership Edge for the coming weeks and months. In other words, the six spirals work both *immanently*, in the moment, to orient us with what to do next; and *transcendentally*, to guide us longterm in our mastery of as transformational leadership.

Over time, it is crucial for us to develop skills and qualities in all of six of the spirals in order to continuously metabolize constant change in the outside world into value within ourselves and our organizations. Each spiral, as well as being a learning-doing loop, is therefore a pillar in my enterprise's curriculum for transformational leadership. By using analytical consciousness to break what is really whole—the integrated being-doing of a transformational leader—we get a full-spectrum leadership model, assessment framework, and curriculum.

However, although they can be seen as distinct spirals, they always remain one fluid movement. They are at once *both* separate spirals in a diverse range of leadership capabilities *and* part of one united way of leading transformationally. We must always remember to see our leadership capability through the worldview of our connective consciousness as much as our analytical one.

Within each spiral there are elements of C-BC and I-AC. I think of the spiral as a double helix that unfolds and expands as it goes from the inner game deep inside an individual right through to the expansive outer game of systemic change. C-BC and I-AC are the strands of the double helix. In every moment and movement of leadership, we are tapping into our capacity to think/act and sense/feel ever more systemically. Each spiral has a different weighting of the two strands depending on whether the focus is more affective-interoceptive or cognitive-behavioral.

At the start of each leadership spiral, our focus will naturally be more within, focused on the blockages and fixations inside us that are preventing us from solving a Transformational Challenge. As we progress from inner world to outer world—moving through team, project, enterprise, and system—the relative weighting between the two extremes changes. For example, when we are most externally-focused—say engaged in leading systemic change—we will primarily be focused on co-creating interventions that solve complex problems in the outer world. This will require prodigious levels of Cognitive-Behavioral Complexity. But even then, we must always remember to check in with ourselves about our own inner conditions and conditioning—and empathically explore how our ideas are landing with people across the system—before, during, and after each intervention.

In the following chapters I briefly lay out the terrain of each spiral and how it can help us in the moment; and longer term over months and years to land adaptive transformation that keep us

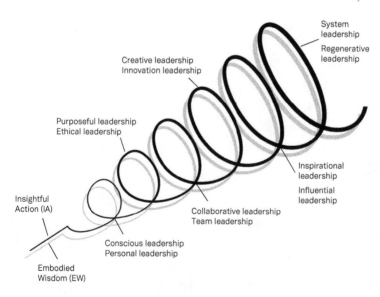

FIGURE 19 *The 6 Spirals of Transformational Leadership*

fitted. Each deserves a book or three of its own. We cover each in much more detail in our Master Transformational Leadership program, which is structured around the 6 spirals.

For now, a few pages should help orient you to the terrain of each spiral. Bear in mind that although I set them out as a linear progression—from deep within our individual bodymind right through to the furthest reaches of the system—we often switch between different spirals during a day. Just like a heroic narrative arc, at the end we return to the beginning: the final loop of systemic change and regenerative innovation returns us back to the individual bodymind of each human in the system (as well as our own).

Transformation is always non-linear by definition. Models and sequences attempt to create sense and simplicity out of a very complex and chaotic reality. The sequence is useful; yet always just a map, not the territory itself.

40

SPIRAL 1: CONSCIOUS LEADERSHIP & PERSONAL LEADERSHIP

The starting point for resolving any Transformational Challenge is to check in with ourselves consciously. In the *immanent* moment, we want to understand whether we are "in pattern," rigid and reactive (even if polite about it); or relaxed, available to new insights, and bubbling up with possible ideas. The key to conscious leadership is to spot protective patterns that show up repeatedly in different situations. We become vigilant for clues in our emotional landscape, felt sense, self-talk, and stories that alert us to the fact that we're stuck in a pattern.

The first step when encountering any Transformational Challenge is not to react with tried-and-tested solutions and best-practice thinking, but to stop; connect inside to reflect, allowing intense emotions and any shock to be processed; and engage with the incoming data and insights completely to find potential creativity within the chaos, and possibility within the problem. This is impossible when we are emotionally attached to old ways of doing and thinking. Like execs at Kodak and Nokia, we cannot see the world afresh with new thoughts unless we feel differently inside.

A crisis, a turning point presented in an intense way, reveals who we (and our business) really are. It will often clarify and amplify our 'personality': our protective patterns and defensive habits. Yet it can also reveal our deeper character, our strengths within vulnerability, if we metabolize the crisis fully. When Transformational Challenges hit, we can find ourselves in C&P Mode, reacting and resisting; or C&C Mode, adapting and transforming.

- Are you reacting to this challenge with outdated protective patterns; or are you feeling free, fluid, and flexible?

- Are you suffering from interoceptive exhaustion, overwhelm, or stress that is locking you into reactive habits; or are you able to show up fully and on fire, working with what is happening to co-create what could be?

- Are you able to own this problem and take it within your bodymind to metabolize it into value; or do you blame others for it, and complain about what a burden or worry it is?

- Are you gripping onto business model assumptions that are outdated; or are you able to relinquish attachment to old thinking and disrupt your business model purposefully before competitors or world events do?

- Are you triggered, defensive, and disconnected, locked in C&P Mode; or are you open and available, grieving and weaving in C&C Mode?

Transcendentally, conscious and personal leadership is about mastering how to lead ourselves through our own transformations so we can then lead others, and our organizations and systems, to land their own transformations. The focus is always about increasing our *palette* of potential and fitting responses to difficult challenges so we don't rely on one or two familiar strengths, within our comfort zone or box, to deal with anything. This is a lifelong process and it is never 'done.' The point is not to reach some mythical perfect state of leadership; but proactively to stretch ourselves to explore new colors, tones, and patterns through every leadership situation we encounter. We explore new leadership archetypes, and experiment with more fitting patterns. This is a conscious *choice*.

It always begins by inhabiting an "ownership mindset" that takes responsibility for the problems we face, and how we react to them; and avoids resisting "learning moments" through blaming, shaming, and complaining. We cannot transform what we do not own. And what we don't own, owns us. When we take any problem within us, by owning it, we are not taking the blame for it. We just recognize that the more creative and adaptive way of resolving it is to metabolize it within us, and this only happens when we are ready to try a different response than the one we would usually use.

At the core of conscious and personal leadership is mastery of transformation *practices*—they are called practices as we must practice them regularly so they are of use when we need them— that allow us to become more aware of, and then change, our state of mind and body in each moment. We must become world-class experts at discerning, decoding, *and then shifting* our own unique bodymind reactions with all their history, baggage, shadow, and potential.

Initially, we start by developing full bodymind awareness around when we are feeling an emotional "charge" that reveals that we are triggered by a perceived threat and so "in pattern." We become increasingly sensitive to the tell-tale signs and signals within our bodymind that show when we are reacting to life (i.e.

switched off); and when we are co-creatively responding to it with fitting ideas and actions (i.e. switched on).

As we become more aware of what is happening within, we can then practice how to *consciously* dissolve even the most persistent and pernicious patterns (that rarely help and empower us); and build new neural pathways that enact new patterns that fit who we are becoming. The archetypal move of conscious leadership is to break through old patterns (habits of sensation, mood, belief, and behavior) and to replace them with new patterns, or "repatterns," that allow us to adapt to the changing world better.

Our minds become clearer, more possibility-focused, and more optimistic (optimism has been proven to have major benefits to our material health, again showing that psychology and physiology are one[32]). We lose our emotional attachments to legacy business model assumptions and old leadership model beliefs, no matter how comfortable and successful they have been in the past. We are free to engage our 'meta-cognition' fully in triple-loop learning to suck the transformational potential from every problem. As we engage in this process, we discover that many ideas turn out to be mistaken and that our knowledge of the world is inadequate. Rather than resist or repress this, we welcome such insights to upgrade our consciousness and adapt our Business models.

We become ninjas, or perhaps break-dancers is a better metaphor, at breaking through protective patterns that once served us but now hijack our best intentions, diminish ourselves and others, and block the changes needed to stay relevant in a fast-changing world. We are able to rapidly spot familiar patterns when we lock into them, and know how to release them in real time to embrace more creative, appropriate responses. We become masters at breaking old, redundant leadership habits and at making new habits that support our ambitions for our enterprise and system.

Each repattern involves us shifting habitual interoceptive and emotional states before editing the assumptions, stories, and self-talk that block creativity in the **head**; and skillful action in the **hands**. This is the inner work of 'healing': a concept that is rarely mentioned in organizations; or in the field of leadership development. As we heal our **hara** and **heart**, we can be more responsive and receptive as opposed to reactive and resistant. Our nervous system becomes more integrated and better regulated; and our bodymind as a whole becomes more harmonious.

A conscious transformational leader knows that her/his **hara** and **heart** has many wounds within from their formative years. We seek to rapidly heal our interoceptive-affective bodymind by constantly processing difficult emotions, releasing old pain memories and feelings of inadequacy, and even transforming wounds of abuse or neglect. We do such concerted inner work precisely because it is the only way to show up in the world with a whole bodymind that feels full; and fully on fire. As transformational leaders, we must be constantly moving ourselves from a hurt heart to a whole heart. This self-transformation also means clearing up any 'messes' we have made when we were in pattern.

I suggest that rather than trying to change everything about yourself that is not serving you, all at once, just focus on *one* thing—which becomes your Leadership Edge—at a time. You don't need to force it. If you engage with life with an open heart and mind—awake to the possibility of identifying your Leadership Edge—you will likely see that, in every period of time, a theme will emerge for conscious self-transformation. Essentially, a particular protective pattern that is no longer serving you will come to the fore in various areas of your life and work. This is then your invitation to transform it into a repattern; and then "integrate" each repattern into your life by embedding new habits in the days, weeks, and months after the excitement of a breakthrough has passed.

In order to learn as fast as we can with each "upgrade opportunity"—the reframe we use for the fails that occur when we use a pernicious protective pattern that is a mismatch for the moment—it is vital that we give ourselves time each week, and ideally each day, to "process" our reactions and to extract the breakthrough potential of each. We need space and time to spot a trigger, decode what was happening in the moment, identify the pattern we were using to protect and control, and release it to embrace a new way of being. This has the added benefit of ensuring that we avoid the potential of the fast-moving world becoming traumatic.

The process of self-transformation speeds up the more we practice it (but only if we always make time, and create space, to reflect and (re)connect with ourselves). Interoceptively, this means coming back into full presence within our bodymind daily. By returning to the sense of stillness that arises when we feel into the very center of our being, we press the reset button on stress and anxiety. Practice coming back into the 'midline' of your bodymind across all 3 dimensions of height, width, and depth—something we call "3D midline mastery." Emotionally, it means processing the frustrations and fears that naturally arise with the ever more intense leadership (and love/life) challenges that occur when we take on more senior roles; and evolve into more mature stages of human development.

If we stop doing transformational inner work, we will likely find ourselves in a crisis before long. Life, love, and leadership crises are inevitable if we stick with outdated patterns to attempt to deal with fresh and emergent Transformational Challenges. If we do not consciously close the gaps between who we are, and who we need to become, to thrive in our emergent life, love, and leadership realities, we will enter breakdown (burnout being a dramatic signal of breakdown). If we are not finding our way back to peace and freedom within—each and every day—because we are failing to seize upgrade opportunities... stress (AKA fear) builds up in our bodymind and we will resort to pernicious and persistent protective patterns to cope. These diminish ourselves and others.

We cannot be conscious, flexible, fluid, and free transformational leaders without taking full ownership of our interoceptive felt-senses and our affective emotional states. It is the primary goal of conscious leadership and self-mastery to maintain a pellucid consciousness within ourselves that allows possibility spaces and creative thoughts to arise even in times of great stress. We actively cultivate our consciousness to be sufficiently clear and calm that the 4 guidances within—instinct, intuition, intelligence, and insight—can be parsed without blockage or obfuscation. Only then will we make both wise and smart decisions in the quotidian moments of choice where our legacy as leaders is laid down.

The transformational leader sees 'self-care' as an essential part of leading and landing future-forward transformation. This is not about narcissistic bliss, middle-class indulgences, or hedonistic escapism. It is about doing what we need to do for ourselves so we can be at our Leadership Edge for others. I invite you to take seriously the development of a self-care strategy that preempts stress and overwhelm; and an embodied wisdom approach that inoculates you against the life, love, and leadership crises that inevitable arise when we fail to metabolize mismatches in the moment. You must proactively take steps if you want to avoid the twin specters of burnout and breakdown! I recommend building yourself various non-negotiable practices within a Personal Resilience Plan that includes some, or all of, the following:

1. Exploring intermittent fasting, which research says can prolong life and boost health

2. Maximizing the quality of nutrients coming into your bodymind. For example, ingesting more fiber and Vitamin D

3. Anchoring into your schedule near-daily aerobic exercise; and regular non-aerobic resistance training

4. Developing stringent 'sleep hygiene' (arising and sleeping at similar times each day, within a bedroom space that feels like a sanctuary)

5. Maintaining clear and sacred boundaries, both digital and relational, that keep your consciousness safe and nurtured

6. Building in recovery time (including pottering about or daydreaming) to recharge your batteries, as top athletes do

7. Ensuring you give yourself near-daily space and time to process the crises, challenges, and emotional strains of your life

8. Developing at least one "reconnection practice" to switch on your heart and feel connection/love within

Meditation, yoga, conscious or ecstatic dance, *chi gong*, *aikido*, transformational breathwork, mindful walking—and a score of others—are all great options for reconnection practices. Over time, reconnection practices will deepen your embodied wisdom and enable you to discern which of the four guidances you are sensing in a moment: instinct (protection), intelligence (control), intuition (connection), or insight (creativity).

41
SPIRAL 2: PURPOSEFUL LEADERSHIP & ETHICAL LEADERSHIP

Each of us faces many Transformational Challenges each day. We see mismatches arise between how we do things and how the world is changing, all the time. Which one do we focus on with our precious discretionary energy? And how do we stay grounded and in integrity as we go about creatively solving such challenges by leading transformations?

Ultimately, we cannot achieve our fullest potential for self and systemic transformation without expanding our level of consciousness about life in general, and our specific life in practice. This means not just becoming more conscious of our inner world, but it also means asking, and attempting to answer, key questions about: the meaning of existence, the role of leaders in this world, and the point of this one short life. These existential questions can be seen as part of conscious and personal leadership; yet over the years, I have located them in their own domain of "purposeful leadership" to give them the importance they deserve.

I define genuine leadership purpose as a deep and authentic caring for people and planet, that orients all our work as a leader (and our career in general) and emanates powerfully from our bodymind whenever we tap into it. Purpose should not be confused with a mere social mission; or a vague desire to do good. It is a genuine *calling* we are compelled to follow that we feel deep within our bodymind. We can only discern this interoceptive-affective calling—that may or may not resolve into a clear 'purpose statement' in our mind (it does not really matter if we have the words for it or not as long as we know the feeling)—once we have cleared sufficient protective patterns away. The protective patterns we developed to get ahead in life—by being rich, smart, and successful—usually stop us being vulnerable and really caring; so they block purpose.

Purpose comes to us most clearly when we allow our heart to be broken apart by the suffering in the world. Rather than allow ourselves to feel dejected or despairing about this suffering, we feel a call to dedicate our lives to resolving it with our work as leaders. The transformational leader understands that when they see and feel, through the lens of purpose, there are massive opportunities for positive social and ecological impact hidden within every Transformational Challenge that is thrown up the threatening VUCA reality.

The transformational leader is unafraid to go on the lifelong journey to find, refine, and fully express her/his purpose in work and business; metabolizing all the inevitable failures of life and leadership into upgrade opportunities for his/her work as a leader. There is a major "purpose dividend" to this: a career with limitless meaning and fulfillment; a grounding in something that feels stable and essential even in dizzying VUCA environments; a limitless wellspring of energy and resilience that never falters; and the capacity to attract and retain the most transformational talent.

However, there is also a "purpose premium" to be paid: To become truly transformational, we have to risk giving up the safety net of following societal rules, parental expectations, and organizational career tracks and *truly care* about people and planet. Leadership purpose can only flow freely up from **hara** to **hands** once we have surrendered major protective patterns about what we 'should' do with our lives/careers and what people (for example, parents whether in reality or in our perceptions) expect us to be. We accumulate such socialized beliefs during our formative years as Contributors and Achievers.

Once we have dissolved the old box that tried to keep us safe by being smart or successful, purpose is free to arise from our **hearts** and **hara** and flow into our **head** and **hands.** Heartfelt, wholehearted caring then pervades all that we do. Purpose is what I describe as "love-in-action": an unstoppable force of connection and compassion that flows out into every decision and project. Purpose causes us to make different choices: from how we treat staff to our use of green energy. Everyone can talk about having a purpose: but if it isn't demanding that we change actions, it is just talk. If purpose does not require us to stop doing things and give up conveniences, then it is just marketing.

When we are out of integrity, "off purpose," we increasingly feel, deep in our **heart** and **hara**, incongruence: a disturbance in our field. When we are congruent—our actions and thoughts are aligned with the open heart of C&C Mode—we feel a jolt of reassurance that we are "on purpose." The sense of shock and even disgust that arises when we are off purpose acts as a powerful fuel to shift our habits toward more ethical behaviors. Over time, and with many experiments, we develop and evolve a clear moral compass that guides our choices; and allows us to be unafraid to be ethical, truthful, *and radically transparent* with team members, collaborators, and customers.

At the heart of the lifelong adventure of purposeful leadership is to joy that comes from refining our life/leadership philosophy in active dialogue with the natural world. As we converse, we clarify our evolving, alive, biodynamic moral compass. This is an expressly philosophical endeavor to raise our consciousness; and to increase our existential intelligence. It is thus a 'spiritual' journey toward increased enlightenment; making our decisions in everyday life from a place of awakened, connected, and compassionate consciousness.

Harnessing Bio-Transformation Theory & Practice—rigorous science woven together with equally rigorous wisdom—we look to the scientific method to give us the best available knowledge about the things we can see and measure objectively. Yet we also become comfortable with the stark reality that, although science can give us rigorous knowledge about the facts of matter, only our *inner* intuitions and insights are reliable guides to matters of conscience.

Thus, we realize that all our business, political, consumer, and relationship decisions must be based on *both* objective 'facts' (data about our citizens, users, customers, and markets) *and* our constantly refined, yet always subjective and intersubjective, moral intuitions. Wonderfully, social science research has shown that this is a powerful (and lucrative) way of making decisions: City traders who use data *and* intuition together make far better returns than those that use just one of these forms of decision making.[33]

Legendary politician Henry Kissinger stated that leaders need to make important decisions without perfect data; and there never is perfect data about the future as it always comes from the past. Kissinger said: "The dilemma of the statesman is that he can never be certain about the probable course of events. In reaching a decision, [s]he must inevitably act on the basis of intuition that is inherently unprovable. If he insists on certainty, [s]he runs the danger of becoming a prisoner of events." Waiting for the 'right' information paralyzes us and locks us into stasis. As transformational leaders, we must often make uncomfortable decisions that impact a lot of people before others would be comfortable to make them. We risk ire and blame from all sides as we do so as many will disagree with our choices, as all leaders find out eventually.

The difficulty comes because we cannot use eternal moral principles—whether from religious rules or rational axioms—from the past to make great decisions in an alive moment that has never occurred before. We have to go where we have most insight into the alive moment: within our own bodymind. This means learning to check in with ourselves—pausing to sense into our biodynamic purpose-driven intuitions about the data and facts on the ground—before make tough decisions as leaders.

Therefore, to be a purpose-led transformational leader, we must take time for regular introspection and soul-searching; especially when we get an interoceptive-emotional intuition that we are off purpose; or out of integrity. This may mean doubling-down on transformational reconnection practices that keep us feeling grounded and connected even as others succumb to fear and despair. It may mean engaging in ideas and wisdom philosophies that deepen our existential intelligence about the purpose of life. And it may mean committing to regular contemplation to find our own truth within.

To become properly and powerfully purposeful—guided by our unfolding purpose as much as desire for profits/performance— we must develop a profound capacity for deep listening to our interoceptive-affective internal guidance: our intuitions and insights. We cannot grasp such inner guidance if our bodyminds are full of the loud clamors of stress, threat, and addiction: all we can sense is protective instinct and controlling intelligence. By returning to transformational reconnection practices, we can quieten the storm within so we can intuit what our embodied wisdom is telling us. Then we can blend intuition with instinct, and insight with intelligence, to make ethical yet effective decisions that are on purpose. This is a Third Way creative tension between *both* data-driven *and* intuitive decision-making.

Sometimes this means *not* making a business decision until our intuition and insight resolves into a firm direction about what to do next that balances purpose with profit; and protection with connection. More likely, we will need to boldly step forward, armed with a little data; plus a deeply felt intuition. We can better make such bold and tough decisions in complex and chaotic 'hot' environments if we rely as much on our inner guidance as we do data about the market or community we serve. This invites us to get serious about refining our intuitive skills; and understanding how to 'test' out our life-affirming intuitions with others to ensure they are not noisy survival instincts.

To deepen your purpose and existential intelligence, I recommend that, as far as your circumstances allow, you purposefully avoid situations that severely lessen your integrity: particularly people and contexts that trigger addictions. If you have to be in such environments, develop strong boundaries to hold your own. Consider investing your precious time into metabolizing any 'failures' and 'crushed dreams' into deeper truths about why you are here; and how you can serve your fellow humans; and the planet we all rely on for health and happiness.

By regularly using reconnection practices to experience connective consciousness, most people will find their way to a truth beyond analysis and alienation: that we are all one, in some ineffable way. Once this discovery has been made, we access a source of love within that animates all genuine purpose. We may spend months and years reorienting our beliefs, habits, and career around the felt sense of an inalienable and unalloyed purpose that reveals itself most when we feel connected within (and facing a crisis without).

With this source of compassionate certitude within, a transformational leader is free to ensure every project or organization he/she leads is rooted in a purpose beyond profit: a business purpose that genuinely seeks to transform human suffering and planetary devastation. We do this without needing a 'business case' to persuade is: it is simply what our world needs to survive, and thrive.

Such a leadership purpose inspires and enables us to engage fully in global existential risks like pandemics, climate change, political instability, depression, and pollution; seismic societal shifts driven by changing generational ideas and ideals; and the exponential technologies of the 4th Industrial Revolution, from AI to blockchain. We know that, as leaders, we can—and actually must—harness the engines of our business or institution to solve problems that matter for the good of humanity (as well as shareholders/stakeholders).

Purpose is the lens of creativity through which we can find our way to building ethical and regenerative business models that are planet-ready and future-positive. Purpose grounds leaders in values, meaning, and caring so they build ethical organizations and service-driven teams. The purpose-led transformational leader knows how to ensure everyone in the team feels like he/she is doing something meaningful for the greater good, and can help the group make quotidian decisions that lead to regenerative outcome—that leave the world better—as well as profitable results.

By reconnecting with our leadership purpose, we generate a strong buffer between a Transformational Challenge—which often shows up in work clothes as an alarming crisis or shocking event—and our response. Purpose, as it is explicitly grounded in compassion, connection, and an abiding sense of love for self and system, absorbs the shock and provides us with an anchor of hope and meaning in the chaos of complex change.

Thus, purpose allows us to process rapidly the grief and anger that often come with crises—appropriate emotional reactions to the loss of old forms of order and safety—and return to a Transformational Challenge with compassion and co-creation instead of frustration and righteousness. We can then focus on a fitting Transformational Challenge; and be free to leave other challenges, or parts of challenges, for leaders with different purposes, skills, and talents.

42
SPIRAL 3: CREATIVE LEADERSHIP &
INNOVATION LEADERSHIP

Once we can show up feeling fluid and free—using our purpose to focus on a specific Transformational Challenge (or element of one)—it is time to generate a creative response rather than a conditioned reaction. We want to invent non-linear next practice to resolve the challenge by transforming what we do and how we do it, rather than knee-jerking back to technical best practice; hoping the problem goes away with linear continuous improvements. This is the domain of creative leadership and the leadership of innovation: solving Transformational Challenges with transformational solutions that adapt our enterprise or unit to the fast-changing world.

Creative leadership is about rapidly making sense of Transformational Challenges and reframing problems into possibilities by casting a new light on them; and then resolving them creatively by experimenting with a palette of adaptive responses. Creativity is as key for future-proofing our own careers as it is our enterprises. Even the smartest AI programs are baffled by things that 6 year olds can do easily: like create a new structure in LEGO or sense that their Mommy is feeling tender and needs a cuddle.

Machines will do algorithmic, rule-based learning better than we ever can. But they won't do rule-breaking creativity anytime soon. And they won't be able to care for the elderly, depressed loved ones, or stressed out and overwhelmed employees. As far as my understanding of both computing and consciousness goes, there will never be such a thing as Artificial Transformational Creativity or Artificial Heartfelt Wisdom.

The creativity we need to understand complex problems—and then solve them with inspired solutions—demands very high levels of both C-BC and I-AC. We need insightful action (C-BC) to make sense of complex problems through different lenses, rapidly shift lenses and frames, and move to a resolution. We need embodied wisdom (I-AC) to be able to give up old frames rapidly, release outdated assumptions eagerly, empathize with users fully, sense into the moment maximally, and have the confidence necessary to move toward a creative solution that we cannot be sure is right (if we were sure it was right, it would be a best practice improvement, not a transformational innovation).

Thus, we cannot break apart complex problems and deliver transformational solutions to them without Cognitive-Behavioral Complexity and Interoceptive-Affective Complexity working together seamlessly.

While everyday creativity and adaptability is, of course vital, in the immanent moments where each problem appears, the great test of transformational leadership is being able to lead and land significant business transformations and disruptive innovations in products, processes, and policies. This means harnessing creativity *strategically* to metabolize Transformational Challenges— which constantly arise due to the rapid changes in the external environment—into value-generating innovations that are then delivered with regenerative business models.

We are using both C&C Mode and C&P Mode at all times to bring creativity to bear on challenging problems; and then refine and optimize ideas so they actually work. Between the two, we can enter what psychologists call creative 'flow states.' Academics, such as psychologist Mihaly Csikszentmihalyi (formerly at the University of Chicago), have interviewed hundreds of sports people, artists, and scientists, and found that many of them have experienced times when their sense of self, time, and space has receded. Instead, they have been fully consumed by the moment: with creativity flowing from them without striving for it.[34]

The creative and innovative transformation leader recognizes that, at some point, best practice in *every* business area will no longer be enough to drive either decent returns or positive social and ecological impact. Mismatches occur that show up as signs and symptoms of fading and failing. We know these as Transformational Challenges. We must be able to see these signs for what they are—an opportunity to transform some area of product, process, or people so it better fits the emerging world—rather than dismiss or deny them as mere technical problems; or diminish them by blaming someone or something else.

Every innovation/transformation process (remember that they are two manifestations of the same underlying movement toward changing things to fit the world better) begins by defining a Transformational Challenge or two by looking through the prism of personal and business purpose. Transformational Challenges *always* emerge in fast-moving systems and markets where changing customer needs, segments, technologies, and realities make old ways obsolete. Each challenge is *always* an opportunity for someone: the creative and innovative transformational leader who can see them for what they are and has the strength to rise to them.

The Business as Usual mindset of good management tends to deny or avoid Transformational Challenges. C&P Mode blames the market; the business context; our competitors. C&P Mode retreats into a comfort zone of technical problem-solving that focuses on symptoms rather than root causes. In C&P Mode, leaders bring in external consultants to look like they are in action but are rarely given enough power to implement genuinely transformational solutions; or they commission a (yet another) report.

The transformational leader knows he/she must get into C&C Mode long enough to recognize each challenge; as well as become curious about all the ways there might be to fully resolve it. We must be able to call time on a particular product or business model and restlessly seek the next-level product or process that can replace it. Yet we must do this all without disturbing the existing business too much. We need to maintain predictable returns and profitability (perhaps actively managing the decline of a product or revenue stream) while giving ourselves the time, space, and permission necessary to disrupt ourselves. This capability lies at the heart of creative leadership. We want to be able to succeed in the present even as we invent a future that lives up to our purpose.

Once we see and own a Transformational Challenge—and willingly take it within our organization by owning it—we must then metabolize the problem into value-creating ideas for new products or processes. This means mastering how to *cause* breakthroughs: opening up transformational solutions that cannot be predicted by extrapolating the past. We transmute changing customer/employee needs, global risks, and new technologies into concrete value. This happens by consciously deconstructing best practice to invent next practice.

There is a dual move here. On the one hand, we bring to the surface and challenge legacy organizational and industry-wide assumptions that are no longer a fit with the world. We identify and release what is breaking down and fading from value. Insight into what is being disrupted, deconstructed, and destroyed is delivered brilliantly by analytical consciousness: taking apart wholes and breaking them down into constituent parts. It is related to the deductive process of science.

At the same time, we must seek what is breaking through so we can encourage it, shape it, and deliver it to market before anyone else does. This means making sense of, and harnessing, "weak signals" of the future in the present. Insight into what is being formed, transformed, and generated is delivered brilliantly by connective consciousness (assuming we can pause, reflect, and connect): taking fragments and nuggets and building them into a coherent, congruent, and creative whole. It is related to the inductive process of science. Future-forward signals of what is possible and what is emerging—that we pick up and call 'insights'—prove that there is a source of (often exponential) value in the future that has yet to be captured with a creative strategy.

We want to spot weak signals of emerging changes that open up opportunities—market shifts, competitor moves, unusual customer needs, and changing team dynamics—and leverage them before other people do; and before crises turn into terminal spirals where there is no longer time to adapt. Crisis and disruption are always opportunities for leaders that can sense what is breaking down and what is breaking through and act on it with transformations that have time to be implemented into the world.

A central ingredient of creative leadership and the leadership of innovation is what I call "smart experimentation": testing out ideas without needing them to be piloted to perfection; in cheap and fast ways with real human beings that provide actionable data and insight; and doing this systematically—scientifically—so we know what we are actually testing for with each prototype and trial we carry out. This means bringing a level of rigor and discernment into creative processes and teams. We ensure that every experiment has a hypothesis to test; and that the variables are reduced as much as possible so we know if the hypothesis is proven or not.

We are working with a Third Way creative (or palintonic) harmony: using C&C Mode to open up new customer insights and ideas; and then improving, refining, discerning, analyzing, testing, and evaluating each with C&P Mode. We are able to get out of Business as Usual mindsets and enter C&C Mode to be curious, open-minded, and quick-to-learn; looking for what is possible within ambiguity. Then we appraise ideas, from others and ourselves, critically and without attachment in a restless search for excellence in C&P Mode. The very latest research backs this: creative leaders and innovators are able to co-activate both Modes simultaneously.

As transformational leaders, we must nurture an innovation culture where diverse individuals can access safe spaces and agile places to be creative. This means generating mindsets, habits, and emotional states that nourish inchoate ideas rather than criticize, control, and kill them off. We want to shift our people from seeing failure as something that is going to cost them their livelihoods and the respect of their peers; to realization that failure (small, cheap, strategic) is the only way to provide the learning we need to adapt and transform.

This is very challenging as most people have protective patterns learned in childhood—and then further conditioned in each moment of every day by efficiency-driven company cultures—to avoid failure at all cost. Instead, creative transformational leaders need to be able to carefully stretch comfort zones so people can risk thinking new thoughts and embrace failure as learning. This kind of "fail-forward" culture, as I call it, understands that when we are forging the future, we have to find ways to fail well; and use all failure as an opportunity to challenge deeply-held assumptions with triple-loop learning.

As creative and innovative transformational leaders, we must develop our capacity to be agile: able to change direction constantly as new data and insight comes rushing toward us without losing clarity, consistency, and focus. We must allow for constant ongoing evolution and creative iteration even as we execute with laser-like intention. Otherwise, by the time we deliver our project, the new product/service/business model will be out of date already.

Transformational execution requires a "palintonic harmony" of *both* intentional and committed action *and* adaptive and emergent behavior. We must always sense and discern when to let go of an idea that is not a fit (or whose time has yet to come); when to park a plan that is just not working; when to postpone any action until we have reflected sufficiently; when to sit *not* knowing the answer so insights and ideas emerge as we grapple with chaos and ambiguity; and when to push our foot to the floor to make things happen today. We must be able to be intuitive and adaptive but also know when to apply pressure and dig inside for more grit, breaking through perceived limitations.

Ideally, we want to cultivate the mindset of a start-up founder with whom the buck stops. There is nobody but us. We want to drive forward execution at pace, fearlessly getting in action to champion change at every opportunity. We don't want to complain about any resistance we encounter to our ideas or get stuck and doubtful when we reach a bump in the road: *all* transformational innovation will encounter inevitable and challenging execution challenges. Instead, we always move to solve problems, creatively coming up with ideas on the fly.

This means we must be able to generate a near-constant source of motivation within us. I have found—through many, many ups and downs—that a genuine purpose is the next-level fuel we need to execute next-level ideas. Purpose allows us to be *both* totally committed to our ideas *and* totally ready to give them up; and have the resources needed to pivot on a dime to find a way to bring our vision to reality. We must be dedicated and devoted to our transformational innovations, but never attached to the fruits of our labor, as the great Indian wisdom text the *Bhagavad Gita* puts it. We must build a 'reality distortion field' to create space in the world for our innovation no matter what the naysayers and doom-mongers think; yet never let our own hubris and *chutzpah* prevent us from learning from failure and feedback.

43
SPIRAL 4: TEAM LEADERSHIP & COLLABORATIVE LEADERSHIP

Before engaging others to execute a creative response to a Transformational Challenge, the transformational leader ensures they are grounded, connected, and feeling their purpose (especially in intense VUCA environments). Awake, conscious, and settled, we are now ready to focus our team/partners/peers/colleagues/collaborators/customers/investors on the tasks at hand.

We will need to help our colleagues break through their own protective patterns and well-conditioned habits; unravel conflicts and misalignments that are stopping creative flow on executing transformational solutions; and adapt team structures, processes, and workflows to support our people *both* to get stuff done without lots of treacle getting in the way *and* ensure that creativity, emergence, and adaptation can occur so that the project is a fit for the future when complete. This is team and collaborative leadership: crucial in the quotidian moments that, taken together, scaffold up to determine the success or failure of every project.

Transformational problem-solving is more about conceptual breakthroughs through deep and penetrating human insight than it is about technological solutions *per se*. Once we have cultivated a transformational solution to a challenge, the requirement for technical expertise usually becomes clear. Gone are the days when we need to be the smartest gal or guy in the team. Today we need to be wiser, not smarter, than our team members.

Our employees should be the technical experts needed to execute (whether in AI, blockchain, or carbon-sequestering). Our job is to have the wisdom needed to know who should be on a team, how to motivate and incentivize them, and how to ensure each individual helps the team to pull together toward a common goal. As we deepen insight into our own embodied wisdom, we develop better emotional and cognitive empathy for others in our teams so we can also support them to transform the protective patterns that are holding them up from delivering transformational outcomes. This is serious, significant, and important 'emotional labor'. It must be treated as such.

We are often going to have to help team members and collaborators adapt their thinking (**head**) and change their habits (**hands**). This, as we know, also means helping them change their emotions (**heart**) and felt senses (**hara**). Mastery of how we help them, empower them, direct them, and sanction them is key. We are going to have to have many difficult conversations and give tough feedback. As emotions drive thought and action, remember to *connect* with your colleagues with cognitive and emotional empathy (and kids/partners/friends!) before you *correct* their behavior with feedback.

If team members enter a blame, shame, and complain cycle, they lose the capacity to be coached and guided. They will be in C&P Mode as they feel under threat; rather than the C&C Mode necessary to listen to feedback, learn, and change. We cannot prevent someone being triggered and we cannot ever control how they react: this is always their own responsibility. It will depend on how much inner work they have done and how much trauma and adverse experience they have had.

We don't ever *cause* people to be upset or angry. But, as transformational leaders, we can *always* own our own capacity to *inspire* safety, connection, and adaptability rather than *inspire* fear, threat, and pain. Before we intervene with any team member or collaborator, we want to settle our own nervous system, regulate our own emotions, and find our own sense of connection.

Before we start coaching, we want to find our inner calm and our sweet spot as a leader. Yet we do not want to beat about the bush either, sucking up precious transformation time because we are fearful of being disliked. We want to be both empathic and caring; but also straight and direct. We want to listen deeply for what people mean, not just what they say; and then tell them our perspective on their performance. The more we master how to guide and intervene with compassionate yet straight and generative feedback, the more team members and collaborators will be empowered to break through outdated patterns and step up to fulfill their potential *for themselves* as opposed to just obeying the rules.

At all times, we want to avoid questioning anyone's core intentions or morality. We have to trust that, in their world, they are doing the best they can. Attempt to adjust their behavior but not judge their character. When having difficult conversations and giving tough feedback, we transmit what psychologist Carl Rogers called 'unconditional positive regard'—no matter how people react to what we say. Easier said than done, but every interaction is an opportunity to practice and build muscle!

Ultimately, *every* human alive needs to take care of himself/herself. While we can care for our team members and coach them to be more empowered and valuable to the team, we can never do their life or career for them. This means careful discernment between being a coach, mentor, and guide; being a manager ourselves that is accountable to the business; being a leader who is a steward of an organization's future success; and being a co-worker who should not have to do therapy for people or solve everyone's personal issues in a professional environment.

We will no doubt encounter colleagues in the workplace who have pernicious and persistent protective patterns that sabotage them each day (after all, every human being does). Some will be outies with overly porous boundaries and find it hard to contain their emotions and ideas. Some will be innies with overly rigid boundaries and so find it hard to express their passion and creativity fully. Some may have significant personality and/or mood disorders.

Weak boundaries flood the workplace with drama, victimhood, and exhausting demands on everyone's attention. Rigid boundaries block the flow of insights and ideas from team members that we need to develop adaptive projects and innovations. Helping people find their own Third Way creative harmony is key to an effective transformation team. This might include suggesting they seek professional support from a therapist or mental health expert to work on their own boundary issues, trauma, and protective patterning.

At the very heart of every transformational team and effective collaboration is a nuanced and wise understanding of the need for *both* individual rights *and* collective responsibilities. We want to cultivate *both* accountability *and* agility: C&P Mode and C&C Mode. We want to create spaces and cultures of psychological safety and mutual trust that afford creativity and adaptation (rights); but never at the expense of personal accountability and interpersonal reciprocity (responsibilities).

This means discerning, in the micro-moments, whether the moment calls for the prioritization of safety because people are feeling stressed or scared; or whether it requires people to step up and be more responsible and complain less. On one hand, we don't want team members walking around demanding to feel good all the time, or to have to be persuaded to do their job properly. Yet neither do we want people walking around repeating best practice in order to please us; or to work hard just to get a bonus when what is needed is passionate creativity and empowered agility.

Ultimately, many moments need a fine balance between rights and responsibilities, between mutual trust and mutual reciprocity. We want to have a creative harmony between individual initiative to get stuff done, with collective sense-making and decision-making when it is appropriate and valuable to deliver the full purpose of a project. We want to encourage people to feel safe enough to bring their whole selves to work; yet also ensure we do not disable them with too much micro-management, feedback sessions, and team huddles.

This means working on our own capacity to "hold space" for others to transform; while not allowing the team to descend into constant self-reflection, trust exercises, and navel-gazing. The aim is always to be building agile yet accountable cross-functional and multi-generational teams whose members contribute fully to deliver ambitious transformational projects.

Longer term, as we build transformational teams around our projects, we want to embrace diversity in our team not because of compliance but because diversity of all kinds (including of mind-set and heartset), brings creativity and divergent thought that are essential for adaptation and transformation. We want to nurture a diverse group with many different perspectives and skills, yet focus them on a common purpose and a shared vision of what transformational excellence looks like.

With diverse cross-functional teams, we have to find ways to harmonize the different needs, ideas, and talents of diverse people without spending hours each day ensuring everyone feels good and that all are aligned. Roles need to be clear while still adaptable; and hand off moments and responsibility areas must be thought about with care, lest we lose either accountability or agility (or both). I highly recommend exploring and evolving adaptive ways to design teams and processes that balance efficiency and control (C&P Mode) with creativity and agility (C&C Mode). This is the subject of my book *Become A Transformational Organization*.

It is critical, in our development of collaboration-generating transformational leadership, to understand that there is a spectrum of different types of collaboration. I outline five types in our work building collaborations: closed; co-ordination; co-operation; collaboration; co-creation. They get progressively more innovative, but also more risky, as we move from closed to open. On one extreme—in closed projects—we essentially tell people what to do and when to do it to deliver. On the other extreme—in full co-creation—everyone is an equal as we innovate together into the unknown.

Our job as leader is to discern which type is appropriate for a given project (and a given moment in a project); and what help people need to adapt their mindset, behaviors, and agreements to fit the type. None of the types of collaboration are inherently better or more valuable than another. They all have different benefits and costs; and they lead to quite different outcomes. Each mode requires us to be a different flavor or shade of transformational leader. When the time comes for genuine business transformations—and it always will—we need to be able to flex between being highly directive and totally open to new directions.

As a collaborative transformational leader, we must always be up for evolving how we ourselves show up in relationships; and the protective patterns that are causing stress and conflict. With lashings of embodied wisdom, we will be acutely aware that we will all bring templates and imprints from past relationships into the present. Any, and every, encounter with another person in the workplace is an opportunity to heal historic disturbances within our relational fields, and update our relationship patterns so they are fit for the future. For example, we might treat our boss like we did our older brother; or a team member as we did our little sister. This past-driven imprint in our relational field will hold the team back from forging the future.

We have to be prepared to do more inner work to transform within: repairing the historic relationships in the memory storage of our bodymind; and then repairing the live relationships afterwards: apologizing where necessary and forgiving absolutely. This level of vulnerability, being exposed without being weak, is a formidable strength to develop. The most transformational talent will see it, appreciate it, and model it themselves. It is utterly natural for all relationships to have ruptures from time to time. Therefore, the team-inspired transformational leaders know how elegantly, generously, and generatively to repair relationships after a 'fall'; and transcend differences to reach ever-higher levels of group coherence.

Pay particular attention to cultivating strong yet semipermeable boundaries. We want to be vulnerable and ready to take on the feedback and perspectives of our team members without taking it personally; while still being 'the boss' whom others must respect and, at times, obey *without comment* in order for transformation to be delivered. We want to allow in insights from our team to transform elements of our own shadow. We want to allow our compassion and kindness to flow out into our teams. Yet we don't want to be uncontained and unbounded, splurging out our emotions or desires. Nor do we want to be rigid, uncaring, emotionally withdrawn.

Above all, we definitely want to avoid developing any form of dependence, co-dependence, or excessive independence that are all remnants of earlier stages of leadership development. As Transformers, we embrace *interdependence*: we honor and nurture the web of reciprocal relationships that make our projects (and life) work; without needing others, or rejecting others, in order to strong and whole.

Trauma-driven fixations in our development can easily lock us into co-dependent relationships in which we *need* our employees to like/respect/applaud us so that we feel good. We cannot need team members to like us all the time. We have to be okay with them reacting in all manner of ways to our ideas, directions, and guidance. Team members will likely react with protective patterns of blame, shame, and complain when they feel threatened, destabilized, or lacking in self-esteem.

Telling people that change is needed, and giving them tough feedback that aims to adjust inappropriate behavior, are likely to trigger employees to dislike us in moments. Such is the life of a leader. We must clearly transmit to others that we do not *need* to be liked; and are comfortable being a leader not a mate or friend. This might mean going out for drinks less often and being less involved in company gossip—without becoming an aloof and hierarchical boss who looks down from on high.

People are people and their protective patterns will inevitably lead to conflict whenever projects are critical and livelihoods are at risk: exactly the kinds of situations with which transformational leaders must engage, and lead their teams through, regularly.

The people-wise transformational leader knows that all and every conflict is a huge opportunity for team transformation. Rather than shy away from conflict (with flight, freeze, and fawn patterns like being 'nice' or avoidant) or charge straight into conflicts (with fiery fight patterns like being right or blaming people), we want to see conflict for what it is: evidence that various C&P Mode protective patterns are fighting for power in a struggle for control. This means that conflict is essentially team creativity waiting to be unleashed. It occurs because people care.

If everyone involved in a conflict can come into C&C Mode, new insights will flow. The way out of conflict is not for any one pattern to win or to 'split the difference' with a weak, vanilla compromise: but for all involved to understand where and why they are being reactive and to see what opens up when they enter a more creative and empathic environment. For it is these self-same protective patterns that are likely locking the team and the enterprise in old thinking, legacy processes, and mismatched business models that are not a fit for the future. Conflict sets us up for transformation, as long as we have mastered how to move through it wisely rather than smartly.

When something is really not working in the team—or the team is dealing with a major loss or shocking event—there are scores of valuable interventions we can lead to restore a team to a more creatively and palintonically harmonious state. All interventions should be designed with deep insight into where our team is at across the four elements: **hands**, **head**, **heart**, and **hara**.

Mindful of the balance between rights and responsibilities, it can be valuable to include the team itself in the diagnosis and resolution of team issues in a spirit of shared responsibility. After all, everyone is responsible for the effectiveness of the team. Crisis and breakdowns are always upgrade opportunities for everyone in the team.

We can lead a "collective inquiry" into what is occurring so everyone in the group can contribute his/her perspective; and everyone in the team can also learn what is needed to learn to step-up. Genuine co-creative dialogues like this are brilliant for rejuvenating team spirit and for solving team issues: but we don't want them to suck all our transformation time. We are leading teams and collaborations not simply for the growth and learning of all (though this is important). We are leading teams to deliver ambitious collaborative goals that nobody could execute on their own.

44

SPIRAL 5: INSPIRATIONAL LEADERSHIP & INFLUENTIAL LEADERSHIP

Once we have a transformational solution worthy of committing a decent chunk of our lives to, we soon realize that the world has rarely been waiting for us to implement it. In fact, most people beyond our core team will resist or reject the unfamiliar in an instant. We have to cut through the noise, chaos, and ambivalence with a compelling and well-crafted vision; and paint a pathway of how all involved can land the possibility we have envisioned with an achievable yet ambitious narrative.

Once we have a potentially transformational idea, innovation, or strategy to future-proof a part of our organization—from a more fitting expenses policy to a billion-dollar business model—we have to get everyone else in the organization and beyond to understand it, buy into it, find their role to play in implementing it, and work together to deliver it. Then we have to get our customer base and stakeholders to use it and pay for it. This is where the skills and qualities of inspirational and influential leadership will help us not just have a bold breakthrough; but actually manifest it in a world that is generally resistant to them.

No amount of genius in our ideas and plans will mean a jot if we can't capture the hearts and mind of others to get them behind our ideas. Many leaders win the war; but lose the peace. Given that manipulative and coercive ways of getting people to support us—through explicit threats of censure, veiled threats of sanctions, or through bribes and promotions—are less effective than ever, we actually have to inspire and influence people to change. We must find ways ethically to get groups of people to change their protective patterns, often developed over a lifetime, and working for them just fine (or so they think).

The essential tool for inspiring and influencing others ethically is story: narratives of the future that show how things could be (and why); and that paint a navigational pathway for manifesting possibility. Stories, whether brand commercials or quick emails to the company, can drive mass behavior change in **hands**. To ensure that happens, they give the **head** rational and logical reasons to change. But people will not pay attention, care about a solution, or be able to overcome their fears of change until the emotional **heart** has been captivated; and the **hara** gripped.

Transformational narratives capture hearts, shift mindsets, and have a call to action designed to deliver the change in behaviors we need to deliver the transformation we envision. Stories are our species' solution for how to transform others without coercion. Otherwise we will fail to overcome the Backfire Effect: the more we try to challenge a strongly held belief rooted in emotions with reason, evidence, and facts, the more believers believe they are right. They double down on their erroneous assumptions (especially, research shows, those with a more conservative outlook). Every transformational leader, entrepreneur, and innovator therefore must become a virtuoso at storytelling if they want their bold ideas and ambitious visions to be actioned.

I see storytelling as two separate, yet related, activities. The first is story-crafting: designing a narrative that meets our audience where they are at and then takes them somewhere higher, better. We painstakingly craft a story that includes all the key ingredients that **hara**, **heart**, **head**, and **hands** need to effect the various changes we want to see that will scale up to land transformation. After that, the second element is story-sharing: how we deliver that story in pitches, talks, brand identities, landing pages, meetings, emails, reports, pitch decks, social media posts, commercials, and more. Transformational leaders must become consummate experts at both skills, while always being aware that a powerful protective pattern is to leverage stories for the wrong reason: to obfuscate, gain affection, and capture attention without a purpose-driven vision.

Story-crafting requires that we can first envision an alternative, valuable, and achievable future to the one predicted by extrapolating trends from the past: a transformed reality that is markedly different from the one that is likely to occur *without* transformational leadership. We must be able to craft this possible future within a "transformational vision" that feels both new and refreshing yet also attainable and familiar. If it is too other-worldly, not many people will connect with it or see themselves in it. If it is too mundane and banal, there is no transformation and there is little value in us holding the vision.

The vision should, of course, come from a strategic and systematic interrogation of the future; and be driven by real and profound insight into existing and future customers'/users'/employees' needs, wants, and yearnings. But it must also be relatively simple, even if we know that simplicity is an artificial construct in a VUCA world. Given that many receivers of our vision may be at a lower level of C-BC than the person who has gone on the journey of complex problem-solving to have a breakthrough—which is *never* a judgment about their intrinsic value as human beings—we must use our intelligence and wisdom to find metaphors and emotive possibilities that render complexity into simplicity.

Finding appropriate ways to communicate transformational ideas and insights is key and often our signal is drowned out by noise, the complaints of protective patterns, the plethora of internal comms, corporate jargon established by the legacy business model, and cultural codes and team shortcuts that obfuscate as much as clarify. We must then be able to turn a vision of how the future could be into a compelling and coherent narrative *structure* that inspires others to get involved.

To design a story that can transform people and our world, the sequence of the story elements is critical. There is a time-proven narrative structure that change-driving stories leverage. If we ignore it or try to improve it, we risk very few people getting what we see as possible. Whether developing a leadership, brand, funding, or team narrative—we usually need all of them to affect transformational change— our story sequence must inspire hearts, elevate minds, and invite immediate action. It must connect emotionally, justify rationally, and make change urgent, compelling, and clear.

Every story structure requires, at a minimum, essential context that explains why the transformational idea or strategy is better than the past and why it is the right fit for this organization to bring to life right now; a clarity of focus and intent, reducing complexity and noise in the system so people of varying levels of Cognitive-Behavioral Complexity and embodied wisdom can see their role and where best to act; and a call-to-action, which explicitly asks people to change their behavior, whether through shifting the allocation of resources or through speaking or acting in a new way.

Once we have developed a story with the right elements and ingredients—perhaps with multiple variants for different audience segments—we then must decide how, when, and with whom to share the story. Whilst some of our communication efforts will be through media, like video and reports, we will at some point have to share our story in person.

This means mastering how to show up with our full potential as inspirational transformational leaders: how best to speak about, and present, ideas that fit our character; and how to be fully present ourselves with people, at ease in our skins. The transformational leader knows never to moan that investors don't get our genius idea, customers don't get how awesome our product is, or bosses don't appreciate our brilliance: instead we own the resistance and refusals we get and metabolize them into a more compelling vision, a clearer and more engaging narrative, and more executive or leadership presence.

How we show up in pitch rooms, meetings, conference calls, and workshops is key. Our capacity to influence others is beyond mere words. It sits, in essence, within the relational field between leader and listener. Inner work we have done to date on ourselves to clear away fixations and distortions in our relational fields will come into its own when we want to inspire and influence others most powerfully. According to studies at UCLA, change in people occurs not so much through the language and intellect but through a deep dialogue between entire bodyminds.[35]

The less we are snarled up with old trauma and patterns in our relational fields, the easier and quicker it is to change people. This is, I believe, a large part of what *genuine* charisma and gravitas are (as opposed to the demagogic and manipulative charm of the narcissistic and phony). To be fully present means that we must be able to break and transform protective patterns that pull us away from presence: such as being distracted by technology, wanting to get to our bit of the meeting, urges to use power to increase our social status, or prioritizing being right over deeply listening.

Incongruities and conflicts within us as leaders will be obvious to perceptive listeners. If we are unsettled by our own story, have seen inconsistencies and contradictions in it, or just don't fully believe in, it will impact our capacity to influence and inspire. If we are tired or jaded, it will spread like a virus to our listeners. If we have persistent self-esteem issues, these will permeate across a room and diminish the power of our vision and narrative. If we are either too arrogant or not confident enough, our audience will sense this and it will cause them to doubt us.

Therefore, there is more inner work to expand again our embodied wisdom: to become ever more compelling, energizing, and electric. We must be able to shine a light on complexity when others are confused, fearful, or cynical; and manage our own resilience so we have the inner resources needed constantly to re-inspire people when they tire or fall by the way. We also may sense hidden agendas, silent worries, and elephants-in-the-room that need to be dealt with before people can listen. Choosing how and when to do this while avoiding shame and blame reactions in our listeners takes prodigious levels of both Cognitive-Behavioral Complexity and embodied wisdom.

Beyond vision, narrative, presence, and genuine charisma there are many other ways to persuade people to join our cause. Scores of books and courses exist that claim to teach the (often dark) art of persuasion. Many of these techniques are not ethical as they require subtle (or not) methods of manipulation: persuading people to do what is not in their genuine best interest to do, but serves our needs instead.

A well-developed moral compass, that we fully embody not just speak about, becomes an essential guide for how to harness 'soft power' ethically to persuade people to make things happen with minimal resistance and maximum energy. If we have not done the inner work to develop such a purposeful and refined compass first—which takes months and years not hours and days—persuading people without manipulation or coercion will constantly be tricky. Tools such as 'reciprocity' and 'social proof' are useful ways to persuade and influence, but we must use them with a whole heart or risk backlashes and off-purpose feelings.

Ethical influencing, like genuine coaching, is always about supporting people to change *for their own longterm best interest* as well as ours, helping them give up comforts and conveniences that their C&P Mode relishes. We want to identify, activate, and cultivate both formal and informal networks up and across our enterprise and system; and then find the right Mode, message, and moment to influence people in different groups to find the Triple Win.

45
SPIRAL 6: SYSTEMIC & REGENERATIVE LEADERSHIP

Any ambitious and purpose-driven transformational vision for an individual enterprise—whether micro-business or august institution—will necessarily seek to shift the dynamics of an entire system. No business is an island, entire unto itself (echoing medieval poet John Donne). Every organization is part of a system. Any transformations within it necessarily impact webs of suppliers, customers, workers, and shareholders within the wider system.

Up to this point, our attention as transformational leaders has focused on ourselves as individuals, our transformation team, and our organization. This final spiral now brings our attention to bear on the system as a whole so that, immanently, we consciously and purposefully seek to impact it positively through the quotidian acts of adaptation and innovation we deliver in our own backyard; and, transcendentally, we consider how we can use our own brief career, and our organization's engines of commerce, to deliver transformative benefits to the systems of which we are part: from the employees and vendors who support us to the customers and communities that buy from us.

Ultimately, systemic and regenerative leadership is about ensuring that we leave humankind and the world *better* than how we found it. We are not just interested in basic Corporate Social Responsibility or sustainability initiatives to minimize our footprint (which is great, but not sufficient for the crises we face). We want to *improve* the systems of which we are part and leave them in a more *regenerative* state to not just sustain, but affirm and encourage, life on this Earth.

Becoming systemic leaders involves shifting our entire frame of reference from feeling and thinking in the straight lines of Industrial Age enterprise—capital>raw materials>labor>industrial processes>product/service>marketing>margin>return on investment—to sensing, feeling, thinking, and acting with a Networked Age systemic view: that is modeled on more circular, web-like, and non-linear relationships between all things.

This worldview understands that our organization is situated within a vast web of life that is interconnected. It is our duty as business leaders, and human beings in the Networked Age Operating System, to leave this web of life better off—in terms of its livability and its ability to cultivate more life—than it was in the Industrial Age, when people assumed businesses and economies could grow without limits, and without negative effects.

We no longer see simple vertical silos and functions, even within a matrix organization, but a vast constellation of humanity, matter, and data that together make up the entire local and global systems; and within which our business plays a role. The systemic leader must be able to switch between both linear and non-linear views at will: constantly zooming in and out of different levels of magnification and resolution to make sense of enormous complexity, which may be challenging our long-term strategy, and then decide what to do about it in a team meeting at 9 am in the morning.

One minute, we need to be able to understand how our products and processes impact the people and things in the systems of which we are part, trying to understand how to reduce carbon across our networks of suppliers and generate a more biodiverse and socially diverse community; and, the next minute, we need to be able to zoom right into the linear and silo-ed detail to suggest a nano-level process or productivity intervention that delivers one small element of our transformational vision.

We must hone our capacity to map, individually and collectively, complex, adaptive systems; and understand the feedback loops, both negative and positive, that shift system dynamics. We want to be able to use, like a virtuoso, tools like systems mapping and scenario planning that serve to help us glimpse the future into the present; and that bring the cacophony of myriad voices from the system to our attention.

Such tools and techniques can help us make sense of chaotic, adaptive, living systems and then anticipate opportunities for systemic transformation *before* crises ensue. Most supposed 'Black Swan' events, like climate change-induced flooding or Covid-19 pandemics, are in some ways predictable—and, at the very least, preparable for—by students of systems thinking. We are all students of systems thinking, no matter our expertise. Beginner's Mind is crucial when intervening in complex systems; and so real peoples' lives.

Systemic and regenerative leaders need to be able to deconstruct and destabilize all claims to truth/power in the system; and ensure systemic inequalities and iniquities are brought into sharp focus. But we also need to be able to swiftly move out of criticism and analysis—in doing so risking our reputations and livelihoods—to actually intervene in the system (even if others are profoundly challenged by this and attempt to bring us, and our projects, down).

Systemic leaders must be able to spot weak signals in everyday life that suggest historic patterns within a system are breaking down; and sense new patterns that are "seeking to emerge" from the system as it unfolds in a biodynamic process of always-becoming. We can then accelerate this process, or mitigate it, through our leadership actions and systemic change interventions.

We want to be able to locate and understand systemic "sweet spots"—where small actions might create outsized impacts—and innovate the lowest cost and lowest friction ways of acupuncture-like stimulation of these sweet spots effectively. Key is to constantly evolve and iterate an arsenal of potent systemic change interventions, ensuring they are driven by real biology and psychology not just wishful thinking.

This means becoming a lifelong learner of systemic interventions and social change movements, constantly updating our toolset and practice-set with critical nuances that can mean the difference between project failure (degeneration) and some kind of success (regeneration). We also want to build muscle in being able to project forward in time the dynamics of a system to understand, as best we can, potential unexpected returns that might make our interventions less powerful, or even detrimental, to the system longer-term.

At the heart of systemic leadership is quickly and effectively making sense of complexity with others in the system, capturing vital perspectives and insights from different areas of the system that are not our own; and then making collective decisions about what to do next in ways that balance collaboration and consensus with action and entrepreneurship.

To make systemic change achievable, we want to be able to surface and understand—rapidly yet compassionately—the worldview of each sentient being, and even concepts like 'money', within the system. We want to empathize with, and in some ways sense-feel within us, each systemic agent's perspectives, motives, wounds, and worries; without becoming co-dependently involved in their narratives and dramas.

Systemic change projects necessarily only work when collaboratively executed with a group of multiple leaders/change-agents. As systemic and regenerative leaders, we cannot afford to waste days and years convening agents of change, and building consensus and alignment within the group. This can dissipate shared intention and collective momentum and lead to failure. But if we do not build a "field"—like a magnetic field of resonance—that holds the diverse group together, miscommunications and misalignments will plague a project; and often lead to its implosion. This takes huge amounts of presence and patience.

We want to ensure that, at all times, we are running systemic transformation projects, workshops and meetings within what I call LOOPPs: Lightly-Engineered, Outcome-Oriented, Purpose-Driven, Practice-Powered Processes. A LOOPP is designed to allow for non-linear breakthroughs at the project level—as well as many individual transformations—without becoming unwieldy and limiting.

Design is crucial. Each engagement in a LOOPP, no matter how small or large, is designed to create a clear outcome that is agreed in advance. The *content* of the outcome is inherently unknowable because it is yet to emerge. But the *class* of outcome can be known if one understands the process of transformation. Without a bias for outcomes, people in a project will often gravitate towards 'interesting conversations' about their favorite ideas with their favorite people. They might remain locked in their comfort zones; or get stuck in exciting but infertile debates that do not move things on.

Therefore each stage of the process has to have definable outcomes that become the designed inputs of the next stage. For example, outcomes can be: a common purpose statement; collaborative give/get agreements; problem definition statements; systems maps; assumption maps; user empathy maps; regenerative business model canvases etc., etc. This allows for a Third Way creative harmony. We design for unpredictable creativity occuring *within* each outcome; and predictable deliverables resulting from progressing forward to the next outcome. We design a LOOPP to afford genuine emergence; through the alternating rhythm of divergence (creativity from C&C Mode) and convergence (discernment from C&P Mode).

If people are left to meet together without excellent design, they will usually connect, chat, and enjoy being together—but very little concrete value will emerge (if tangible outcomes are desired). With too little design, there can be too much chaos. Participants can be triggered into Control & Protect Mode, attempting to project their view of the world, and their vision for the future, onto the chaos to try to lessen the amount of complexity they must cope with. This reduces useful outcomes. However, too much rigidity and forcefulness in the process also triggers Control & Protect Mode: people feel coerced and trammeled; and this reduces creativity.

So a process should be engineered lightly by a central design team, at the core, to be the "minimal viable structure" needed to elegantly deliver concrete and specified outcomes—with every workshop or meeting—whilst allowing for surprise and serendipity. We want to bring in contributors to share their genius and insights from their location in the system and make the most of their time; without them feeling dishonored or controlled. We want to maintain play and fluidity whilst delivering in a timely and high-quality way for funders, participants, and the world.

I suggest that all systemic and regenerative projects should be grounded in something bigger than any individual organization or leader. Such a common purpose orients everyone to a shared source of possibility: ideas and insights coming from the future to shape a regenerative present. The kind of common purpose we want in systemic transformation generates a strong field for self-organization.

A common purpose is the animating force of an unfolding spiral—the project we are leading—that also acts as a 'limbic bond' in real time relationships. A limbic bond is a term some scientists use to describe a strong relational field between the **heart** and **hara** of two, or more, people. Common purpose might be crafted into words but it is more important that it is felt within everyone's bodymind. The purpose should allow each of us to dissolve our protective patterns in the moment; and so allow authentic co-creation and dialogue. It is the responsibility of the transformational leader to help find it; and then keep it alive and ensure it is expressed.

Finally, every LOOPP should be practice-powered. Personality issues and interpersonal problems will distort outcomes rapidly; and rob us of scant time. Therefore the leader must ensure that all contributors are committed to doing their own inner work (of freeing themselves from patterns). Each individual should be encouraged—and expected—to engage with reconnection and transformation practices that are designed to open their hearts and minds; and free them from limiting beliefs and conflictual habits. Our role as leader is to ensure these boundaries are clear and maintained. Then the group can achieve congruence; enter elusive co-creative flow states safely; and then maintain them.

We therefore must be incredibly discerning—without being afraid of seeming to be elitist or dismissive—about whom we invite into the LOOPP; when we invite them in; and what we expect of them. Ideally, we don't want to have to constantly check back on people using hierarchical power; or get caught in endless interpersonal issues and irresponsibilities. We want to be able to challenge anyone, and at any time, without causing needless conflict with clumsy coaching. This means choosing, designing, and convening wisely, as well as smartly.

To be a truly transformational leader, we must *consciously* develop ourselves to the level of systemic and regenerative leadership. Otherwise we can never drive transformations beyond the level of our team, or enterprise. Becoming a transformational leader who can conceive of, and execute, regenerative innovations that transform systems takes the highest levels of both Cognitive-Behavioral Complexity and Interoceptive-Affective Complexity.

In terms of Cognitive-Behavioral Complexity, we need to be super sharp to make sense of the vast flows of people, stuff, and ideas that make up a system; and the sheer complexity of complex, adaptive, living systems. We have to be able to cognitively grok how a system can shift to become more regenerative; and have the Get Stuff Done skills to make (the) shift happen. But systemic genius is not enough. In fact, without matching smarts with development of embodied wisdom, we can easily get overwhelmed by the complexity of systemic change; or become arrogant and intervene without suitable humility. This can have us act, and react, in inappropriate and damaging ways.

With emotionally immature delusions of grandeur, we might believe that we can fully understand and 'control' a system with our planetary-level intellect or our techno-utopian interventions. We might forget that every abstracted data point in the system is a feeling, sensing, concerned citizen of the world who must be respected and honored. We might attach, emotionally, to single solutions, interventions, models of change, or technologies; and discount other peoples' perspectives and actions as stupid or irrelevant.

We might become paralyzed by fear of the Law of Unexpected Returns and end up retreating from any action, afraid to risk our reputation and livelihood in case we make mistakes or people doubt our intentions. We might end up with beautiful cognitive cathedrals of systemic insight—and libraries full of maps, models, and algorithms—while being totally unable to convene a group of stressed, yet committed, human beings to take responsibility for, and then guide with their actions, a system to a more regenerative state.

High levels of Interoceptive-Affective Complexity, embodied wisdom, allow us to discern when and how to intervene in a system. I-AC allows us never to fall into the pattern of being righteous about our systemic ideals; or judging those in the system who we believe pollute, persecute, resist, or just don't get it. An enhanced capacity for empathy, both cognitive and emotional, helps us gain key insights into "resistors" and "accelerators" of systemic change; how to engage and influence them effectively; and how to orchestrate complex sequences of interventions and interactions to shift hearts and minds.

We honor *all* perspectives, and proactively look to build bridges between different camps without privileging one. We actively choose to 'love' everyone in the system, whilst never staying silent about, or encouraging in any way, behaviors and beliefs that diminish our humanity and endanger our work. This is as much a biological imperative as a moral one: 'abusers' in the system will change their mindsets and habits most effectively if they feel safe and sense that they are held with unconditional positive regard.

With C-BC and I-AC fused in a Third Way palintonic harmony in our **hara**, **heart**, **head**, and **hands**—congruent and integrated—we create the optimal conditions and contexts for personal and systemic change. We are inclusive of all views in the system, even those we find painful or distasteful. We have the courage and conviction to stand up for people who are being repressed or marginalized by dominative hierarchies; yet we never succumb to the dictatorship of forced flatness and consensus. We hold and host generative spaces—acting as an amplifier and accelerator of others' talents and skills—without this always being visible or appreciated. We build a sense of belonging in the group, finding ways to weave together disparate change agents (who often won't agree) into a cohesive and coherent whole, grounded in a common purpose.

Aikido-like, we harness human resistance to change to propel people toward transformation. We subtly, yet sometimes emphatically, micro-coach and mentor individuals elegantly to upgrade their beliefs and transform their defenses—helping people overcome collaborative glitches that are blocking creative flow, inspiring them to leap over dips in energy and moments of despair, and always stabilizing them when the chaos and complexity are almost too much to bear—even if they don't thank us for it. Truly interdependent, we take on all feedback without neurotically questioning our own integrity.

As this is happening, we can shift our attention to people in systems and sense the mood of it before moving to resolve issues. We always remember that we are part of the system and need to act fully and with commitment rather than just wait for perfect data or for the ideal moment: neither ever come. We exist in a creative tension between humility (who do we think we are to lead systemic change?!?) and hubris (who do we think we are to not step up and lead systemic change?!?). Confident, courageous, and willing to take wise risks, we show up fully to serve whatever is seeking to emerge as we listen individually in our hearts—and collectively in circles—often in silence, to the whispers of the system.

We do all this while stubbornly guiding the system as a whole toward a regenerative vision through concrete action. We orchestrate the sequencing, and support the collaborative execution, of systemic transformation strategies; and ensure they are adapted to fit the changing landscape. By fusing instinct, intuition, intelligence, and insight within us, we do our best to de-risk systemic interventions and promote actions and movements that will bring the system into a more thriving state; while being fully aware we might be catastrophically wrong. We are totally at peace with this possibility.

Ever more free from egoic fixations and resistance, we challenge our assumptions and cognitive biases with alacrity to let go of old ideas so we can forge Triple Win solutions that not only deliver profit but also improve and restore the habitats in which we play. We *naturally* want to step out of extraction and accumulation and toward contribution and collaboration.

We are happy to give up a lot—whether industry reputation, great wealth, or convenient flights to our holiday homes—to fulfill our potential as leaders of systemic change. No longer tossed around by the damaging and diminishing actions of others— and the vagaries and uncertainties of the VUCA reality—we are instead like wise, stable oaks that stay grounded and generative even in the most extreme storms. Thus, we are back, full circle, where we started—conscious leadership—as if for the first time (*pace* T.S. Eliot). Except, having been through a complete spiral of transformational leadership, we are both wiser and smarter, ready to meet the next challenge of our times.

46

LEADING TRANSFORMATION IN ANY HUMAN SYSTEM

Every leader on this beautiful, fragile Earth is faced with rapidly evolving digital technologies, disruptive social changes, and global existential risks from damaged systems. There is no one-size-fits-all strategic solution to deal with these complex challenges. The nature of the VUCA world means there's no easy template for transformation that a consultancy can peddle and a Board can execute with certainty. In fact, the opposite is true. Each organization, with its unique history, geography, nationality, culture, business model(s), and people models, has to live into its own answers. It must go on the *journey* of metabolizing external changes into value within the organization. To do this, each must find the adaptive pressures that are most severe and pressing, quite literally; and discover and define the Transformational Challenges that are most ripe for resolving. In other words, each organization must, in the immortal words of poet Rainer Maria Rilke, "live the questions now."

However, C&P Mode craves predictability and safety. When we are in it as leaders, we want transformational change; but we want it in a risk-free and linear way. This is an oxymoron. We want to guarantee to our investors that we can deliver predictable returns on investment by tweaking the algorithm or the production line with best-practice technical solutions and continuous improvements with margin gains; but we also want them to believe we are adapting and transforming effectively for the future.

We want to do exactly what we have already done, using thinking that we already know—just a bit better—to solve emerging customer needs and market failures, rather than engage in the risky but rewarding journey of transformation. We like to use machine metaphors and machine thinking—efficiency upgrades and productivity gains—to solve technical problems but watch as linear optimizations start to fade and fail. If we cannot break out of C&P Mode for long enough, what we thought were 'safe,' incremental improvements lead to decline. What we do, and how we do it, starts to fade from relevance. Instead of predictable growth, we get symptoms of failure to adapt. I call this pathway the Breakdown Decline.

The Breakdown Decline charts the journey of a leader, or her organization, when we remain locked in C&P Mode: blaming disappointing results, slowing growth, or talent problems on market conditions or competitors rather than owning them and metabolizing them into new value. It shows what happens when

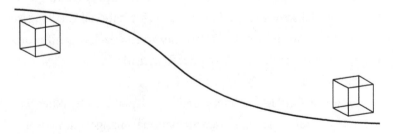

FIGURE 20 *The Breakdown Decline*

we cannot give up old ideas, perhaps because we are emotionally attached to them as they made us strong and helped us succeed in the past; when we attempt to escape the transformation imperative and seek our way back to a yesterday that no longer exists; and when we maintain a narrative about our failure to adapt that casts us as 'right.'

The Breakdown Decline shows what happens when we try to cling onto an old reality rather than embrace inevitable change . . . and find a way to be great in a different way; a path that doesn't involve returning to a mythical past that worked for few (which historically has meant older, richer, whiter, 'maler' folk). The Breakdown Decline shows us visually that we simply cannot continue to do what we have always done, endlessly tweaking the legacy model, and expect to stay relevant and valued in times of rapid change.

All enterprises and systems are made up of *people*—whether staff, customers, citizens, or stakeholders—who have a wet, messy, and complex biology underpinning their thoughts and feelings. People don't change in a linear way as machines do. We are, by nature, unpredictable and non-linear. It's this very unpredictability that allows for breakthrough thinking and genuine transformation: from the invention of language to the discovery of quantum mechanics.

While there is no simple, single silver bullet for how to transform such enterprises and systems—and their biological and psychological wetware—there is a *proven* pathway that every organization and leader can follow that, so far in my experience, always delivers appropriate, responsive, and fitting transformational solutions to every Transformational Challenge. Every leader can learn to lead himself/herself, their teams, and entire organizations into and beyond transformation *by choice*. I call this non-linear, deeply creative, and profoundly conscious pathway of problem-solving The Transformation Curve.

The Transformation Curve appears to be what German scientist and writer Johann Wolfgang von Goethe called an *ur-phenomenon*: a blueprint that underpins *all* transformative change in organisms and organizations that are reliant on biology—life—for their existence. Goethe, who promoted a competing scientific paradigm to Newton, based on empathic connection as opposed to analytical separation, neatly summarized the biological elements of being seen on the Transformation Curve: "Basic characteristics of an individual organism: to divide, to unite, to merge into the universal, to abide in the particular, to transform itself."

Unlike the predictable straight line of continuous improvement and profit growth that C&P Mode (management) mindsets desire, to lead and land lasting positive change we must instead embrace a J-shaped curve. Instead of progressing incrementally upward from an initial state, with things getting slowly and safely 'better' in a linear and algorithmic way, we first head *down:* disrupting ourselves by unpacking the problem and embracing the chaos of possibility. Only artificial, man-made machinery works in straight lines.

47
THE TRANSFORMATION CURVE

The Transformation Curve maps how human biologies—and so all *human*-populated enterprises, institutions, and systems—move from mismatched, outdated solutions to future-positive, planet-ready solutions as effectively (but not always efficiently) as possible.

We first jettison outdated thinking, behaviors, and emotional states before we then discover more adaptive solutions that fit the emerging world better. We spot, and then relinquish, what is breaking down first, before we can find and accelerate what is breaking through: weak signals of the future-value in the present. These transformational ideas and solutions take us even higher than we were at the start, delivering exponential value and impact.

The personal, strategic, and societal innovations that are the outcome of a journey along the Transformation Curve include some of the original properties of the old reality; but they transcend the old with new emergent features. Thus, by leading ourselves and others across the Transformation Curve, we build new and more appropriate "higher-level" or "higher-order" solutions that fit the changing world better.

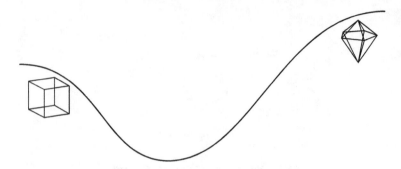

FIGURE 21 *The Transformation Curve*

This allows us not only to survive when we encounter intense evolutionary pressures; but to metabolize threats into value-generating ideas that allow us to thrive *because* of the evolutionary pressures. We can, if we follow the logic of The Transformation Curve, wrestle from the jaws of chaos fundamental breakthroughs in people, products, and processes that ensure we come out of all crises having learned from them; and co-evolved through them.

Out of confusion flies triumph. From constraint arises creativity. Within the chaos, genius is forged.

The Transformation Curve seems to be a fundamental blueprint for how breakthroughs burst forth from the world and—as we rigorously embed and embody novelty in our nerves, thoughts, and processes—become true transformations. The J-shaped curve seems to signal something important . . . something essential; even eternal. It shows up fractally: each Transformation Curve can resolve into smaller journeys of transformation as we zoom down into what is occurring at deeper levels in a system.

You can see the telltale trace of a J-shaped curve in how start-ups turn venture capital into creative solutions that drive 100× returns; right through to how seeds turn their stored energy into leaves that can capture the power of the sun's rays. Political scientist Ian Bremmer, in his book *The J Curve*, shows that as a country moves from dictatorship to democracy, it first encounters disorder and chaos. Yet even at the level of an individual, we see the same: people get worse before they get better when learning challenging new skills. No matter what scale of human endeavor we look at—from the creation of energy in exothermic reactions to the creation of nations in our globalized world—we see the same Transformation Curve appear.

The structure of the Transformation Curve can be summed up like this: if we want to create something that is more ingenious, adaptive, complex (to fit more complex environments), and creative than that with which we started—in other words, we want to lead our system toward and through a transformation that allows us to thrive more—we have to be prepared to enter a strategic and systematic breakdown first. The old has to melt (down) before the new can be smelted. Things have to disintegrate before we turn the corner and rise, phoenix-like, with a better idea.

If we want a product or policy that excels, we must first engage with the possibility (though not necessarily the reality) of its opposite: complete disassembly and disruption. We have to risk what we have for what we could have. We have to give up the safe predictability of old patterns for the adaptive unpredictability of new ones. To solve our important Transformational Challenges and usher in a transformed world order, we must first accept the Leadership Invitation, heed the call of adventure, and leave the old world behind.

I first encountered this kind of transformational journey in the work of the historian of science Thomas Kuhn. He demonstrated that science does not progress in an incremental, linear path toward absolute Truth. This kind of learning occurs, of course, as scientists slowly fill in the gaps in a theory or model in an incremental way. The same is true of transformation and innovation in an organization: once we have had a transformational vision of what is possible, lots of incremental and more linear change needs to occur to deliver it.

Kuhn demonstrated, in his landmark book *The Structure of Scientific Revolutions*, that when science undergoes a 'revolution'— for example the transformation from Newtonian mechanics to quantum mechanics—it does so in a non-linear way. This depends as much on the imagination within the consciousness of the scientist (leader) as it does on the cold, hard data.

To describe what happens when science undergoes a major transformation, Kuhn came up with the notion of a 'paradigm.' He suggested that all scientific (and business) activities, from switching on an MRI scanner to pipetting a chemical solution, happen within a paradigm: a way of thinking about the world that makes sense of it. In other words, scientific knowledge is developed within a set of assumptions, just as a product or sale program is developed within a set of business model assumptions.

Scientific and economic knowledge is discovered through objectively investigating nature; but every data point only makes sense from within a subjective paradigm in our consciousness. Therefore, the lens through which we look, our meaning-making frame of reference, distorts as much as it reveals. Idealism and materialism are both true; stretched in palintonic harmony.

During Business as Usual, one scientific paradigm rules over all, just as it does in a market. But data start to show up that don't 'make sense' from within the ruling paradigm. At first, these contradictory results are rejected as 'anomalies'; since they do not fit the paradigm, they are discounted. This is the same in business. Market leaders at Kodak and Nokia discounted anomalous signals in consumer mindsets and behaviors because they did not fit the rules for which their entire business model was optimized.

However, when anomalies build up, transformational leaders (whether scientists or innovators) discard the old paradigm and co-create a new one that fits the new data better. The data points are remixed into a new theory/business model that transforms everything we thought before. Some leaders, the old guard, find these transformations tough; even if they invented the new way of doing things.

With the famous EPR paper, Einstein co-proposed big ideas that were instrumental in the revolution that ended up in the powerful theory of quantum mechanics. But he was conflicted in his paradigm, in his consciousness, until the day he died by the core truth of it: that there is randomness at the heart of the universe. Likewise, Nokia invented the smartphone, and Kodak the digital camera, but failed to double-down on their transformational solutions in matter because of reticence with letting go of old paradigms in their consciousness.

We can prevent these failings from happening to us with transformational leadership. If we are prepared to transform our own consciousness in **hara**, **heart**, **head**, then we can transform the material worked with our **hands**. We can usher in the transformations that are seeking to emerge in our paradigm, our system, through transformations in our self.

Every organism, and every organization, must find a way to stay relevant through transformation along the Transformation Curve; or they will slide down the Breakdown Decline. These are the only two choices. Breakdown of the old occurs on both paths. However, it can happen to us, and we will fade. Or we can encourage the breakdown and adapt to a better state. Charles Darwin, toward the close of *On the Origin of Species*, puts it like this: "better adaptation, in however slight a degree to the surrounding physical conditions, will turn the balance." Adaptation helps us stay fitted with environment.

48

THE TRANSFORMATION DIFFERENTIAL

Although *fitness* is vital for competition and survival, I believe that *fitted*ness is equally important for individual and organizational thriving. We need *both* to be competitively fit to maintain our edge with efficient best practice; *and* always maintain our fit with a dramatically changing world by exploring next practice. Fittedness is not about being good or bad; better or worse. These moral dualities dissolve with genuine wisdom. Fittedness is about discerning, without falling into dualistic judgement, whether a thought, feeling, or action matches or not with the world around us.

Do our ideas fit the world as it is becoming? Do our actions fit the realities of the Anthropocene Age? Do our habits fit with a flourishing and regenerative ecosystem? Do the stories we tell ourselves fit with who we want to be? Do the assumptions at the core of our organization fit the 3D future? Do our persistent moods and hidden traumas fit with the family life, and team spirit, we yearn for most?

We must all live, love, and lead in a constantly evolving world. A recent series of studies by evolutionary theorist Prof. Umesh Vazirani, at U.C. Berkeley, used computers to explore how evolution works.

His research suggests to me that nature values both efficient fitness and creative fittedness. Nature loves high-performance species. They *fit*: strong, competitive, and so survive. They make it, where others do not, to pass on their genes. But nature also loves variety and diversity, which allows more *fittedness* as the world changes. If our genes are fitted—by being perfectly tailored to a particular ecology—when the outside world changes (as it always does eventually), then a genetically more varied species is better able to adapt.

The fittest may survive. The fitted—those of us who lead continuous transformations to adapt to a ceaselessly changing environment—can go beyond mere survival and thrive. Control & Protect Mode, which sees parts, has proven with science that these parts—species and individuals within species—compete with each other for scarce resources to survive. Create & Connect Mode, which sees entireties, intuits that the whole thrives through collaboration and synergy. For example, our bodymind works in intimate collaboration with the bacteria of our microbiome, which collectively contributes more genetic material than our cells do to our whole body.

We can no longer operate a disempowering business model that punishes our customers for being human (for example, Blockbuster's late fees making c.75% of its profits) in a world that is becoming radically more empowered. We can no longer solely care about profit in a reality where purpose and sustainability are even driving mammoth huge hedge funds and pension funds to divest of stocks and shares that don't take this seriously. We cannot offer luxury products for parading around town if people in those towns have reconnected with what's really important after a pandemic.

We must match the environment within which we find ourselves; and be ready to adapt to environments that are coming. This principle was brought to light by William Ross-Ashby, a psychiatrist (mastery of the inner world of consciousness), that became a systems theorist (mastery of outer world of matter). In the 1950s, he formulated the Law of Requisite Variety. Also known as Ashby's Law, it states that an organism/organization must have the same level of variety *within* it as is found in the external environment. In other words, an organization can only cope with the spectrum of challenges that arise in its ecosystem if it has a palette of responses that are as varied and creative as the problems it must solve.

In static, and statist, markets, an organization does not need much variety—diversity, inclusion, empowerment, creativity, purpose, innovation, co-creativity, etc.—within to succeed. In fact, the Industrial Age exploded into every home because it *reduced* variety inside companies so that every box of cereal or porcelain plate was identical to any other. This reduced production and transaction costs. Standardization of sizing and components was vital to scaling once-prohibitively expensive products and services to billions of people. People liked their beer, or hotel room, to feel the same wherever they were.

'Variance' was eliminated from production lines, and rules—encoded in best practice management procedures/policies— ensured risks were minimized and outputs maximized. But in the rapidly-changing VUCA context, old rules are often maladapted to emergent realities. Then best practice starts to kill the next practice that organizations need to stay fitted with customers and technology. Variance is another term for thinking differently and adapting in real time. The word 'art' originally meant 'to fit together; to join.' The art of leadership is, in some very real and profound way, about staying creatively fitted not just competitively fit.

In fast-moving markets and dramatically-changing environments, we have to allow much more variance, creativity, and diversity of thought inside our teams and cultures. The world is massively more varied and complex than it was even twenty years ago. So Industrial Age management theory and practice that limits variance, creativity, and agility is leading most modern organizations to fade; and many to fail: they are becoming increasingly irrelevant. Most multinationals are underperforming given their abundant access to different forms of capital. Industrial Age management thinking, with transactional management at its core, is no longer working optimally in the digital, disrupted, and damaged reality. It is struggling to keep major enterprises competitive and innovative in the marketplace—and attractive places for employees to spend the majority of their time and energy. In fast-changing markets, which are changing faster than most organizations are, only transformational leadership can deliver the continuous transformations that are needed to fit, and perhaps even forge, the future as it comes hurtling toward us.

We fit. Or we fail. We transform; or we decline. Our ideas and actions either fit the moment (what I call "FiMo"); or they mismatch the moment (what I call "MiMo"). This is glaringly obvious when we turn to one of the biggest problems facing our species: diseases such as obesity, type 2 diabetes, heart disease, and depression. Our actions are MiMo. We are not eating, exercising, moving, and working in a way that fits how are physiology works. There is a mismatch between how we evolved (to hunt and forage for food, running, and walking long distances burning calories in the process) and how we live now, where we have access to extremely energy-rich foods at the click of a mouse; or the opening of a fridge door.

Daniel Lieberman, an academic at Harvard University who writes about the evolution of the human body, says that most of us will die from such 'mismatch diseases.' I believe that most of our organizations will die from mismatch business models and operating practices. To prevent this from happening, we cannot just do more of the same—faster, cheaper, more, better!—and expect different results. We have to disrupt ourselves and release the old so we can then rise to thrive as we make our way up the steep learning and execution side of the Transformation Curve. Nothing is forever, especially a business model, product, or process. At the core of Buddhist wisdom is the truth that everything—success, stock prices, market hegemony, leadership power, and our life—is impermanent. We can embrace this and guide our constant adaptation. Or we can resist it, and suffer.

In any given moment, we all have a conscious choice to see the digital, disrupted, damaged world through C&P Mode as a triple threat . . . or to switch on into C&C Mode and see it as a triple opportunity. Each moment is a bifurcation point: follow a Transformation Curve or ignore the signs and symptoms and see if we ride it out on a Breakdown Decline. The bottom line is that in this fast- and furiously-changing world, no product, process, or person stays successful for very long. Everything is forging or failing the future; and without continuous transformation we get stuck in the past.

If we are stuck in the past, then we underperform, disengage, get frustrated, and experience lots of stress. But if we switch on, we realize that the rapid change in the outside world is opening up continuous spaces for transformation: both within our organizations and beyond, in the sectors and systems of which we are a part. Organizations do not fail because of lack of intelligence, but because they can't let go of old mindsets and perceptions long enough to be on the right side of history. Yet if we ensure our organization takes the road less traveled, a journey along the Transformation Curve, we will be rewarded with the "transformation differential":

the exponential difference in outcomes between unconsciously managing our own decline and consciously leading our own transformation.

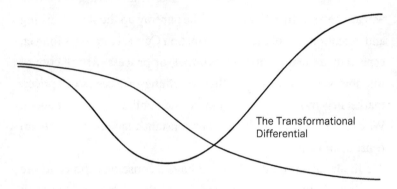

The Transformational
Differential

FIGURE 22 *The Transformation Differential*

49

BTTP GEM 7: THE SEVEN STEPS OF THE TRANSFORMATION CURVE

Although the process of transformation is utterly fluid and non-linear—from the moment of awareness that something feels like mismatch right through to final delivery of a breakthrough solution into the world—there are key moments on the Transformation Curve that can be identified as discrete steps. By understanding these steps both cognitively and emotionally, you can better lead yourself, teams, organizations, and system to the next step; and beyond.

I usually suggest that there are seven classical steps of the Transformation Curve, although this can be more or less depending on the context and the scale of the transformation. The steps can be *analyzed* through the lens of Cognitive-Behavioral Complexity and seen as a change 'process'. This would be the case in language-based 'games' like strategy or coaching. We label this process the 7 Ps. However, experienced through the lens of Interoceptive-Affective Complexity, a bodymind feels 7 Rs. This might be the case in a healing experience or in a spiritual awakening workshop.

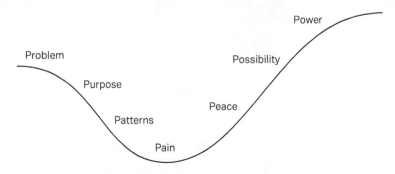

FIGURE 23 *The 7 Steps of the Transformation Curve*

The 7Ps and the 7Rs are simple different ways of describing the same transformational journey or pathway. Both are *always* happening at the same time as there is only one unified bodymind. The label simply corresponds to what we *pay attention to*: cognitive-behavioral processes or interoceptive-affective experiences.

The 7 steps in BTTP Gem 7 are fractal and can be described in different ways depending on the scale: whether they relate to an individual's transformation; that of a group or team; or as they pertain to an entire organization undergoing a business transformation or innovation processes. As above, so below: the motto of the medieval alchemists; Isaac Newton had this maxim on his desk.

Here I have set out the 7Ps as they pertain to an individual leader who is seeking to transform themselves in advance of transforming his/her organization or system (a far more detailed journey can be found in my book *Switch On*):

Problem: We start by pulling ourselves out of automatic reactivity to an issue once we spot the tell-tale signs and symptoms of a mismatch/MiMo. These signs are in the outer world; and within our inner world (feeling stuck, stressed, or suffering). We take time and space to get some perspective. We reflect and connect in order to identify and define Transformational Challenges that we want to break through. We consciously avoid the seductions of seeking 'easy' technical problems that can be solved with existing knowledge and skills; or repeating what worked in the past. We ensure that we focus on Transformational Challenges that are driven by environmental pressures forcing us—inviting us—to adapt.

Switching out of blame, shame, and complain, we own the Transformational Challenges fully; and then emotionally and cognitively bring them 'inside' us as individuals. Avoiding narratives that make us appear right, we see each Transformational Challenge as a bifurcation point: an opportunity to proactively choose the Transformation Curve pathway rather than allow a Breakdown Decline to continue. We own the problems rather than letting the problems own us. We take them within so we can metabolize them into value through adapting our products, processes, and people.

Purpose: As soon as we sense identify Transformational Challenges, we reconnect with our purpose. By reawakening to the intense richness of our connective, love-fueled, heart-led purpose—and reminding ourselves of our calling as a leader—we ground ourselves with stability no matter the complexity and chaos. We stop stressing and reacting with knee-jerk solutions; and, instead, rest in the safe space within. We are anchored, tethered, to something bigger than the frustration and the fear; and the pain and the heartache.

This allows us to move through the transformation process safely—with confidence in any eventual breakthrough outcome— even although we know it will mean disassembling and disrupting our own patterns. Our purpose enables us to stay together as we allow things—assumptions and addictions—to come apart.

With purpose boosting our courage, we penetrate past the symptoms and signals of fading and failing to choose which Transformational Challenge we want to focus on this time: one that *really matters* to ourselves, our organization, and the systems we touch.

Rather than concentrating our limited leadership capacity on problems that matter little in the overall scheme of things, we devote our discretionary effort and life force to solving meaningful problems: challenges that, when resolved, will create major dividends in terms of a reduction of suffering (impact) and an increase in thriving (value).

Patterns: Having harnessed our purpose to open our hearts and minds rather than allow them to close in fear and frustration, we consciously, fearlessly, and attentively identify the habitual protective patterns with which we currently react that still leave a Transformational Challenge unsolved. Each pattern is made up of: **hara** (felt sense); **heart** (emotions); **head** (beliefs/thoughts/assumptions); and **hands** (behaviors).

We recognize without shame or resistance that if the protective patterns were fully fitted to the fast-changing world—an adaptive match for reality—then there would be no Transformational Challenge. We clarify the triggers in the external world—people and events—that stimulate our reactive protective patterns. This generates spaces between stimulus and response. We slow reactivity and open the possibility of a creative breakthrough.

Pain: We reflect on the underlying pain or wounding that the protective pattern is designed to stop us having to experience again. It is not essential to clarify the pain fully in words as long as we can make sense of it. This means distinguishing underlying fears, anxieties, and traumatic memories that lock the pattern in place. We explore the perceived needs that the protective pattern was designed to meet, and look with clear eyes at whether those needs are being met optimally.

We explore whether the pattern is serving us fully or sabotaging our potential, causing different pain. We clarify the gain from the pattern as well as the pain. We see if we can penetrate to the hidden order of things and spot the initial imprint/template of the pattern: when and why it developed. By understanding the pattern's role as a defensive force against further wounding, we can judge whether we still need it. By joining the dots like this, we can make sense of seemingly crazy or frustrating beliefs and behaviors.

Peace: No longer resisting or repressing the past, we can now accept who we are and how we have arrived here. This means fully honoring a sabotaging protective pattern as absolutely essential to have made it this far. Having found reliable ways to feel safe and connected, we can accept who we have become but also know that we can choose to be much more. This is the time fully to feel, process, and then *release* underlying pain, trauma, fear, wounding, and stress within.

No longer locked in by pain, we can break out of even the most persistent and pernicious protective patterns; and looping protective patterns such as addictions to work, social media, substances, power, control . . . or simply being right. The more connected we feel, the more safe we will be to release old trauma that has not been processed; the more empowered we will be to dissolve outdated neural pathways that are no longer needed to defend us; and the quicker we can melt away protective habits that are sabotaging ourselves and our organization's potential.

Possibility: No longer stuck repeating old patterns that were locked in by historic pain, we can now open up adaptive and fitting creativity in the present. No longer gripped by fear and stress, we see the Transformational Challenge for what it always is: an opportunity to forge the future without limits. We have said 'yes' to all that has been and now we say 'and . . . there is better way.'

With peace within, we are free to respond to the challenge with agile, imaginative solutions rather than automatic knee-jerk reactions. We enter creative-flow states, alone and with colleagues and collaborators, where fresh insights and bold ideas rush into our mind. We are fully alive, reborn in transformation, because we are fully metabolizing problems into possibilities.

Dramatic changes in our environment are being metabolized and alchemized within: into creative solutions—for customers, employees, stakeholders—that resolve emerging pain points and fulfill emergent needs. Unshackled from history and legacy, we innovate and invent amazing possibilities that can drive exponential value creation. We have disrupted best practice and led ourselves to generate next practice.

Power: We now wire this inchoate creative response into our bodymind, consciously shaping new neural pathways that turn an imaginative experiment into our dominant habit. We hack the process our bodymind uses to develop protective patterns to embody our breakthrough repattern. We attentively transform inspiration into action by building new habits and processes that manifest exciting possibilities in concrete form. What fires together wires together: the more we practice a new, more empowering repattern, the more rapidly we will rewire our nervous system.

Understanding that nerves don't fully rewire overnight, we maintain commitment to the transformation until we fully land a positive change in ourselves and our world. We stabilize positive and courageous emotional and interoceptive states in **hara** and **heart**. We embed new thoughts and beliefs into our **heads** by shifting meaning-making frames, editing explanatory narratives, and refining our leadership philosophy. We then do different things during our day with our **hands.** As we behave, think, feel, and sense ourselves into a transformation, the Transformational Challenge is resolved with concrete solutions that change ourselves, our enterprises, and the systems we touch.

Perhaps the most powerful aspect of the Transformation Curve is that, once we've embodied a transformation personally, and perhaps embedded a transformation into our organization, we realize that there are other Transformation Curves in which to engage: to solve other Transformational Challenges in other areas. And so the process starts again. Expanded and inspired, we seek the next Transformation Curve to ride . . . and repeat.

50

THE CONNECTION SOLUTION

You might have noticed that the key inflection point on the Transformation Curve—when we turn the corner between old and new, breakdown and breakthrough—is reliant on feeling *connected*. This should not be a surprise. Biological science has shown us that if we want to *do* things differently, we have to *feel* differently, too. We have to find ways out of fear and stress if we want to concretely step up with our full leadership potential.

If we have the same emotional states and feelings dominating us, we will likely have the same thoughts and the same actions. There will be no transformation. But if we become masters of the emotions flowing through our bodyminds, the more we become masters of our leadership capability. The more we master our emotional relationship to change, challenge, and crisis, the more we master our mindsets. Then we can enter the right Mode for the moment and positively impact our teams, organizations, and systems.

To achieve radical *behavioral* agility—the ability to adapt in real time to a changing world and lead transformations within it—we need radical *emotional* stability. Your *emotional* relationship to intense challenges (including those in your past) will in a large part determine how transformative you are as a leader, because your emotions play such a dominant role in determining the Mode you are in. If you want to inspire your employees more, be more collaborative, become a better storyteller and so more influential, conceive of transformational innovations, achieve ambitious sustainability goals, or take part in shifting an entire system to be regenerative . . . then you have not just to spot protective patterns cognitively, but to release them emotionally.

To shift reliably between C&P Mode and C&C Mode, relinquishing pernicious and persistent protective patterns in the process, we need to feel safe. This, categorically, is healing. As we self-heal, we become ever more whole, able to use the full spectrum of responses to any given stimulus, no matter how initially stressful. *Holy*, *whole*, and *heal* all come from the same etymological root. There is no wholeness without healing. And healing is a little bit sacred.

We have to find a way to feel safe within ourselves. Even if our managers, Board directors, investors, and colleagues are awake to the importance of safety, nobody can make us feel anything within. Others can inspire safety within us. But we always generate the safety ourselves. I have discovered, through many years of trial and much error, that the most reliable source of psychological and emotional safety is a feeling of connection. I mean a felt sense of connection to ourselves, to others, and to the world around. Connection is the solution to feeling stuck or stressed within. It is the gateway to transformation.

Connection is the only infallible way to get on track for transformation and unlock any form of stuckness in leadership situations. We cannot become the most creative, collaborative, and inspiring leader that we know we can be without regular access to such connection. Nothing else can substitute. I cannot use science to prove to you that the Connection Solution is attainable by you; and of primary value to you. Objective science designed to study physical matter cannot prove what exists within our subjective consciousness. However, over millennia, millions of people have found out this truth for themselves through practice: transformational practices that reconnect the heart. So I invite you to practice and prove it to yourself.

The experience of connection is the only experience more powerful than our fear memories, traumatic wounds, and the constant threats of modern-day anxiety and stress. Therefore, the experience of connection is the only thing that I believe can reliably and regularly secure us sufficiently within ourselves so that we can release old protective patterns; and achieve transformation in the outside world.

A sense of connection shifts us from a state of threat to a state of safety. It creates a sanctuary—a refuge—within our inner world that can ensure we feel safe no matter what is happening outside us. The safer we feel, the more we can release the emotions that are holding in old patterns of behavior. We can pull up the emotional anchors that are keeping us stuck in ever-diminishing circles of ineffectiveness; and we are thereby freed to invent new ways of being that fit the moment better. The more stable our connection is, the less reactive we are; and the more creative we become.

The more connected we feel, the more our **hara** and **heart** can resist destabilizing emotions and instead feel consistent stabilizing emotions: passion, purpose, empowerment, curiosity, trust, belonging, togetherness, and self-worth. The more connected we feel, the more we can enter the **head** and **hands** C-states (like creativity, curiosity, connection, collaboration, care); and the less we enter the F-states (like fight, flight, freeze, fawn, fornicate, faint).

The question then is, how do we feel a reliable sense of connection within? There are scientific answers to this question; and philosophical ones. In fact, for thousands of years, the great preoccupation of many philosophers—especially within the 'wisdom traditions', whether ancient Greek Stoicism or Chinese Taoism—has been answering this very question.

The outcome of this sustained experiment in truth-seeking—carried out by thousands, if not millions, of wise folk—is that when we meditate, dance ecstatically, or empathically bond with nature, we can reliably reach a sense of connection that feels more true than any other human experience. This sense of connection has been given many different, and often more exotic, names: 'belonging', 'fullness', 'emptiness', 'love'; as well as *Advaita*, *Brahman/Atman*, *Ein Sof*, Emptiness/Form, Buddha-Nature, thusness, Oneness, VALIS (the name sci-fi writer Philip K. Dick gave to this Vast Active Living Intelligence System), or the Tao.

Whatever we call it connective unity has no opposite. Thus we come full circle and return to BTTP Gem 1: the unity of object, subject, and the universe.

The sense of connection to all things is an expressly 'spiritual' thing. However, don't get me wrong. As I go to great lengths to show in my 'metaphysical memoir' *Spiritual Atheist*, this does not require any religion, whether established church or New Age cult. The feeling of connection is accessible to everyone if they commit to reconnection *practices*: from meditation to yoga, from breathwork to ecstatic dance. It is utterly secular yet totally spiritual at the same time. It requires no dogma, Bible, or priest (although it does help to have some words, and principles, to make sense of it).

The feeling of connection that arises within connective consciousness is a reliable and stable 'truth' that can be experienced by all with practice. When we experience a live connection to life itself, what some call the 'universe,' we feel a sense of love within. I believe love is the metaphor we humans use to describe the feeling of oneness and unity. This love then allows us to experience old pain and trauma in a safe way, and eventually let go of it. Love within provides us with what attachment theory calls an 'internalized secure base' so that we can heal trauma and stress to become more whole. Wholeness inside leads to wholeness in our teams and enterprises.

Rather than seek security in others, which is what happens in co-dependent relationships, we build safety and groundedness within. We can then experience this connection/love in our relational fields—and so collaborations—with others in genuine interdependence. Because the connection/love we find within is self-generated and self-discovered, it is unlimited and totally unconditional.

This kind of connection/love is the only thing I have ever heard of, or experienced myself, that is bigger than our fear and therefore strong enough to transform our protective patterns. If we don't feel this unconditional, universal, spiritual love, then there is nothing bigger than ourselves into which we can release our pain, disappointments, and troubles. We are stuck with them. We need connection to heal our hearts and achieve lasting serenity and equanimity in the face of even the toughest challenges.

Even if we have not experienced much biographical trauma—acts of omission and commission like neglect and abuse in our childhood—we will suffer inside as long as we consider ourselves separate from the world. Separation—the sense of alienation and atomization that arises in useful but limited analytical consciousness—is the ultimate source of all our suffering. This is because it drives lack—I have less than they do; I need something outside of me—and so endless and unquenchable desire.

The Buddha points this out in the Four Noble Truths: desire for safety, for power, for fame, for money is the root of all human angst. Therefore, the only way to relieve the suffering is through unity: connection/love. With the 7th gem of BTTP, we return to the 1st: the principle of a unified bodymind. It is not just united within itself; it is united in some ineffable, but practically experienceable, way to all that is: the one universe we are all part of.

Most of our emotional baggage, which drives our maladapted leadership patterns, comes from not getting connection/love in the way we wanted it in the past. Few of us grow up receiving the connection/love/safety we want in exactly the way we want it. This generates an unstable attachment to others and to the universe of which we are part. We can only heal such pain if we repair the loss in the same domain in which the original disappointments occurred. That domain is love/safety/connection. Love is the ultimate solvent to melt down pain that is holding us back.

By using connection/love as a *context* to explore difficult *content*, we can bring up any fear and pain memories safely within our consciousness. With the universe at our back, we can let go of trauma—usually with a long exhale—rather than repress the sadness and frustration. Tears may flow. This is an entirely appropriate response—childlike not childish—to *really* feeling grief, loss, and pain from the past (or shock from intense events in the present). In this way, pain can always be transformed into possibility: serenity in our hearts, clarity in minds, infinitude in our potential habits.

In order to let go of emotional baggage like this, the stuff that stops us from being confident, creative, and compassionate, we have to feel the feelings that we have repressed so they can be released from our bodymind. Healing has to be done where we feel things, in our entire bodymind. Therefore, as PTSD pioneer Bessel van der Kolk makes clear, we must paradigm-shift out of the medical model to fully transform trauma.

We must be able consciously to change our psychology of **head** and **heart** as well as our physiology of **hands** and **hara** to transform. Attachment researchers Alan Sroufe and Daniel Siegel put it this way: "it's possible to develop a secure state of mind as an adult, even in the face of a difficult childhood. Early experience influences later development, but it isn't fate: therapeutic experiences can profoundly alter an individual's life course."[36]

When we practice returning to connective consciousness, from analytical consciousness, we develop what influential psychologist and Sufi teacher A. H. Almaas calls 'basic trust': trust in the inherent nourishing support of the universe. He likens this to finding a sustainable sense of being held—the secure attachment of John Bowlby—that we all want and deserve. We start to trust that, despite the sorrows both everyday and extraordinary—whether the early death of loved ones or the collapse of our organization in an economic crisis—the universe is there to ensure we learn, develop, and become more whole as leaders.

It is not always about enjoying this or feeling good about it. The universe is agnostic about this. The system just promises us that—if we feel connected enough to let go of pain, trauma, and stress—we will receive new ways of thinking and feeling about life, love, and leadership. We will have breakthroughs. If we embody and embed the breakthroughs, we will be transformed. This is the royal road to transformational leadership.

When we make time to connect and reflect, we actually become more productive, more effective, and faster. Rather than getting stuck in outdated patterns that prevent us from being agile, we can rapidly let these go and try out new patterns. We can experiment with new ways of thinking, and acting, that might help our organization become better adapted to the fast-changing environment. It is false economy to keep pushing, and pushing, and pushing—getting emails done, nailing urgent tasks—if we're feeling emotionally fraught. We need to find time, ideally that day, but certainly that week, to reconnect within and lead ourselves along a Transformation Curve.

A rapid way to feel a sense of connection—rather than a sense of protection—is through altering our breathing. Breathing is a reliable way *consciously* to influence our autonomic nervous system. Most of the functionality of our sympathetic and parasympathetic nervous systems happens outside of our control, whether it is blood pumping faster or the shifting of energy systems. But our breath is a place where our conscious abilities and unconscious systems intersect.

In the 1970s, Dr Herbert Benson at Harvard Medical School realized that deep breathing can elicit an equal and opposite response to the stress response. He called this the relaxation response. I call it the reconnection response. By breathing deeply into our belly, we slow our heartbeat, lower our blood pressure, and encourage full oxygen exchange.

In such moments, our vision expands. We can see more holistically, more of the whole field; and can take different perspectives. As we relax into deeper breathing, our homeostatic state shifts away from adrenaline and cortisol and toward hormones like oxytocin and acetylcholine (the hormone of learning). Sensors in our lungs then send information through the vagus nerve to the brain; which then sends signals back to the heart to slow it down. The key to maximizing the reconnection response is the exhale.

As neuroscientist Lucy Norcliffe-Kaufmann of NYU confirms: "Vagal activity is highest, and heart rate lowest, when you're exhaling." In a study, researchers discovered that we can calm ourselves optimally by breathing six times a minute. I suggest 4-5 seconds of inhale; 5-6 seconds exhale. Strangely, or rather not, this is how many people breathe during relaxation meditations.[37]

A challenge we have to overcome within modern society is that our ideals of the perfect body—with a nice chest and a tight belly—promote chest breathing rather than belly breathing. When we breathe primarily into our chest, we activate the intercostal muscles in our ribs, rather than our diaphragm, which can *increase* tension and anxiety. To Connect & Reflect, at your desk or in the restrooms during a tense moment at work, it is important that you really allow your belly to relax and take deep breath from your belly. Even three deep breaths can hack you to switch out of C&P Mode and into C&C Mode. *You can breathe yourself into a breakthrough.*

Deep breathing like this has been shown to activate the key areas of our cerebral cortex that we need for higher-order thinking, higher-quality ideas, and wiser being. A recent study showed that people who meditated and relaxed for 30 minutes a day had significantly enhanced creativity.[38]

51

LEADING TEAMS ALONG THE TRANSFORMATION CURVE

The Transformation Curve journey is applicable to any area of leadership and organizational change; as well as any area of life, love, and relationships. Leading ourselves through a transformation to embed and embody new habits that resolve persistent problems is a great challenge. Leading other people across an organization, with all the inevitable moments of fear and confusion inherent on the journey, is the greatest challenge for the transformational leader. This is very much Business as Unusual.

To recap, management science developed in a period of relative consistency when the external world an organization had to fit to was stable, predictable, familiar, and clear. We were taught by an Industrial Age school system, and trained in Industrial Age management, to push projects forward with the right answer : best practice. We were told to shut down complexity, chaos, and uncertainty as fast as possible; and de-risk business planning to return predictable profits or performance to shareholders, donors, or government owners.

Now we find ourselves leading people and enterprises in VUCA environments—having to make business decisions every day in the face of political instability, economic turbulence, climate emergencies, mental health crises, and pandemics—which invites us constantly to transform what we do and how we do it . . . by transforming how we feel, think, and act as a team. What???!!!!

On top of this, we have neural hardware that hasn't changed much since the Stone Age, while our social and cultural evolution has 'progressed' from feudal agriculture to hyper-modern AI-driven realities. Additionally, our brain feels uncertainty and complexity in the same place, and with the same intensity, as physical pain. This tends us toward repeating reactive patterns just at the moment we need adaptive responses.

Research has shown that teams put under time pressure make way more errors than those that aren't.[39] Stress increases our discomfort with ambiguity. The need for quick 'closure,' by making a decision, increases when we are rushed, bored, or tired. Older adults—the kind many of us are as we lead organizations—use less effective decision-making strategies in unfamiliar situations; and use less diverse information when making decisions. Men, when their bodymind is flooded with testosterone (like in tech-bro or macho organizational cultures), make more 'incorrect shortcuts' when making decisions.[40] We have a bias toward speed, scale, and efficiency; not adaptability, flow, and effectiveness!

What is common to most transformation journeys is the likely resistance to the process people will demonstrate. Change can elicit feelings of fear and even pain; and most of us don't like to own our own experiences. Instead, we want to blame, shame, and complain, pushing responsibility for our stress and displeasure onto the people around us: especially the leader who is attempting to lead transformation.

The more we help our people understand what the Transformation Curve entails, the more they can get with the program. Initial resistance can give way to intense excitement: at the possibilities and the newness, and the better fit we will have with the world. However, there will be many moments where they want to retreat, and try and climb back up the left side of the curve to when things appeared safe and good.

There will be moments where they will want to force closure on a solution or answer before one arises, locking back into their training to solve technical problems fast. There will be moments where they want to speed up, or reduce the intensity of, the transformational experience because it is threatening to overwhelm them with uncertainty. We have to be ready for all this and more.

This is the time for us to build transformational leadership habits that enlighten, empower, and enable teams to stick with transformation. We must find ways to generate resolve and resilience so that the team, and the enterprise, make it through. There can be no genuine transformation without completing this journey.

The great news is that, in my experience helping all sorts of organizations and leaders ride the Transformation Curve, better fitted transformational solutions *always* arrive if we are courageous enough to release the old and continue past the turn of the curve. We must give our teams and collaborators absolute certitude that there will be a profound breakthrough waiting for them if they keep going.

This is as much about showing up with full, grounded, embodied leadership presence as it is making the journey feel safer through seemingly linear plans, workshops, and tools. Without transformational leadership, those in a team/system who are experiencing the breakdown of the old—which is often accompanied with a sense of anomie and even terror—will likely knee-jerk to try to return to the old ways just to get out of the uncertainty.

The elemental truth of the Transformation Curve is clear: when transforming anything, things appear to get worse (unlearning, disruption, disorder) *before* they get better. It is the nature of things and the nature of nature. But if we stick with it, things do always get better! We have to help people *willingly* enter this period of self-disruption, releasing old ideas and habits, otherwise transformation cannot occur. For a transformational leader, it is more important to help people relinquish the old than it is invent the new.

Our first priority is to get them to the bottom of the Transformation Curve for, when they are there, innovative solutions will flow. The challenge is helping people let go of old assumptions and successful best practice long enough for fresh insights and creative ideas to have space to arise, incubate, and take shape.

Once breakthroughs have erupted at the bottom of the curve, we must then inspire strength and resilience in the team as we go about the tough work of implementing and integrating new ideas into Business as Usual. We will usually encounter enormous resistance and disillusion as we go, as few people have been waiting breathlessly for our team's brilliant innovations.

On each of the 7 steps, the team will likely feel and think in ways that, when experienced many times over, become somewhat predictable. Therefore, we can anticipate, and so dampen down, team fears and anxieties; and reign in excesses of exuberance when people might lock down on a solution too soon or run away with half an insight.

At the start, there will usually be initial inertia, or denial that there is a problem. Watch out for denial, dissociation, depression, discord, and displacement. People may feel the mismatch between enterprise and ecosystem as increasingly frustrating, and so be reactive. They may feel trapped, stuck, and scared. With connection to a collective purpose, this can be rapidly dispelled, giving way to excitement around what is possible with transformation/ innovation. As teams knuckle down to engage in Transformational Challenges, fully owning them as possibilities-in-disguise, passion and entrepreneurial energy often arise.

Further down the left side of the Transformation Curve, authentic empathy for users stimulates fellow-feeling for, and curiosity about, the human beings we serve with our products and services. Attuning to the genuine pain of humankind opens up a sense of unity and belonging. Open-mindedness allows exciting insights to arise that feel fascinating and important.

However, as we descend to the bottom of the Transformation Curve, it's normal to experience periods of intense doubt and anxiety. The deeper we go, the more we realize that we don't have an answer to the problem yet. For leaders, this presents a challenge as we're used to being in control; and have been paid, up to now, immediately to have solutions when asked for them. Yet here we are, toward the bottom of the Transformation Curve, and everything seems confused. There is no clear strategy, no pre-existing formula, and we might feel that we're coming apart at the seams—both as leaders and organizations—as we self-disrupt our own thinking and models.

Thus initial enthusiasm and excitement can quickly give way to the habitual C&P Mode craving for instant, safe, 'right,' risk-free linear solutions as teams realize they are going to have to give up cherished notions, and seemingly 'safe' activities, in order to engage in true transformation. People can start to ignore or de-emphasize Transformational Challenges and instead lock back into known and knowable technical problems. In these moments, people may want to retreat back up the left-hand side of the Transformation Curve and halt the transformation that is occurring.

But the nature of transformation is that we can never go back to how things were. As we've seen, the world is changing so fast and so dramatically that what worked even a decade ago will not work in the future. Therefore, the only alternative to a Transformation Curve journey is the Breakdown Decline. Getting teams and senior leaders to grok this, without getting stuck or shutting down, is crucial for the transformational leader.

As we enter the deepest parts of the Transformation Curve, we must surface and challenge the core assumptions that the business or organization relies on for strength and certainty. This can trigger a desire to shut down and withdraw. It can even prompt senior leaders to can the project altogether. They will generate a false narrative that makes this seem smart and sensible; when really it was just driven by fear. If we haven't been able to hold space for senior managers to transform without blame/shame/complain, and have found it tough to influence them with a compelling narrative, ruffled feathers can lead to all sorts of protective patterns erupting. With skillful leadership, we can allay fears and quiet down anxieties; and get things back on track.

Distress diminishes and flashes of insight start to arise. This usually excites everyone and can lead to extraordinary creative and co-creative flow states that people remember for life (and yearn for ever after). In stepping out of our collective comfort zone, we make way for rushes of energy, intuition, and creativity that come with true transformation. We often experience such ideas and epiphanies as a 'subliminal uprush,' according to a contemporary of William James, pioneering psychologist Frederic W. H. Myers. I have experienced such uprushes on countless occasions; as well as guided many others to have them.

If we can get our team right to the bottom of the Transformation Curve, where confusion and creativity reign, "Ah-Ha!" moments will burst into hearts and minds as we glimpse the future in the present. As a confused 'which way is up?' feeling dissipates, teams enjoy a sense of expansion, hope, and possibility. This is the upwards trajectory of the Transformation Curve. Turning the corner, people feel elated and inspired, sure they have found unique and valuable ideas of how to envision a better future.

However, great excitement about what's possible can bring great anxiety about whether we can handle the change, and land the transformation. As people leave team huddles, workshops, and away-days, doubts set in as analytical consciousness struggles to make sense of the novelties that came from connective consciousness. Away from allies on the transformation trail, C&P Mode patterns can block transformational ideas from unfolding to their full potential. Legacy processes can ensnarl projects in treacle. The organization's immune system may well attempt to kill breakthroughs, or shrink them back into comfort zones. This can also result in transformational leaders being sidelined, dismissed, and diminished in subtle or emphatic ways.

Legacy beliefs and assumptions can even return at this stage with a vengeance: one last noisy "hurrah!" of regressive thinking even as the writing on the wall makes it clear that old assumptions and models are on the wrong side of history. Our new ideas and intuitions may not be well received by others who have not gone on the journey: this can trigger deep frustration, anger, and even despair. How can others not buy into the transformation when I've made myself so vulnerable? Why is change so hard for them to embrace? Why don't these people just get it?

We must remember that letting go of old ways is difficult. Others still see us through the old lens. What seems like an obvious insight to us is not so obvious to others who have not been on the Transformation Curve we have been riding. Leading with influence and narrative power brings people with us.

If we still have the resources and conviction to push our transformational ideas forward, in the last steps of the Transformation Curve, the need for executional brilliance and constant experimentation will test our leadership to the max to keep our team going, learning, evolving. Transformation does not happen overnight. The integration of new ideas into an organization, new behaviors into processes, and new products into markets takes months and years; not days and weeks. An almost inevitable lack of recognition and appreciation demands we must be able to ceaselessly generate resilience and confidence in the team.

Finally, if we do manage to support our team to land a transformation into the system, many may want to take credit for it. Some may want to make it appear like it was obvious and inevitable (when nothing could be further from the truth). These are all more triggers that we can metabolize to become ever-wiser leaders.

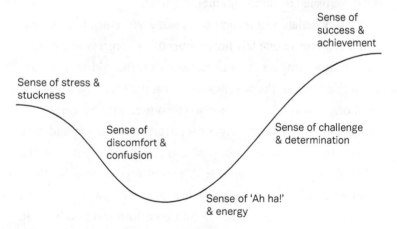

FIGURE 24 *Typical Experiences On The Transformation Curve*

52

THE IMPORTANCE OF EMOTIONAL SAFETY

On the Transformation Curve, it is normal for team members to encounter feelings, emotions, and memories that most would not consider 'normal' in the workplace. This is very much Business as Unusual. People can find this immensely challenging (as well as invigorating). We are asking people to come out of their comfort zones: protective patterns they developed to be safe! A transformational leader must recognize that the box/comfort zone/protective pattern has an important evolutionary role and survival function.

To transform an organization—whether through innovation in products, processes, or people—we must first honor the strengths of the patterns that maintain the status quo. Once C&P Mode feels seen, heard, respected, appreciated, and safe, we can look to bring them into C&C Mode to help the enterprise adapt and transform. The key to this is to help people feel safe—in ways that they feel emotionally as well as recognize cognitively—*before* we encourage people to begin the journey of transformation. We must always meet people where they are—and value and validate their patterning—before we start to take them somewhere new . . . where they will be required to give some of it up.

Transformational leaders understand that all protective patterns—their own or the groupthink that reduces insights and innovation in the organization—serve a function. With this level of compassion—that comes from insight into the biology of connection and protection—we have a *much* greater chance of leading people into the right Mode for the moment. If our capacity as transformational leaders is in many ways determined by our emotional relationship to change, then it makes sense that the capability a team has to drive innovation and change is related to the team's emotional relationship to change, uncertainty, and risk.

I've known this for years but never had any evidence to support this experiential insight. However, this truism is now backed up by an extensive research program undertaken by Google, which spent over 5 years studying 250 attributes of over 180 teams trying to discover the secrets that drive high performance (which at Google means creativity, innovation, and adaptation, as much as execution and hustle). The key factor they identified turned out *not* to be IQ, salary, education level, or past success (as they had assumed it would be). The key factor is 'emotional safety' or 'psychological safety.'

Psychological safety can be measured by asking people whether they feel that they are punished (in some way) when they make a mistake or criticized for challenging the status quo.[41] When people feel psychologically and emotionally safe, they are not locked into C&P Mode trying to protect themselves from threats, or control the chaos. Instead, with safety, they feel free to enter C&C Mode where they can have new thoughts, invent new possibilities, and build new habits.

Paul Santagata, Head of Industry at Google, has said: "in Google's fast-paced, highly demanding environment, our success hinges on the ability to take risks and be vulnerable in front of our peers." Their outer game of innovation, adaptability, and agility is utterly dependent on their inner game of safety, trust, and sense of purpose. Writing in the *Harvard Business Review*, Laura Delizonna from Stanford University states that "psychological safety allows for moderate risk taking, speaking your mind, creativity, and sticking your neck out without fear of having it cut off—just the types of behavior that lead to making breakthroughs."[42]

If you want teams with fluid agility, transformational capability, and radical adaptability then you need to find ways to hold space for your team members to feel safe and 'in it together'; while still demanding impeccable execution and ensuring the exacting standards needed to succeed with transformation and innovation.

This idea that the *context* in which we work and live determines the *content* of that work and play was made clear by psychologist Donald Winnicott. He suggested that the quality of the 'holding environment' that a caregiver provides a child, physically and emotionally, is critical in development. If there are disturbances in the holding environment, then the child will develop fixations and neuroses: pernicious and persistent protective patterns.

Just as a good therapist must provide a safe holding environment, or container, for a person to resolve their issues, a transformational leader must hold a 'safe space' for team members to drop damaging patterns of C&P Mode in order to boost the creativity and collaboration of C&C Mode. As the leader "holds space" for genuine trust and safety, team members can engage in personal transformations that allow them to break through their own limits and so deliver organizational and system transformations.

Although it is always tempting (to our C&P Mode) to drive change by focusing on the 'visible' elements of behaviors in **hands** and mindsets in **heads**, a transformational leader understands that it is the 'invisible'—and so hard to measure and engage with—elements of **heart** and **hara** that require the most investment for transformation to actually land.

53

THE EDGE OF CHAOS AND THE ART OF THE POSSIBLE

A transformational leader knows that the journey of transformation has many unpleasant moments within it. We must be ready to put our entire being on the line to get people past the bottom of the Transformation Curve and inspire them up the other side. On every Transformation Curve we will have to lead people through the "edge of chaos": the moments in every transformation project where we have maximum creativity—and so also maximum confusion. The adjacent possible is being entered. Possibility spaces are opening.

This is the moment where the old patterning has broken down but the emergent possibilities are yet to arise clearly and definitively. It is where disaster or victory can emerge, depending upon a palintonic creative harmony between resolve and vulnerability: to allow what is seeking to emerge to rise up, past shared assumptions and habits, into our collective and connective consciousness. We support the change that is 'wanting' to occur—without the stressing or striving that block creativity. Back to Lao Tzu: "doing without straining is the way of the wise."

Stuart Kauffman, a biologist who works on complex systems at the University of Calgary (and external professor at the Santa Fe Institute) suggests that the complex living systems that are best able to adapt—whether companies or individual brains—are those poised at the edge of chaos. They exist on the border between creative chaos and total disorder. They are *both* flexible, diverse, and open, *and* focused, intentional, and committed. We want to become confident in leading at the edge of chaos. We want to be comfortable with our organizations existing permanently at (or near) the edge of chaos, too. There is a word for this: being 'chaordic'.

We appear to have evolved to be the most chaordic species in the known universe. We have two powerful brain networks that afford us *both* order/convergence (C&P Mode) *and* disorder/divergence (C&C Mode). We are amazingly good at both structure and variance. We can exist in both analytical and connective consciousness. A neuroscience study suggests that a healthy, integrated brain actually cycles many times a second between states *at the edge of chaos.*

As the great philosopher Friedrich Nietzsche wrote: "One must still have chaos in oneself to be able to give birth to a

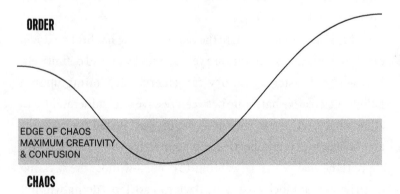

ORDER

EDGE OF CHAOS
MAXIMUM CREATIVITY
& CONFUSION

CHAOS

FIGURE 25 *The Edge of Chaos*

dancing star." We have a self-organizing, self-creating, 'autopoetic' bodymind: it creates itself anew every moment, building new cells and replacing old ones at the edge of chaos while still maintaining a clear structure and order. Our autopoetic self is able to drive systems and societies to ever more complex states because of its unique and innate capacity to ride the Transformation Curve *by choice:* flexing between the two Modes to enter creative chaos; and then integrative order.

Human beings, with our insanely complex bodyminds, are oases of chaordicity in a universe tending relentlessly toward disorder through the process of entropy. As we become more transformational as a leader, we can transform anything at the edge of chaos. We can push past any limitations to reorder the world as we envision it. Every vision, when manifest, becomes a better fitting form of order up the right-hand side of the Transformation Curve.

However, the great teaching of the Transformation Curve is that we have to be able to let go of old ideas, patterns, and structures before we get the cool new innovations. We must be able to let things come apart, toward maximum chaos, without allowing our team, or enterprise, to fall apart. We must hold them together at the moments of peak uncertainty, and hold space for everyone in the team to adapt and create without the stress and overwhelm just being too much to bear. We need to allow the team time and space to really reflect on the problem.

If they jump in and try to solve it too quickly, as C&P Mode is wont to do, they will inevitably find solutions to the wrong problems, using old ways of thinking and outdated approaches unsuited to the becoming world. By allowing teams time to connect and reflect, they can understand the space in which the problem operates, whether that be existing or new customers, partners, vendors, suppliers, stakeholders, or citizens.

As a team descends down the left-hand side toward the edge of chaos, confusion and discomfort reign. Mob behavior and crowd panic can spark out of nowhere. C&P Mode gets alerted to perceived threat. It craves coming out of chaos as quickly as possible. This shows up in various "anti-transformation tropes" which attempt to protect us from the pathway of transformation and the intensities of the edge of chaos.

The first anti-transformation trope is what I call the "escape fantasy": the notion that things will be better in a different function/company/country/system. Individuals and even whole teams may want to escape the inevitable need for transformation. They might think that if they go to a different company, move to a different sector, or head a different department, things will be better without the need for transformation. While this escape fantasy might work in the short term, once the fun and excitement wears off, people will show up the same as before. The old blockages and protective patterns will likely still be there and the challenges will still exist.

The second anti-transformation trope is the desire to 'make X great again': a return to a fantasized time when everything worked and the team/company/country was strong and in control. At the systems level in society, it means returning to a time of perceived nationalistic and ethnic power. This is what Polish journalist Ryszard Kapuscinski calls the desire to return to a "Great Yesterday" rather than do the hardest thing in life, which is to transform ourselves to forge a Greater Tomorrow.

Even though the historic moment that people want to return to was only good for some people, it can be cast—often by demagogues who fire up people's pain to benefit their own agenda and ambitions—as a halcyon age of order and power in today's relentless chaos. In organizations, this shows up as a bolt back

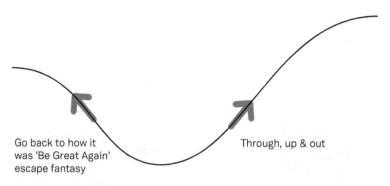

Go back to how it
was 'Be Great Again'
escape fantasy

Through, up & out

FIGURE 26 *Through, Up & Out*

toward the illusory safety of the old Industrial Age business model.
Yet it totally ignores the fact that such models are in decline.

This can stimulate a third anti-transformation trope: the desire
for 'strong' men and women to return the system to some form of
stability at the expense of human freedom. Employees and citizens
might prefer (yet another) dictator to the pain of uncertainty on
the journey to self-organization and true democracy. This means
people giving up on their own empowerment in order to have an
authoritarian leader secure them with (illusory) power over the
chaos.

Transformational leaders are very strong within; but know never
to fall into the role of the pre-modern strong man. They share their
compelling vision and narrative to forge a better tomorrow; but they
know that no human alive can dictate a genuinely transformational
solution to others because colleagues/citizens have to go on the
journey together to live the questions themselves.

In today's complexity, a neat solution (especially one that looks
a lot like the past) is an illusory mirage: tempting but unattainable.
Brexit, a US-Mexican wall, a merger and acquisition with a rival:
none of these will solve the Transformational Challenges of the age.
They will just defer them.

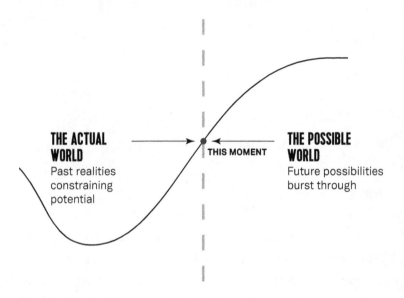

FIGURE 27 *Actual World & Possible World*

The transformational leader must empathize with all the fears and anxieties that underlay these three tropes—as well as ensures the team/enterprise/nation can go "through, up, and out" to find a higher-order solution through genuine transformation.

As we travel down, through, and up out of the Transformation Curve, transformational leaders can—mysteriously and perhaps mystically—bring the future into the present. By releasing old assumptions, intense defensive instincts, and pernicious protective patterns, we somehow allow future-forging insights to come 'through' our bodymind...and out into the world (where they can set about regenerating our creaking and tired systems).

Brilliant quantum physicist David Bohm came up with a way of understanding how this might occur, in nature, by proposing that in complex, adaptive systems, like our universe, there is an 'Implicate

Order' and 'Explicate Order.' In the Implicate Order, everything is connected together in some way. Everything is possible. I call this the Possible World, which we can gain access to within connective consciousness. Creative possibilities then 'unfold' into the Explicate Order, tangible reality that I call the Actual World. We understand this reality best through analytical consciousness and science. The transformational leader transmutes or transports potentialities from the Possible World into actualities in the Actual World.

Many artists, musicians, writers, and innovators talk about this transmutation or transportation in various ways. Creators can only use metaphors to describe aspects of connective consciousness with analytical consciousness. The celebrated South American novelist Isabel Allende, who has sold over 50 million books, says of her creativity: "I'm not the one who invents the stories; I'm like a radio that picks up the waves. Somehow, if I move the dial very carefully, I'll pick up the wave and get the story. But the story doesn't belong to me; it's somewhere out there floating."

She's not alone. Writer after writer, artist after artist, scientist after scientist has claimed they are not the source of their creativity. The great composer J. S. Bach said, "I play the notes as they are written, but it is God who makes the music." Legendary French anthropologist Claude Levi-Strauss said: "I don't have the feeling that I write my books . . . I have the feeling that my books get written through me."

I have witnessed time and time again, in workshops and coaching sessions with thousands of people, that everyone can feel newness and novelty arise through them, as if from nowhere. I believe we are, in some way, 'channelling' ideas: acting as a conduit for newness to come into being as we consciously and purposefully unfold content from Bohm's Implicate Order to shape the Explicate Order.

It appears that human beings are the *only* organisms that can consciously and purposefully tap into Possible World to accelerate problem-solving in the material Actual world (although animals from dolphins to crows can creatively solve problems, too): we can *choose* to open up our minds and our hearts on the Transformation Curve to funnel ideas from the future into present, and execute them brilliantly with entrepreneurial fire and rigorous diligence.

However, it is very easy for our notions about what is 'right' to cloud up this process and stop the flow of ideas from Possible to Actual Worlds. We have to remain a clear channel for ideas to come through us without the distortions of our protective patterns warping reality. Then we can proactively support what is seeking to emerge from the Possible World and manifest this novelty in the Actual world of projects and processes.

We exchange knowing 'the answer,' as if there is a single silver-bullet solution to all our challenges; to knowing the process and practices that will find us every solution we need. We rest in the knowledge that transformational solutions will flow through the channel once we are in the right place/space to receive them. We have to help our teammates and colleagues do the same, otherwise their cherished but outdated notions will block the channels of team creativity. Likewise, unresolved interpersonal issues, team resentments, traumatic memories of failures in the enterprise, power plays, and status moves by senior managers will all block the flow with heavy, dense sediment that stops creativity and connection.

From such insights, the true role of transformational leaders in our time—this shared Metabolization Moment—appears to emerge. If my felt senses and intuitions are accurate, a Regenerative

Renaissance is seeking to emerge from our crisis-hit world. Thus our purpose as transformational leaders becomes purified and clarified: to support, encourage, and realize this transformation through our quotidian work in our teams, organizations, and communities. We don't have to be at the front and center: just playing our part leaving our part of the system better—less suffering of life; more affirmation of life—than how we found it. We channel relevant insights and ideas from the Possible World into the Actual World with our entire bodymind.

We *must* ground this most sacred of mundane processes in 'purpose'—love-in-action—otherwise we risk implementing breakthroughs like the poison gas Zyklon B (that scaled up mass murder at Auschwitz); or the drug-trafficking innovations of El Chapo. Without love-fueled purpose to orient us, we will follow the logic of advanced capitalism: galvanizing billions of dollars—and enormous amounts human effort and ingenuity—to solve the supposed 'unmet needs' of consumers at scale. Purpose allows us to see that most of capitalism's current innovations are designed to solve the desire for more comfort and convenience of the few; rather than alleviate the genuine pain and suffering of the many.

Our crisis-hit world really does not need any more problems solved that are about convenience and comfort as opposed to resolving the vast amount of stress and suffering of the people; and our planet. To lead transformatively means consciously co-creating, with life itself, transformational solutions *to our greatest human challenges.*

This is a constant dance of problem and possibility. The ideas and intuitions we need lie pregnant in every interaction as long as we can flip out of C&P and into C&C Mode (and back again to execute). Then we can align with our nature, and human nature, by channeling suffering-reducing ideas into the world.

The idea that a human being can align with nature is the core teaching of many wisdom traditions: from Western Stoicism to Eastern Taoism. As connective and empathic scientist William James suggested, genuine spirituality is about sensing that "there is an unseen order and the supreme good lies in harmoniously adjusting to that order." If we engage in dialogue with the Possible World, through transformational practices that quieten the noisy mind and elevate our creative intuitions, we will usually come to understand how to serve best whatever is seeking to emerge.

This helps us lead the transformations that are most needed in ourselves and our organizations. This is nothing to do with prayer to a personal god. It is the leader engaging in a co-creative relationship with life, the universe, itself. Transformational Challenges are the invitation, the initiation call, to co-create. Systems scientists call them 'strange attractors': that guide a system to self-organize towards a more complex, creative, and fitted state.

Without compassionate and connected transformational leaders that understand how to guide organizations and societies through deep transformation—particularly how to secure people when they are at the edge of chaos so that they don't revert back to old patterns, like racism and rage, to feel safe and in control—things are going to get a lot tougher. This is why we transformational leaders must fearlessly bring the full power of connection/love to our people.

This means well and truly stepping out of the "love closet"—if we are in one—and allowing biodynamic, loving purpose to flow into our work, our organizations, and our systems. We consciously heal our hearts—allowing them to become whole through repeated gulps from the well of connective consciousness—so we can lead wholeheartedly. This elixir of transformation is accessible 24/7/52 within our own Create & Connect Mode. All we need do is stop… and practice reconnection through whatever technique we choose.

If we do this with passion, conviction, and discipline, we can reliably enter the most intense states of connective consciousness. In "Extreme Connect," our everyday awareness of objects, people, and life/leadership problems falls away. All that is left is what wisdom traditions call Pure Consciousness or Total Presence. This is the Connection Solution as its most potent: the quintessential mystical experience whispered of by shamans and sages for millennia.

In the last decade, there has been a flood of scientific research into such altered states and their healing potential. Respected universities, such as Imperial College and Johns Hopkins, have found that psychedelic plants and substances can generate such states. They have been shown to be potent in healing PTSD (Extreme Protect states becoming looping patterns?), reducing the fear of dying from cancer, and rapidly transforming treatment-resistant depression.[43]

As you have come this far on the journey of mastering transformational leadership with me, you may be interested to know that we call such substances "Consciousness Medicines." Just as medicines for matter treat pain and disease in the body, Consciousness Medicines seem able to help treat pain and *dis*ease/unease in the mind—if people do the inner work necessary to embody and embed the insights and intuitions that arise within the experiences. This is categorically not the same as using them for hedonistic indulgence. Just as with pharmaceutical medicines, one would want to use them when they can make a concrete difference to one's consciousness (that is to say, when one needs healing/'wholing'); and, of course, never abuse them.

Indigenous people the world over use Consciousness Medicine to realign the tribe with their environment—when mismatches arise between the people and nature. Do note that recent scholarship has firmly suggested that the shamanic use of Consciousness Medicines has traditionally been about realigning the entire tribe with their ecology; not about the healing of the individual's personal trauma, which appears to be a Western hybrid/invention.[44]

I sense that Consciousness Medicines thrust those that take them into the edge of chaos—in a non-negotiable manner that avoids the usual resistance and anti-transformation tropes that block such ingress. The taker can then bring back insights and ideas from the Possible World that might help them resolve the Transformational Challenges (in life, love, and leadership) that they face in the Actual World. One can seemingly use Consciousness Medicines to enter C&C Mode to heal, listen, reconnect, imagine, and invent... and return to C&P Mode to turn inspiration into concrete actions that regenerate our world.

Clearly, this will work most successfully when the taker engages in significant embodiment and repatterning practices that *integrate* the insights and ideas discovered in altered states firmly into the wetware of their bodymind; and the structures of the body corporate/politic that they lead. Although I neither recommend nor object to the use of Consciousness Medicines—we must all make such choices with full ownership and self-mastery—there is an emerging 'psychedelic renaissance' with a resurgence of interest in their benefits from leaders, entrepreneurs, and investors.

However we choose to do it, transformational leaders have no choice but to cultivate a pellucid and lucid consciousness, free from blockages and distortions. If we achieve this liquid form of awareness, we can master the elemental dance of transformational leadership: consciously and confidently transforming our own consciousness so we can transform our organizations to fit the world as it changes. We then become what the Taoists call a *Zhenren*: a True Man.

The Chinese ideogram for *Zhenren* brings to life someone who is always in continuous transformation yet always staying rooted: in purpose, in connection, in the Tao. The power of the True Man comes from mastery of their own consciousness rather than from exerting power and control over the world. Creativity flows from them precisely because they have no pernicious and persistent protective patterns keeping them rigid and resistant. The True Man, the truly transformational leader, is willing to change anything and everything about themselves and their organization in order to create a flourishing future for all.

The Stoics called such a person a Sage. To them, becoming a Sage was the aim of *all* philosophizing (the loving of wisdom). The transformational leader, as Sage, is totally human and grounded in this world, yet is, at the same time, as expansive as the entire universe. Such a transformational leader is poised at the edge of chaos: channeling ideas and innovations from the Possible World into actualities in the Actual World… at breakfast, lunch, and dinner through their own biodynamic bodymind.

If we choose to become a *Zhenren* or Sage—even if the state of transformational flow only lasts a few minutes a day—we are always alive and awake to what is always possible in the moment. We are natural born Transformers, leading people in, through, and out of the edge of chaos.

54
CONSCIOUSLY TRANSFORMING INTO TRANSFORMERS

We know that environment we live, love, and lead in is getting ever more complex. This is unlikely to ever stop. To stay fitted with it, we must become ever more complex, too. To follow Ashby's Law, we have to match the complexity of the environment with our complexity as leaders. Our consciousness must be upgraded and evolved to match the VUCA world within which we find ourselves. This means engaging purposefully in transformations of our Cognitive-Behavioral Complexity and Interoceptive-Affective Complexity so we can move 'up' the 5 stages of leadership development to become genuine Transformers.

Although we are *always* on one or more Transformation Curves of various intensities and importances in various areas of our life and work, when we move from one *stage* of leadership development to another, we move through life-changing transformations that disintegrate and reorder our entire self-concept and its relationship to the world. We have minor key and major key Transformation Curve journeys; and each has a theme that we usually only realize in 20/20 hindsight (although I have noticed that clues do show up in seeming coincidences and serendipities). Major key Transformation Curve journeys last a few years and see us inhabit and stabilize ourselves in a new stage of human development.

As we embark on major key Transformation Curve journeys, hopefully more conscious than we were in the past that these shifts can and do occur, we have to allow ourselves to come apart without falling apart—particularly if we are responsible for leading teams and enterprises as we change ourselves. Major key Transformation Curve experiences can be extraordinarily challenging as we struggle to release, receive, and renew ourselves even as we deliver proposals, maintain KPIs, and keep others feeling safe.

As developmental stage psychologist Robert Kegan makes clear that "the shift from one self to the next can be painful, protracted, and life-disordering." We need to give ourselves the safety and self-care necessary to become the change. Psychological safety, the holding environment we generate for ourselves, is what Kegan calls an "evolutionary bridge, a context for crossing over" as we transform from one stage of development to a more realized stage.

To arrive at each transformational leadership development stage, fully embodying the wisdom and habits and embedding the cognitive frames and schedules, we must successfully navigate a major key Transformation Curve journey. Each requires us to relinquish something on the left-hand side of the Curve that we thought was essential to our survival; but we realize (as we increase our cognitive and emotional complexity) was simply a protection or control that once served but we now no longer need. Once we surrender it, we can receive new 'superpowers'; polishing areas of our underlying character that have remained hidden or distorted by our protective personality.

There are transformation hacks and unlocks to speed things up; but there are zero shortcuts. The Transformation Curve must

FIGURE 28 *The Transformation Curves For The Five Stages of Transformational Development*

be lived through. Each transition is a rite of passage that we have to go through, live through, and embody fully before we can move to the next stage. Trying to skip stages or jump to a 'better' place can only end up in disaster. As we engage wholeheartedly in this process, we have to find time and space to resource ourselves fully and stay resilient, all the while doing Business as Usual. The importance of rigorous resilience protocols is crucial. If we don't know how to stop, resource, reflect, and recharge—and instead stop our resilience and self-care routines because we are so darn busy—we will likely get stuck and stressed, returning to pernicious protective patterns that are always available in our neural pathways when tired, destabilized, and tense. The twin specters of breakdown and burnout will come haunting.

To go from being a Contributor to an Achiever, we relinquish victimhood and a sense of being put upon in order to receive ownership and a sense of gritty responsibility. These open up the capacity for excellence in a profession; and so achievement in society. We must watch out for a regression back toward self-centeredness; and the ever-seductive sirens of blame, shame, and complain. A transformation hack is to heal our relationship with ourselves so we experience the self-love we need to really connect with others (without co-dependency and distorted boundaries). The theme of this Transformation Curve seems to be trust in, empathy for, and connection with other humans. Vulnerability is a powerful unlock.

To go from being an Achiever to an Innovator, we must relinquish social conformity and ideological certitude in order to receive the insights and ideas that turn into successful innovations, that challenge the status quo, whether in business or civil society. We must watch out for a regression back to seeking the approval of others; and the disempowerment that comes from needing to be helped. A transformation hack is to heal our relationships with our parents—and other formative influences—so we can be truly independent *without* rejecting anyone or anything. This confidence, not arrogance, allows us to embody an innovative vision fully until it becomes realized. The theme of this Transformation Curve seems to be confidence in, and resolve to deliver, our unique vision. Commitment is a powerful unlock.

To go from being an Innovator to a Transformer, we must relinquish any unresolved cravings for power, profit, and recognition in order to receive our leadership purpose; and the infinite intuitions and insights that flow from a healed heart. It is this daily connective creativity which regenerates the enterprises we lead; and the systems we touch. We must pay attention to a possible regression back to being a power-hungry control freak; a desire to be famous and/or infallible; and the allure of wealthy comforts and conveniences. The transformation hack I have found most useful here is devotion: the kind spoken of in the Indian wisdom classic, the *Bhagavad Gita*.

By devoting all our work and efforts back to the universe of which we are intrinsically part, we can quell any lingering attachments to fame and fortune. We can swap out power over people for power to support their transformation. This move requires that we heal our relationship to the universe we are part of: so we trust that said universe gives us what we need—not what we desire—to keep

NOW LEAD THE CHANGE

growing, thriving, and expanding our transformational potential. The theme of this Transformation Curve seems to be mastery of both self-transformation and systemic change: i.e. virtuosity in transformational leadership. Purpose is the key.

Conjecturally, as I have not lived through it myself, to go from being a Transformer to an Elder, I imagine we must relinquish ambition and willpower—giving up leading projects from the front and center to take our place in the circle—in order to receive the wisdom we need to heal our communities; and pass on without fear. Perhaps we must look out for a regression back to wanting to be at the center of things. From studying the lives of others, it appears that a transformation hack is to surrender everything we thought dear until we release our attachment to life itself. We ride the ultimate Transformation Curve as we pass on and away, hopefully having lived fully our one short life as a transformational leader.

Folks, it's time to evolve. That's why we're troubled. You know why our institutions are failing us, the church, the state, everything's failing? It's because, um – they're no longer relevant. We're supposed to keep evolving. Evolution did not end with us growing opposable thumbs. You do know that, right? There's another 90% of our brains that we have to illuminate.

Bill Hicks, Comedian

EPILOGUE
THE GREAT TRANSFORMATION &
A REGENERATIVE RENAISSANCE

As the 3D Futures Framework makes clear, as well as having to engage with radically-emergent digital technologies and dramatically-changing customer needs, four major global, yet intensely local, crises are calling us, inviting us, demanding us to lead the change; *now*: The Industrialization Crisis. The Inequality Crisis. The Illness Crisis. The Identity Crisis.

The deaths, economic meltdowns, and political chaos generated by the microscopic SARS-CoV-2 virus are amplifying the Transformation Imperative and accelerating the Leadership Invitation within it for us all. We entering a full-scale meltdown of the modern world. We are in a "modernity emergency." Even one of the richest financiers (and philanthropists) on Earth, billionaire Ray Dalio, said in February 2020: "[t]he world has gone mad, and the system is broken . . . All systems should evolve. We all need to evolve."

The ideogram for 'emergency' in Chinese has two characters: danger and opportunity. One choice is to further attempt to shore up the profit-maximizing, innovative, and convenient—yet climate-polluting, unequal, unhealthy, and conflictual—reality we have right now. Yet the dangers of this route towards existential collapse are clear. If we choose to continue on a mass breakdown decline as a species—a Grand Decline if you like—towards obsolescence as we repress, ignore, or deny the Transformational Challenges we all face, the symptoms of failing the future within each of the four crises will be exacerbated.

Research has shown that seemingly permanent and immutable individual and organizational patterns in complex systems become susceptible to transformation right after major shocks destabilize them. In a study of 850 international conflicts that arose between 1816 to 1992, 75% of them ended within 10 years of a major destabilizing shock.[45] So we can seize the opportunities within climate change, current and future pandemics, and economic shocks to wake up to the dangers of the emerging four crises; and lead ourselves and our organizations to new and better-fitting possibilities. I have dubbed this the Great Transformation.

By playing our unique part in such a whole-system transformation, we will also future-proof our careers, our organizations, and our shared, yet fragile, world. There is nothing moral in whether we choose this breakthrough or a Breakdown Decline. It is simply a matter of adapt; or die (out). But if we talk and worry about it, but do not take action, we will leave it too late. Then we will not have enough time to make the Great Transformation stick.

Seen from the lens of transformational leadership, the dangers and existential risks we face—and technologies and innovation opportunities we can seize—are material world realities that are calling us to upgrade our consciousness within: to wake up; switch on; and step up. Given that the hardware of our neural architecture is relatively fixed—and that the material world is a crystallization of our shared assumptions and priorities—the place to focus on to initiate the Great Transformation is upgrading the 'software': our consciousness.

If we penetrate to the hidden order of things, beneath the four seemingly distinct crises in concrete reality is a *single* set of assumptions in our shared consciousness that are *not* adapted to the future that is rushing toward us. We have a collection of 'noble lies' about who we are, what the purpose of life is, why businesses exist, how businesses innovate, and what government exists to do, that are locking us into ever-decreasing circles; and ever-depleting cycles. These noble lies have us run Industrial Age patterns in a world that can no longer cope with Industrial Age processes, business models, and consumption behaviors.

Underlying the dangers that face us right now—including the challenges brought further to our attention by the Covid-19 pandemic—are assumptions that appear to be emotionally 'right', comfortable, and convenient to our analytical consciousness:

- Fierce competition for scant resources is natural and normal
- Growth can continue forever because there are unlimited planetary resources
- Meritocracy is empowering and essentially true
- As the rich get richer, their wealth trickles down to all, improving everyone's lives
- Human beings are like machines, built to be productive and efficient
- Productivity gains are more important than presence, caring, and connection
- Consumption of stuff/brands is highly meaningful and necessary
- Different races, ethnicities, classes, genders, and orientations have differing worth
- Private property is an unalienable right

- We are separate from nature, can control it with our genius, and have a right to extract whatever we want from it

These assumptions work together to generate an outdated corporate, economic, and political model that is becoming an existential threat to our entire species (and thousands of other species too). The Covid-19 pandemic is simply accelerating and amplifying the threat.

We are therefore not simply facing four crises in matter. We are actually suffering from a "metaphysical emergency" in our consciousness. The philosopher (and my colleague) Tomas Björkman states that "all the crises of the world stem from one underlying meta-crisis—our collective inability to handle the increasing complexity of our world."

The suffering that so many of us are experiencing—rich and poor—is a symptom of an essential mismatch between the outdated assumptions many of us hold about life, love, and leadership; and the context we find ourselves in. There is a poor fit between how we 'do' life; and the complexity of our societies/the global ecosystem. We do not have enough 'requisite variety'—creativity and connectivity —in our consciousness to match the variety all around us.

This is a modernity emergency: we are trapped in the modern separation between science/reason and wisdom/intuition. Most, if not all, of our social and environmental problems—from individual depression to social inequality; from local floods and to global pollution—are rooted in the domination of connective consciousness by analytical (or separation) consciousness. Our capabilities for caring, creativity, empathy, and connectivity have been downgraded to junk; and, where they are valued, they have been instrumentalized by modernity to serve the pursuit of productivity and profit.

Our entire world is organized around Control & Protect Mode (analysis, separation, competition, order, information, profit, performance, metrics); and actively suppresses, even denigrates, the realities of Create & Connect Mode (connection, caring, compassion, imagination, insight, purpose, presence, meaning). If we want things to change—if we want to stop climate change-driven societal collapse, ensure children do not live in grinding poverty, prevent deaths of despair and addiction, and stop our world exploding with identity-driven conflicts—we have to reorganize our communities, companies, and countries around a balanced, and accurate, understanding of human nature.

We can only bring about the Great Transformation in our concrete, material reality by resolving our modern metaphysical emergency in our collective consciousness. Any lasting solutions to the Four Horsemen of the Anthropocene Apocalypse must engage with our modern metaphysical assumption that we are alone, isolated, and disconnected. For it is this sense of separation and atomization that maintains paralyzing trauma, drives relentless competition, feeds the addictions of consumer capitalism, and encourages internecine conflict.

As prescient ecologist Lynn White Jr. wrote back in 1967, before we realized just how big the four crises are across our economies and ecologies: "Since the roots of our trouble are so largely religious, the remedy must also be essentially religious, whether we call it that or not." If our hearts yearn for a Great Transformation—and our minds want a Regenerative Renaissance in business and society—we must become radically curious about, and committed to, upgrading our individual and shared consciousness.

This is, and always will be, a spiritual thing. (I do not like the 's' word, as it obfuscates as much as it enlightens, but it has to do for now.) Only a transformation in our foundational metaphysics to appreciating our spiritual hearts as much as our scientific minds can ensure that we treat nature, and each other, with compassion, dignity, and care.

If we believe ourselves to be separate and alone producers/consumers that must compete in a zero-sum game to perform and make profits—with limitless resources to use, and no issues with waste (carbon, microplastics etc.)—then the four crises will continue to worsen. It is only if we reconceive of humankind as interdependent co-creators that are profoundly interconnected with nature that we will be able to collaborate on win-win-wins that can bring about a Great Transformation and a Regenerative Renaissance.

As so many of our shared ills come from a disconnection from nature, at the heart of the Great Transformation is therefore a reckoning, reconnection, and reconciliation with the natural world. Human beings have long thought of themselves as separate, and apart, from nature. This separation, driven by the split between subject and object that arises in analytical consciousness—and then encoded in the Western mind by Biblical religions—has given us much. It has allowed us to develop mathematical, scientific, and technological abstractions—and industrial processes and customer-driven cultures—that have saved and improved material lives; made for much fun, adventure, and joy (from flights to festivals); and protected us from many of nature's most extreme threats: whether smallpox or tsunamis.

Yet the separation between us and nature has become a schism that has disconnected us from the truth: we not only rely on nature for everything we humans have, but *we are actually intrinsically and inherently part of the natural world.* Nature is what gives us all life; and the intuitions and insights that guide us on our leadership journey.

When we ignore this, and churn out carbon into the atmosphere to feed consumer addictions, we put at risk our species' position in the great web of life. At best, we drive ourselves onwards towards living in a devastated world. At worst, we are sleepwalking our way into the extinction event of *Homo sapiens sapiens*. As we stride further towards our demise, we are sinking further into feelings of social atomization and unbearable loneliness; and anxiety, depression, and stress.

By reconnecting with nature—truly, madly, deeply—we will find the insights and inspirations we need to reorient our leadership activities and organization's business models so they fit with nature . . . and actually regenerate it. This intimacy with nature will help us ensure our creativity—as well as our beautifully modern capacity to scale ideas with technology—work in service of connection, compassion, and care.

This is a subtle but profound shift. We want to shift from a totalizing societal focus on protection and control; to being in a creative harmony between connection and protection; and between creativity and control. In Taoism, this radical transformation in our consciousness—that can then ripple out into societal concreteness— is brought to life in the elegant figure of the wise sage Lao Tzu wandering atop a mighty oxen. The powerful muscles of insightful action are in the service of embodied wisdom. Currently the oxen of our collective egos sit atop our shared humanity.

We can all rebirth. rewild, and reground our own consciousness so connection/love is equal to, if not more important then, protection/control. This might then recalibrate capitalism and the current world order. This recalibration—definitely *not* a violent or conflictual revolution but a radical transformation none the less—starts with a re-orientation in our consciousness.

As transformational leaders, we can find secular—yet profoundly spiritual and transformative ways—to reconnect ourselves with each other, and the planet itself, to bring about a Regenerative Renaissance. (Because of the appropriate separation between Church and State, religious pathways are more challenging in organizations.) Without using the Connection Solution, we cannot reliably heal our own wounds and transform our own addictive, extractive, and accumulative patterns; let alone help others give up comforts and convenience to align with the limits of our one planet. Only healed hearts avoid hurting other people and the planet we all rely on.

As Bio-Transformation Theory & Practice tells us, major changes in our external world originate in such transformations within our conscious hearts and minds. The onus is on us to transform ourselves first, where we are at, so we can ensure our enterprises and institutions fit the fast-emerging realities on the ground. As the example of Nelson Mandela illustrates: if we don't change but expect others to, nothing much can or will change.

If we want to continue to have outsized profits, luxury conveniences, and asymmetric power whilst wanting the world to become more sustainable and regenerative then we have missed the point—and we have squandered the Leadership Invitation. Transformation of our world is led by transformation of ourselves.

The start-point is always us leaders. The best/only way a leader can tackle any of these crises—and change their corner of the world no matter how modestly or magnificently—is through the transformation of the products, services, policies, procedures, processes, business models, and delivery models of their enterprise. Changes in our reality only occur when organizations—from multinationals to Mom and Pop stores; from tech 'unicorns' to political movements—change what they do, and how they do it.

As we know, changes in organizations only occur when the people within them change how they behave. And changing the people who work within, fund, and buy from an organization always starts with us leaders: we must sense, feel, think, and act differently in order to bring about concrete changes in organizations that then generate lasting and positive transformations across climate, equality, health, and community.

When we engage in a wholehearted reconnection with nature—with a vulnerable and open body as much as curious and open mind—we find our way back 'home'. We realize that our mind and body are one unified whole; and our bodymind is united with the natural world/universe. All is one. All for one.

This is Bio-Transformation Theory & Practice (BTTP) Gem 1. A sense of unity and connection—and the tangible healing of trauma that can come with it— allows our hearts to break open with the suffering of people and planet. Purpose emanates freely from such a heart. A Jewish wisdom saying is that 'there is nothing so whole as a broken heart'.

In some ways, we need interoceptive-affective heartbreak to motivate us to lead and land transformations with our cognitive-behavioral brilliance. We shift from just intellectually and morally understanding that our systems are breaking . . . to emotionally and somatically *feeling* the breaking apart within.

A ripped plastic bag floating in the sea—or the sight of a malnourished child with bruises from abuse—hurts us in the fleshy fragilities of our heart as much as concerns us morally in our mind. Broken hearts—that we tend to and heal within—allow openings through which our love-fueled purpose flows. As we fully accept our shared fragility and inevitable demise—and witness, without flinching, the death and devastation that is all around us—we find invincible strength within.

Many of us have been forced to reflect on our life and business model by the dangers and oddities of a global pandemic and accompanying economic crash. We have a clear opportunity right now to wake up, switch on, and step up to the four crises that threaten us all.

Another opportunity will arise in future when climate change, inequality, rising ill-heath, and political instability conspire to generate another major threat. But the longer we wait, the more will suffer. Just as tens of thousands died from severe Acute Respiratory Distress Syndrome brought on by Covid-19 because governments and businesses were not adapted to the quite predictable threat of a pandemic, many more will die—and live in chronic suffering—if we allow climate change, inequality, ill-health, and identity wars to continue to ravage human society. Rather than react with fear and frustration—or protest or denial—to the crises we face, we can face them head on without needing them to be bigger or smaller than they are.

By switching consciously from Control & Protect Mode into Create & Connect Mode (BTTP Gem 2), we can unpack and process our protective patterns, own our part of the problem, and build concrete solutions in our enterprises that resolve our shared crises. We metabolize the suffering of people and planet into purpose and passion in our work. We seek out the weak signals of the future in the present—in nature as much as in society—and build around them regenerative business models that reduce the usage of raw materials and return clean outputs back to the planet.

We develop transformational innovations that nourish the human families and communities that work for, and buy from, us. Above all, we become compelled to challenge—responsibly yet radically—the logic of constant economic growth and the assumptions that underpin it. As we choose to find our way to connective consciousness more frequently—the alluring wilds within as much as those in landscapes upon which we walk—we can be bolder yet wise and generative leaders of a recalibration of capitalism.

This can and will only happen when we master *both* connective consciousness *and* analytic consciousness; *both* our capacities for creativity *and* our ability to control and order; *both* Control & Protect Mode *and* Create & Connect Mode; *both* profit *and* purpose; *both* glorious imagination *and* genius execution; *both* individual ingenuity *and* collective intelligence. This is BTTP Gem 3.

At the very center of the Great Transformation is the recalibration of capitalism away from extreme focus on order/control/extraction/accumulation into a form that balances protect/control/profit with connect/create/purpose. Our generation of transformational leaders can deliver this Highest Common Factor creative harmony that encourages *both* individual profit from hard work *and* manifests a shared purpose that delivers collective wellbeing.

We can bring together both conventionally right-wing ideals of individual responsibility, national identity, and entrepreneurial flare; and conventionally left-wing ideals of shared rights, global solidarity, and social equality.

Millennia of experimentation has proven that we can *all* find our way to connective consciousness and the imaginative exuberance of Create & Connect Mode even when faced with dangers, emergencies, and crises. The only other universal experience that arises in threatening moments is fear/anger/rage/outrage—and we know where these get us. While it might seem easier to be cynical about the power of connective consciousness to make concrete change in social systems, it is much more useful to realize what transformational leaders *par excellence* Mohandas Gandhi, Nelson Mandela, and Martin Luther King Jr all believed in one way or another: love is the most important leadership principle.

Love is the start and end point: the alpha and the omega. This is because love allows our tender, vulnerable, yet epically strong hearts to temper our smart minds with compassion, empathy, and care.

Love enables us to leverage the intelligence, science, and technology of Control & Protect Mode for the aims and objectives of Create & Connect Mode. Purpose is the bridge of this Third Way harmony.

As legendary revolutionary Ernesto 'Che' Guevara said: "At the risk of seeming ridiculous, let me say that the true revolutionary is guided by a great feeling of love. It is impossible to think of a genuine revolutionary lacking this quality."

The Covid-19 outbreak—and the resulting socio-economic meltdown—has magnified the importance and urgency of the moment exponentially. It has opened up a huge choice for all of us to enact the Great Transformation to a Greater Tomorrow now; or ignore it and attempt to return to a (mythical) past that, clearly, did not work for many (if any). We are in the turning point now.

When the world turns upside down, we all have a choice: 'normality' or transformation; power or empowerment; profit or purpose; control or connection. The path we choose as individual leaders will determine our shared future. We are all faced with a once-in-a generation—perhaps even once-in-a-species—opportunity: to transform our own leadership senses, feelings, ideas, and habits (BTTP Gem 4) so we can transform our businesses and so change the systems we rely on to be life-affirming and regenerative. The rebirth within can generate a rebirth outside us: a Regenerative Renaissance.

To be explicit: the key to recalibrating capitalism and so bringing about a Regenerative Renaissance is a global network of individual transformational leaders who have a trauma-healed **hara** that opens up a spiritually-awakened, purpose-emanating **heart.** This transformed relationship to life, leadership, and society affords such leaders a wise, as well as smart, **head** to make effective decisions, invent future-forward business models, and craft inspiring stories. Such a mindset allows leaders to drive forward productive and efficient—but also compassionate and caring—habits and behaviors with their **hands**.

I believe that Plato suggests, in his *Republic,* that only such truly transformational leaders—those who no longer want to rule with Control & Protect Mode, but instead seek to inspire with the insights and ideas from Create & Connect Mode—should be given the power to lead society. He realized that only people that have spent years engaging in reconnection practices and experimenting with transformational tools—that he expressly saw as 'spiritual'—can push themselves to the stage of consciousness of a Transformer (BTTP Gem 5). It is only Transformers that can being about a Great Transformation to realize a Regenerative Renaissance.

The feminist psychologist Carol Gilligan suggested that love for others and our planet is only unleashed in the most *developed* stages of humankind. It is only the Transformer who has the requisite humility, wholeheartedness, and purposefulness to stop *themselves* leading change from within their pernicious and persistent protective patterns. Such patterns will always cause pain and suffering eventually. The Transformer maintains themselves in the biological and psychological midline between the two modes of consciousness: harmonizing hubris and humility—and profit and purpose—in service of changing our one shared world.

As transformational leaders who have become Transformers, we can all bring about a radical—but not violent and needlessly disruptive—transformation in the material world when we are inspired by huge, healed hearts full of unalloyed love. With love in our hearts, we can reconfigure, rewild, and recalibrate advanced capitalism rather than seek to destroy it (which is both impossible and misguided).

We can choose to devote our one, short, yet exhilarating lives to the removal of human suffering through a Regenerative Renaissance underpinned by purpose-driven organizations and life-affirming business models. We do this not because of what we can get, but because of how much we can give.

As political leaders, business leaders, entrepreneurial leaders, community leaders—or simply leaders of our own lives—it is time to wholeheartedly accept our unique Leadership Invitations. Then can we can work through the six spirals of transformational action—BTTP Gem 6—with every issue we are faced with. Moving through the spirals, we expand from self to system—and back again as we grapple with intense Transformational Challenges.

Rather than react with outrage, denial, or despair to issues, we can respond with heart and mind attuned to co-creativity, not just control. We then avoid enacting the smart, yet predictable, patterns that attempt to maintain our most cherished assumptions, rather than relinquish them in favor of transformation. Without expanding our consciousness like this, we are likely to try to control a crisis; treat it as a technical problem with known solutions; minimize the existential threats; and focus on a return to 'normality' (also known as the status quo) as quickly as possible.

This is what happened in the financial crisis of 2008-2009. We wasted a great crisis—a global transformation challenge—by flooding the financial system with cheap money that prevented unsustainable—in every sense—business models from having to transform and adapt. Therefore we lost the opportunity to reshape and recalibrate our global socio-economic model. We instead settled for more of the same; just a little different (like markets being propped up by Quantitative Easing).

Society—and by that I most poignantly and pointedly mean us leaders—collectively ignored the transformation invitation. Most of us tried to return to a Great Yesterday—of enormous corporate profits, dizzying rises in share price, blossoming authoritarian power etc., etc.—rather than consciously choose to move to a Greater Tomorrow by going "through, up, and out" the Transformation Curve bearing genuinely transformative solutions (BTTP Gem 7).

No leader can solve *all* of the four crises alone and instigate a Regenerative Renaissance. No one intelligence, no matter how powerful or smart, can transform any major crisis or emergency. No single multinational company, government, or even supranational entity—especially when organized hierarchically as most are—has the systemic capability, collective integrity, or political legitimacy necessary to usher in the Great Transformation alone.

Instead, we must rise up together and convene and cultivate collaborations of many transformational leaders. This means pooling our combined insight, ideas, resources, and power around a common purpose and shared vision of what is Possible that can then become Actual. Complex problems in complex, adaptive living systems need to be solved with matching levels of collective sense-making and collaborative creativity.

As I complete this book, the novel coronavirus is ably demonstrating that we are truly only *one* species connected materially and psychologically across our shared planet: if the poorest nations and lowest-income groups in society are struck down by the virus, then the world is at risk. What is good for all is good for each one of us. All is one. One for all.

If we upgrade our own consciousness as leaders and hone our capacity to land transformation in the material world of our enterprise—using the 7 Gems of Bio-Transformation Theory & Practice—we can then join what musician Brian Eno calls a 'scenius': the collective genius that emerges when we work together with other masters—virtuosi—of transformational leadership.

Our potential as a global network of Transformers is dependent on each of us having impeccable self-mastery. Otherwise personality conflicts and interpersonal issues stemming from unresolved wounding and trauma always—eventually—block the collective flow of co-creative ideas and symphonic action. We all have part of the solution; we can all see part of the elephant. We must share what we sense, feel, see, think, and act in useful ways to rise to the complexity of the crises we face.

The future is waiting for us to each to open up our channel to become a choir that, as one, is able to sing the new song, the new dream, the new narrative of humankind without our noisy fears and frustrations ruining it all. Possible futures are rushing toward you as you read this. If you and I can come together, steering our own enterprises towards adaptive transformations as we work together at the level of system, we can co-realize the Great Transformation.

The resulting Regenerative Renaissance can include all the best innovations of humankind; while being able to *consciously* transcend the persistent and pernicious protective patterns of previous stages of human evolution that are no longer a fit; or fit for purpose. This means we can pick the best; and leave the worst, as Lene Andersen explores in her punchy book *Metamodernity: Meaning and Hope in a Complex World.*

We can harness the best of pre-modern Tribal O.S. to find our way (back) to an intimate relationship with nature and build generative communities of mutual aid—and local trade—that fulfill our yearning for simplicity, authenticity, narrative expression, and belonging; while losing strong-man leadership, barbarity, disempowering myths, naive certainties, identity-driven violence, and xenophobia.

We can harness Institution O.S for its elegant legal entities and structures that provide us stability and security; and the capacity for innovations and investments in other places and spaces; while losing the nationalistic, religious, colonial, and class-based oppression/suppression that diminishes and demeans other people and our planet.

We can optimize the liberating reason, scientific rigor, creative entrepreneurship, and ingenious innovations of late-modernity's Enterprise O.S.; while losing cut-throat competition, *faux* meritocracy, and extractive greed that together lock those without capital, knowledge, or power out; and push the world towards rampant inequality and ill-health and environmental destruction and devastation.

And we can make use of the co-creativity, collective wisdom, peer-power, and regenerative thinking of Network O.S.; while losing the forced flatness, technocratic globalization, deconstructive nihilism, and reduced rootedness that can come with it.

As the Operating System of our world is changing, and a new Operating System for humankind is emerging, we can build upon it transformative "apps": business models, policy models, democratic models, and social models. We can challenge the assumptions at the heart of our unsustainable business models and social systems (that are already in decline); and replace them with future-forward, humanity-empowering, planet-regenerating insights (that are starting to break through).

Be warned though. The exact nature of a regenerative capitalist system and transformed liberal order—both of which lie at the heart of the Great Transformation to a Regenerative Renaissance—cannot be predicted by anyone; for that would just be Control & Protect Mode believing it has the answer based on the past. There are many different variants on offer, depending on the light of our shared purpose and the skillful means of us leaders.

Without a refined and purified collective purpose—and truly transformational leaders at the helm of business and society—we could easily find ourselves dealing with 21st Century forms of neo-fascism (crony capitalism, nationalist isolation, expelling foreigners); and/or 21st Century forms of neo-communism (statist capitalism, controlling technologies, and harsh authoritarianism).

We must all live into the Great Transformation with eyes, minds, and hearts wide open. We must all reshape our lives, companies, institutions, and communities by unfolding the Possible world into the Actual world in a biodynamic way. This means following the logic of the Transformation Curve; and trusting in transformation!

That said, although we don't yet know the recipe or the name of the cake, many of the ingredients we need for a Regenerative Renaissance already exist. As we know, a transformed future will always include, yet transcend, the old order as we find ways through the edge of chaos; and up and out of the right-side of the Transformation Curve. We must find a more complex, creative, and fitting order that matches a 9-billion-people-yet-1-planet reality. I sense that a Regenerative Renaissance, led by truly transformational leaders, will bake together ideas like:

- Consciousness (purpose, happiness, relationships) becoming as important as matter (profit, productivity, performance) in society and business
- A renewal of globalization, with the focus shifting to the mobility of ideas and relationships (consciousness) as opposed to simply labor and capital (matter)
- Slow, patient, and humble capital that is far less interested in material scale, exponential returns, and rapid exits (i.e. 'unicorns'); and far more interested in sustained and sustainable positive impact (e.g. 'zebras')

- Authentic purpose at the core of all organizations (that is realized with concrete changes in business practices and investment in employee and user wellbeing)
- Increasing development of sustainable, prosocial, and regenerative asset classes for capital to be invested in
- Distributed ownership models—like co-operatives, social enterprises, and BCorps—that allow users/citizens/workers to share in the rewards and decisions as well as the risks and effort
- Peer-to-peer transmission of services such as education and healthcare
- Compassion, kindness, and connective wisdom as important as knowledge, skill attainment, and accreditation in education, adult learning, and employee training
- Legal rights for the planet/nature (e.g. Bolivia and Ecuador)
- Sharing economies that benefit all sharers; and many more co-living communities
- Participatory design and diversity in decision-making (e.g. Citizen's Assemblies)
- Decentralized organizational structures (e.g. Decentralized Autonomous Organizations (DAOs) and holocracies)
- A wealth of diversity in organizations—with the dissolution of all pay and power gaps
- Transparent and accountable decision-making, with refined intuitions becoming as important as data in organizations
- Local direct democracy (e.g. Flatpack Democracy), local currencies (e.g. Lewes Pound), local supply chains (e.g. onshoring) and local city-scale innovations (e.g. CityLab)
- Regenerative agriculture; and the rewilding of land and communities
- Biodegradable materials and biodegrading organisms

- A permanent shift to renewable and low-carbon energy sources
- Variously colored New Deals to regenerate the social compact between the liberal order and citizens
- Circular and net-positive supply chains with baked in carbon sequestration technologies
- The closure of tax loopholes; and the removal of off-shore tax statuses
- The uncoupling of GDP growth from carbon (e.g. doughnut economics); and a recalibration towards measuring human wellbeing as well as GDP
- The proactive 'degrowth' of planet-polluting and humanity-diminishing industries
- The leverage of transparency technologies like tokens and the blockchain; and emancipatory technologies like AI and nanotech in ethical, and so less profitable, ways

The moment for the Great Transformation is upon us. We are in the bifurcation now. By becoming aware that we are in a metaphysical emergency—which brings with it great despair and great hope—the transformational leader can consciously lead and land lasting, positive, non-linear, and so unpredictable transformations in their products, services, and business models; that scale with the transformational innovations of other leaders to land a Regenerative Renaissance together.

There are limitless opportunities to create exponential value for self and system in this digital, disrupted, and damaged world. The only limitations we have are our own habits of thought, action, feeling, and sensation. We can all become limitless if we master our selves; our consciousness. Virtuosos at transformational leadership are the stem cells of our global community that can bring about the Great Transformation to a Regenerative Renaissance.

It will be messy, challenging, and really, *really* hard. But there is a Triple Win to be had in every future-proofing transformation: a win for our careers; a win for our organizations; and a win for our crisis-hit world.

We can all support each other to enact the Great Transformation in everyday life without delay: to take risks by speaking from a (healed) heart in meetings; to question outdated business model assumptions with purpose; and to respectfully challenge the status quo with wisdom. We can all bring the empowering and caring intuitions and insights we feel about our users and employees into conversations and workshops. We can all identify major Transformational Challenges that our business or institution can take ownership of and share these with our managers and Board.

Now is not the time to hide our brilliance away; nor to carry on with the old controlling and protecting behaviors of the past in an attempt to get back to Business As Usual in a Great Yesterday. Instead, our profoundest duty is to develop ourselves to be virtuoso transformational leaders that guide others—consciously and purposefully—across the Transformation Curve one team, function, business unit, and organization at a time. Then we play our full part in bringing about the Great Transformation as quickly as it is needed; and with as little pain and suffering as possible.

It starts here and now: you are the one that you have been waiting for. Everything you need is within your bodymind and the networks of which you are a part. You were born to transform yourself and your system.

As you read this sentence and soon put this book down, you are in literally in a bifurcation point within your career, your organization, and our world.

Will you give up comfort and convenience to receive upgrades to your consciousness that maximize your potential as a transformational leader . . . or will you retreat, deny, ignore, dissociate, or numb the suffering?

Will you attempt to maintain Business As Usual 'normality' . . . or forge the future by taking part in the Great Transformation to a Regenerative Renaissance?

Do you prefer the challenge of future-proofing your career and our crisis-hit world; or the seeming comfort of maintaining a status quo that looks certain to land us all in ever more pain as individuals, organizations, and as a species?

The choice of which path you take from here is always yours: protect, control, and attempt to maintain the old 'normal'. Or connect, create, and unfold the next level. There is nothing moral in this choice. But it will lead to very different outcomes for you, for me, and for our children. As always, there is a Triple Win.

So I invite you directly, right now and right here as you read this, to accept your Leadership Invitation. You are invited to the greatest show on Earth: to usher in the Great Transformation and bring about a Regenerative Renaissance.

Will you join me to lead the change, now?

If you would like to become a virtuoso at transformational leadership—please do join me on the next cohort of Master Transformational Leadership. It would be an honor to be with you on your journey.

www.switchonnow.com/leadership

FREE READER OFFER

As a truly valued reader, we are offering a valuable tool to support you as a Transformational Leader.

THE 6 SPIRALS OF TRANSFORMATIONAL LEADERSHIP: ENQUIRY

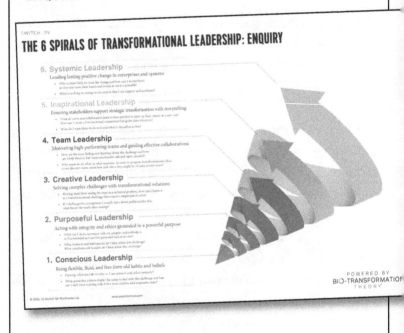

It contains a series of powerful coaching questions to use in any moment to drive transformational outcomes—from the inside out.

You'll get your free PDF at: **www.bit.ly/so-nltc**

When you sign up, you will also receive invites to read future books in advance of publication.

SWITCH ON FURTHER

If you want turn inspiration into action—moving from ideas to making concrete change happen in your life and work—join us on one of our transformation programs for thriving life and relationships:

www.switchonnow.com

facebook.com/switchonnow

www.medium.com/switch-on

If you want to go deeper into the practice of personal transformation, explore my book *Switch On*.

If you want to go deeper into the life and leadership philosophy that underpins my work in transformational living and leadership, explore my book *Spiritual Atheist*.

NOTES

1. Heifetz, R.A., Grashow, A. and Linsky, M. (2009). The practice of adaptive leadership : tools and tactics for changing your organization and the world. Boston, Mass.: Harvard Business Press.
2. Li, J., Gong, X., Wang, Z., Chen, R., Li, T., Zeng, D. and Li, M. (2020). Clinical features of familial clustering in patients infected with 2019 novel coronavirus in Wuhan, China. Virus Research, p.198043.
3. Bechara, A. (2000). Emotion, Decision Making and the Orbitofrontal Cortex. Cerebral Cortex, 10(3), pp.295–307.
4. Liu, S. et. al.. (2012). Neural Correlates of Lyrical Improvisation: An fMRI Study of Freestyle Rap. Scientific Reports, [online] 2(1). Available at: https://www.nature.com/articles/srep00834 [Accessed 9 May 2019].
5. Jung, R.E. (2013). The structure of creative cognition in the human brain. Frontiers in Human Neuroscience, 7.
6. Fox, K.C.R. and Christoff, K. (2018). The Oxford handbook of spontaneous thought : mind-wandering, creativity, and dreaming. New York, Ny: Oxford University Press.
7. Rochford, K.C., Jack, A.I., Boyatzis, R.E. and French, S.E. (2016). Ethical Leadership as a Balance Between Opposing Neural Networks. Journal of Business Ethics, 144(4), pp.755–770.
8. Bonta, B.D. (1997). Cooperation and competition in peaceful societies. Psychological Bulletin, 121(2), pp.299–320.
9. Lucchesi, S., Cheng, L., Janmaat, K., Mundry, R., Pisor, A. and Surbeck, M. (2020). Beyond the group: how food, mates, and group size influence intergroup encounters in wild bonobos. Behavioral Ecology, 31(2), pp.519–532.
10. Jung, R.E. (2014). Evolution, creativity, intelligence, and madness: Here Be Dragons. Frontiers in Psychology, [online] 5. Available at: https://www.ncbi.nlm.nih.gov/pmc/articles/PMC4107956/ [Accessed 20 Oct. 2019].

11. Nāgārjuna and Kalupahana, D.J. (1986). The philosophy of the middle way = Mūlamadhyamakakārikā. Albany, N.Y.: State University Of New York Press.

12. Fredrickson, B.L. (2001). The role of positive emotions in positive psychology: The broaden-and-build theory of positive emotions. American Psychologist, 56(3), pp.218–226.

13. Danziger, S., Levav, J. and Avnaim-Pesso, L. (2011). Extraneous factors in judicial decisions. Proceedings of the National Academy of Sciences, [online] 108(17), pp.6889–6892. Available at: https://www.pnas.org/content/108/17/6889 [Accessed 2 Feb. 2019].

14. DiSalvo, D. (2009). Forget Survival of the Fittest: It Is Kindness That Counts. Scientific American Mind, 20(5), pp.18–19.

15. Simmons, A.N., Fitzpatrick, S., Strigo, I.A., Potterat, E.G., Johnson, D.C., Matthews, S.C., Van Orden, K.F., Swain, J.L. and Paulus, M.P. (2012). Altered insula activation in anticipation of changing emotional states. NeuroReport, 23(4), pp.234–239.

16. Palmer, C.E. and Tsakiris, M. (2018). Going at the heart of social cognition: is there a role for interoception in self-other distinction? Current Opinion in Psychology, 24, pp.21–26.

17. Inesi, M.E., Lee, S.Y. and Rios, K. (2014). Objects of desire: Subordinate ingratiation triggers self-objectification among powerful. Journal of Experimental Social Psychology, 53, pp.19–30.

18. Eisenberger, N.I. (2012). The Neural Bases of Social Pain. Psychosomatic Medicine, 74(2), pp.126–135.

19. Mitchell, C., Hobcraft, J., McLanahan, S.S., Siegel, S.R., Berg, A., Brooks-Gunn, J., Garfinkel, I. and Notterman, D. (2014). Social disadvantage, genetic sensitivity, and children's telomere length. Proceedings of the National Academy of Sciences, 111(16), pp.5944–5949.

20. Waldinger, R.J. and Schulz, M.S. (2010). What's love got to do with it? Social functioning, perceived health, and daily happiness in married octogenarians. Psychology and Aging, 25(2), pp.422–431.

21. Kishida, K.T., Yang, D., Quartz, K.H., Quartz, S.R. and Montague, P.R. (2012). Implicit signals in small group settings and their impact on the expression of cognitive capacity and associated brain responses. Philosophical Transactions of the Royal Society B: Biological Sciences, 367(1589), pp.704–716.

22. Campanario, J.M. (2009). Rejecting and resisting Nobel class discoveries: accounts by Nobel Laureates. Scientometrics, 81(2), pp.549–565.

23. Blair, H.T. (2005). Unilateral Storage of Fear Memories by the Amygdala. Journal of Neuroscience, 25(16), pp.4198–4205.

24. McKinsey & Company. (2009). The irrational side of change management. [online] Available at: https://www.mckinsey.com/business-functions/organization/our-insights/the-irrational-side-of-change-management.

25. Baumeister, R.F. (2018). Conquer Yourself, Conquer the World. Scientific American Mind, 27(1s), pp.36–41.

26. Durlak, J.A., Weissberg, R.P., Dymnicki, A.B., Taylor, R.D. and Schellinger, K.B. (2011). The Impact of Enhancing Students' Social and Emotional Learning: A Meta-Analysis of School-Based Universal Interventions. Child Development, 82(1), pp.405–432.

27. Tugade, M.M., Fredrickson, B.L. and Feldman Barrett, L. (2004). Psychological Resilience and Positive Emotional Granularity: Examining the Benefits of Positive Emotions on Coping and Health. Journal of Personality, 72(6), pp.1161–1190.

28. Goffee, R. and Jones, G. (2004). What Makes a Leader? Business Strategy Review, 15(2), pp.46–50.

29. *Kegan, R. and Lisa Laskow Lahey (2009). Immunity to change : how to overcome it and unlock potential in yourself and your organization. Boston: Harvard Business School, Cop.*

30. Kohlberg, L. and Hersh, R.H. (1977). Moral development: A review of the theory. Theory Into Practice, 16(2), pp.53–59.

31. Gilligan, C. (2006). In a different voice : psychological theory and women's development. Cambridge ; London: Harvard University Press, [Ca.

32. Lee, L.O., James, P., Zevon, E.S., Kim, E.S., Trudel-Fitzgerald, C., Spiro, A., Grodstein, F. and Kubzansky, L.D. (2019). Optimism is associated with exceptional longevity in 2 epidemiologic cohorts of men and women. Proceedings of the National Academy of Sciences, [online] 116(37), pp.18357–18362. Available at: https://www.pnas.org/content/116/37/18357 [Accessed 14 May 2020].

33. Goleman, D. (2014). Leading for the Long Future. Leader to Leader, 2014(72), pp.34–39.

34. Mihaly Csikszentmihalyi (2009). Flow : the psychology of optimal experience. New York: Harper [And] Row.

35. Schore, A.N. (2014). The right brain is dominant in psychotherapy. Psychotherapy, 51(3), pp.388–397.

36. Granqvist, P. et. al., (2017). Disorganized attachment in infancy: a review of the phenomenon and its implications for clinicians and policy-makers. Attachment & Human Development, [online] 19(6), pp.534–558. Available at: https://www.ncbi.nlm.nih.gov/pmc/articles/PMC5600694/ [Accessed 20 Nov. 2019].

37. Bernardi, L., Sleight, P., Bandinelli, G., Cencetti, S., Fattorini, L., Wdowczyc-Szulc, J. and Lagi, A. (2001). Effect of rosary prayer and yoga mantras on autonomic cardiovascular rhythms: comparative study. BMJ, 323(7327), pp.1446–1449.

38. Ding, X., Tang, Y.-Y., Tang, R. and Posner, M.I. (2014). Improving creativity

performance by short-term meditation. Behavioral and Brain Functions, 10(1), p.9.

39. Zavala, A.M., Day, G.E., Plummer, D. and Bamford-Wade, A. (2018). Decision-making under pressure: medical errors in uncertain and dynamic environments. Australian Health Review, [online] 42(4), p.395. Available at: https://www.publish.csiro.au/ah/ah16088.

40. Habak, C., Seghier, M.L., Brûlé, J., Fahim, M.A. and Monchi, O. (2019). Age Affects How Task Difficulty and Complexity Modulate Perceptual Decision-Making. Frontiers in Aging Neuroscience, 11.

41. Frazier, M.L., Fainshmidt, S., Klinger, R.L., Pezeshkan, A. and Vracheva, V. (2016). Psychological Safety: A Meta-Analytic Review and Extension. Personnel Psychology, 70(1), pp.113–165.

42. Cauwelier, P. (2019). Building high-performance teams through team psychological safety. Research Outreach, (108), pp.62–65.

43. Pollan, M. (2019). How To Change Your Mind : the new science of psychedelics. London: Penguin Books.

44. Caiulabate, B. and Clancy Cavnar (2014). Ayahuasca shamanism in the Amazon and beyond. Oxford ; New York: Oxford University Press.

45. Jones, D.M., Bremer, S.A. and Singer, J.D. (1996). Militarized Interstate Disputes, 1816–1992: Rationale, Coding Rules, and Empirical Patterns. Conflict Management and Peace Science, 15(2), pp.163–213.

CPSIA information can be obtained
at www.ICGtesting.com
Printed in the USA
LVHW042317120123
737038LV00001B/75